G000123044

Especially for:

_____

From:

_____

Date:

_____

DAILY
WISDOM
for Men

2018
Devotional Collection

BARBOUR BOOKS
An Imprint of Barbour Publishing, Inc.

© 2017 by Barbour Publishing, Inc.

Print ISBN 978-1-68322-242-2
Special Edition ISBNs 978-1-944836-15-3; 978-1-944836-13-9

eBook Editions:
Adobe Digital Edition (.epub) 978-1-68322-519-5
Kindle and MobiPocket Edition (.prc) 978-1-68322-520-1

Published by Barbour Books, an imprint of Barbour Publishing, Inc., P.O. Box 719, Uhrichsville, Ohio 44683, www.barbourbooks.com

Our mission is to publish and distribute inspirational products offering exceptional value and biblical encouragement to the masses.

Member of the
Evangelical Christian
Publishers Association

Printed in China.

Each new year brings fresh hope for the future and new opportunities to do your best and as 2018 begins, your hopes may be high. But just as often, the turning of the page is accompanied by concern and even apprehension. Many of last year's headlines were troubling, and the news in the financial columns wasn't always good. This may leave you worrying about the year ahead.

But Jesus said, "I have spoken to you, that in Me you may have peace. In the world you will have tribulation; but be of good cheer, I have overcome the world" (John 16:33 NKJV). Down through the ages, the followers of Jesus Christ have been called to "hold firmly to the word of life" (Philippians 2:16 NIV), and to trust in the Lord to breathe strength into their spirits and see them through difficult days. Jesus has spoken to you, and you can have peace!

This book's purpose is to supply you with a daily dose of encouragement, faith, and perseverance by revealing God and His ways to you. It's our prayer that as you take a few moments each day to meditate on the Lord, you'll be drawn closer to Him and walk in His footsteps throughout the day.

May the words of this blessing be upon you: "The Lord bless you and keep you; the Lord make his face shine on you and be gracious to you; the Lord turn his face toward you and give you peace" (Numbers 6:24–26 NIV).

START WITH GOD

*Now the LORD spoke to Moses and Aaron in the land
of Egypt, saying, "This month shall be your beginning of
months; it shall be the first month of the year to you."*

EXODUS 12:1–2 NKJV

The Lord instituted the Passover (a seven-day celebration of Israel's deliverance from slavery in Egypt) in March/April of every year, and it was to become Israel's New Year. In his commentary on these verses, Matthew Henry writes, "Note, it is good to begin the day, and begin the year, and especially to begin our lives, with God."

You probably head into this new year with a number of resolutions in mind. You want to lose weight or get in better shape, read helpful books, tame your tongue, get out of debt, volunteer for good causes, or become more organized.

All of these are worthy goals, but for the Christian, they should all flow from putting Christ first. You lose weight to honor God who dwells in the temple of your body. You read more to nourish your mind. You tame your tongue to be a better witness. You get out of debt so you can be free to invest in the kingdom. You volunteer because you want to show people the love of Christ.

As you consider the changes you want to make this year, ask yourself how putting God first in each change will glorify Him. Take time to listen to the Lord and ponder His Word.

TEACHING OBEDIENCE

Therefore go and make disciples of all nations, baptizing them in the name of the Father and of the Son and of the Holy Spirit, and teaching them to obey everything I have commanded you.
MATTHEW 28:19–20 NIV

Christians are called to make disciples, to baptize them, and then teach them to obey everything Christ commanded His disciples. While the American evangelical church places a high priority on making converts, discipleship is less of a priority.

In a study of 2,930 American Protestant churchgoers conducted by Lifeway, only 42% said they intentionally spend time with other believers in order to help them grow in their faith. The other 58% have a truncated view of the Great Commission, and ultimately, the Gospel. At the 2015 *Turning America* conference in Springfield, Missouri, David Barton, the president of WallBuilders, made the following observation, as reported by *The Pathway* newspaper.

"We've changed the way we looked at the Great Commission," Barton said. "Rather than teaching everything He taught us, which would change the culture, we're just going after 'fire insurance.'"

If you aren't already discipling somebody, you probably know men at work, school, or church who are baby Christians. Invite one of them out for coffee this week and ask to hear his story. Find out what he's struggling with and offer to disciple him, either formally or informally, by walking him through the scriptures.

LOVING OTHER BELIEVERS

*We [Paul and Timothy] always pray for you, and we give thanks
to God, the Father of our Lord Jesus Christ. For we have heard of
your faith in Christ Jesus and your love for all of God's people.*

COLOSSIANS 1:3–4 NLT

As God's people, you are called to exhibit love for everyone,
including your enemies, but you have a certain affinity for other
believers—an instant bond, no matter how long you've known
them. You're united in Christ and that bond is thicker than blood.

Paul wrote to the Colossian church that he wanted them to
know how thankful he was for their reputation of loving all of
God's people. We can't be certain how Paul and Timothy heard
this information, although some commentators speculate that
it was passed on by Epaphras (vs. 7). We also don't know how
they expressed this love, but it undoubtedly involved acts of
kindness and mercy because love includes action, and you build
a reputation for things you do consistently.

How is your church viewed by other Christians who have
never stepped foot inside one of your worship services? Do other
believers see your church at local events, praying and serving
alongside fellow believers? Does your church reach out to other
churches in your city during their time of need? Does your church
celebrate with other Christians? If not, what simple steps can
you take to change that?

MORNING MEETINGS WITH GOD

My voice shalt thou hear in the morning, O Lᴏʀᴅ; in the morning
will I direct my prayer unto thee, and will look up.

Psᴀʟᴍ 5:3 ᴋᴊᴠ

When David penned these words, he was probably surrounded
by his enemies (see vs. 6, 8)—perhaps during the reign of King
Saul. No matter what the circumstances, David made a point to
meet with God every morning. He was intentional in turning
his face toward heaven and directing his voice toward God, being
confident that the Lord would hear him.

On this day, he reminded God about his character—how
He didn't take pleasure in wickedness (vs. 4). He also reminded
God that the foolish would not stand before him (vs. 5). But
David knew he wasn't perfect either. David was resolute in
communicating with God every morning, not because he was
without blemish or fault, but because he knew God was merciful
(vs. 7). So, he approached Him in the morning time with a
healthy dose of fear, knowing he deserved judgment, but trusting
in God's mercy.

What does your morning routine look like? Does it include
approaching God, knowing He will hear you? Do you come
before Him with a proper amount of reverent fear, no matter
what the circumstances? Or do difficulties, business, or sloth
keep you from meeting with Him? Even if you're surrounded
by enemies, God will hear you. You're not alone.

SPIRITUAL PROSPERITY

*Better is the poor who walks in his integrity than
one who is perverse in his lips, and is a fool.*
PROVERBS 19:1 NKJV

The man who walks in his integrity is satisfied at the end of the day. He's done an honest day's worth of work, treated people well, and comes home to a meal that no king would necessarily desire, but it fills his stomach and he's thankful for it. He has nothing to be ashamed about. He's put forth his best effort and tomorrow is another day.

The man who is crooked, however, is foolish. He speaks lies and cuts corners to get ahead. He mistreats people for his own gain. He dines extravagantly and drives fancy vehicles. His conscience bothers him from time to time, but he rationalizes his actions, telling himself that everybody does wrong things. He covers up his sins and falls asleep scheming about the next day.

Not surprisingly, the Hebrew word for *integrity* in today's verse can be translated as *prosperity*. So, better is the poor who walks in his spiritual prosperity than the one who is perverse in his lips. That would seem to indicate a spiritual divide between the person who spends time tending to spiritual matters versus the person who spends time scheming to get ahead.

Proverbs 19:1 doesn't really speak about middle ground, nor about the middle class and its values. So ask yourself which side of the spectrum you're currently cultivating.

GOD'S REVELATION TO MAN

Now after Jesus was born in Bethlehem of Judea in the days of Herod the king, behold, wise men from the East came to Jerusalem, saying, "Where is He who has been born King of the Jews? For we have seen His star in the East and have come to worship Him."

MATTHEW 2:1–2 NKJV

Many Eastern Christians, as well as some Western believers, celebrate Epiphany today—a holiday which commemorates two events in the life of Jesus, both of which center around His divinity: the day the Wise Men visited the newborn king in Bethlehem and the day John the Baptist baptized Jesus.

According to timeanddate.com, "In some European countries, such as the Czech Republic and Slovakia, children dress as the three kings and visit houses. In their roles as the kings, or wise men, they sing about the [day of] Jesus' birth and pay homage to the 'king of kings.' They are rewarded with praise and cookies."

In Poland, Christians celebrate "Three Kings Day" with parades across the country. Some liturgical traditions in the West use specific prayers you can find online that would be a great addition to your family's celebration this year.

However you choose to celebrate, do so heralding the revelation of God to man, who stooped to our level by appearing in the flesh to save us. Contemplate that marvelous truth today.

A VALUABLE EMPLOYEE

Be diligent to know the state of your flocks,
and attend to your herds; for riches are not forever,
nor does a crown endure to all generations.
PROVERBS 27:23–24 NKJV

Shepherds need to be experts in the way their animals are bred, sheltered, fed, jugged (separated with their mother for a period after birth), mixed, weened, dewormed, and even how they play, if the shepherds want to make sure their animals thrive.

Just as shepherds need to be diligent about the state of their flocks, the scriptures call you to know the ins and outs of your occupation. You ought to know all of your industry terms and their nuances. As you grow and immerse yourself in your occupation, you should develop knowledge about what will work and what won't. This will make you a valuable asset to your employer, as well as give you some financial stability.

In so doing, you'll set yourself apart from other employees who are simply punching a clock to earn a living. A few of them might also follow your example of diligence. Your boss will certainly take note, at least. But most importantly, you'll be fulfilling your calling as set forth in Colossians 3:23–24 (NKJV): "And whatever you do, do it heartily, as to the Lord and not to men, knowing that from the Lord you will receive the reward of the inheritance; for you serve the Lord Christ."

PRESERVED FOR THE KINGDOM

Love the LORD, all his faithful people! The LORD preserves those
who are true to him, but the proud he pays back in full.
PSALM 31:23 NIV

In today's verse, the psalmist, King David, explains the benefit
of faithfulness to the Lord: He preserves you.

But in what sense? Don't bad things happen to faithful
believers? Certainly, you know believers who have died in car
accidents, suffered from cancer, or been victims of violence.
While God does sometimes intervene in certain cases but not in
others, the psalmist isn't referring to the here and now as much
as he is speaking of the eternal.

Bible commentator John Gill makes this observation in his
Exposition of the Entire Bible: "[T]hese he not only preserves in a
providential way, but he preserves them in a way of special grace;
he keeps them. . .from the evil of sin; from a total and final falling
away by it; from the evil of the world, so as not to be drawn off
from Christ and his ways, either by its frowns or flatteries; and
from the evil one, Satan, from being destroyed by him and his
temptations; and these are preserved safe to the kingdom and
glory of Christ. . ."

Spend some time this morning thanking God for preserving
you, in spite of your unworthiness. And then set your mind and
will on being faithful to Him.

WHO WILL TRUST YOU?

*So if you have not been trustworthy in handling
worldly wealth, who will trust you with true riches?
And if you have not been trustworthy with someone else's
property, who will give you property of your own?*
LUKE 16:11–12 NIV

An NBC news report said federal inspector general agents caught
at least 60 federal workers cheating on time sheets or skipping
out of work without permission since 2012, costing taxpayers
more than one million dollars over a three-year period.

You've probably worked with people who took extended
breaks, stole items from the company, or fudged reports to make
themselves look better. Maybe you've even done it yourself. In
Luke 16, Jesus addresses the ramifications, and they go far beyond
an employee putting himself in jeopardy of termination. Jesus
wants to know, "Who will trust you with true riches" if you can't
be trusted to faithfully perform worldly matters?

True riches is a reference to the Gospel, or as some commentators call it, "the riches of grace." A dishonest person, Christian
or not, will never be trusted.

"If we make Christ our own, and the promises our own, and
heaven our own, we have that which we may truly call our own,"
says Matthew Henry in his *Commentary on the Whole Bible*. But how
can you expect God to trust you with these if you don't serve Him
with your worldly possessions, of which you are but a steward?

OPEN YOUR HOME

*God has given each of you a gift from his great variety
of spiritual gifts. Use them well to serve one another.*
1 PETER 4:10 NLT

When Peter penned these words, the destruction of the Jewish temple and nation were at hand (1 Peter 4:7 NLT). With persecution imminent, Peter wanted believers to maintain their focus. He wanted them to be earnest and disciplined in their prayers, while loving one another, and opening their homes to one another (verses 7–9). Finally, they were to serve one another by using the spiritual gifts that God had given them.

Are you concerned that the end of the American church and nation may be at hand? Are you angry about it—getting caught up in heated political exchanges, sometimes even with fellow believers? Is your bitterness poisoning your heart, affecting your attitude, and rendering you ineffective in your witness? Listen to Peter's advice. Open your home to fellow believers. Pray with them. Study with them. Laugh with them. Weep with them. Serve them using your spiritual gifts.

If you aren't sure about your spiritual gifting, talk to a leader at church to help you identify it. And then begin to exercise it. You'll notice a difference in your attitude as you minister to fellow saints. And you'll make a greater impact for the kingdom of God as unbelievers see your love for other believers in action.

DON'T WAIT

*Farmers who wait for perfect weather never plant.
If they watch every cloud, they never harvest.*
ECCLESIASTES 11:4 NLT

If you've ever glanced at the annual edition of *Farmers' Almanac* (not to be confused with *Old Farmers' Almanac*, which also predicts weather), then you know how specific it gets regarding a prospective planting schedule.

Based on predicted weather patterns, the almanac lists what it believes will be the best days for planting fall potatoes, turnips, onions, carrots, beets, leafy vegetables, peas, squash, corn, beans, peppers, tomatoes, cucumbers, peas, cantaloupes, and more. It also lists days it foresees as *barren*—days that are best left for killing plant pests or doing chores around the farm.

But do farmers actually use these almanacs to determine their planting schedule? A 2016 *Country Living* article about the topic cites a study that says "just 18 percent of farmers use a farmer's almanac when planning their crops." Apparently, many farmers believe the truth of today's verse. If they wait for perfect weather, they'll never plant.

In the next two verses (vv. 5–6), Solomon says a person can't understand the activity of God, and that it's best to "plant your seed in the morning and keep busy all afternoon, for you don't know if profit will come from one activity or another—or maybe both."

The Christian life is one of diligence. It leaves no room for procrastination. What do you need to plant today?

SPEAK NO EVIL

Remind them to be subject to rulers and authorities, to obey,
to be ready for every good work, to speak evil of no one,
to be peaceable, gentle, showing all humility to all men.

TITUS 3:1–2 NKJV

Titus, who was converted to Christianity under Paul's preaching (Titus 1:4), was of Greek descent (Galatians 2:3), and therefore was a Gentile by birth. He traveled with Paul on occasion (2 Corinthians 8:23; Galatians 2:1), and when they visited Crete, Paul decided to leave Titus there to appoint elders in every town (Titus 1:5).

As Titus began to organize the church there, Paul wanted him to remind believers to be subject to rulers and to be peaceable, gentle, and humble toward all men. This was no easy task, given the history and culture of Crete. Adam Clarke makes the following observation in his *Commentary on the Bible*:

> This doctrine of obedience to the civil powers
> was highly necessary for the Cretans, who were
> reputed a people exceedingly jealous of their
> civil privileges, and ready to run into a state of
> insurrection when they suspected any attempt on
> the part of their rulers to infringe their liberties.

How quick are you to consider running into a state of insurrection when you suspect rulers might be infringing on *your* liberties? Do Paul's words in today's verses convict you? How might obedience to civil authorities earn a hearing for the Gospel?

HIDE THE WORD

*Therefore, putting aside all filthiness and all that
remains of wickedness, in humility receive the word
implanted, which is able to save your souls.*

JAMES 1:21 NASB

James, who was probably writing primarily to Jewish converts to Christianity who were dispersed abroad (James 1:1), wanted them to understand that their trials could produce lasting spiritual results because the testing of their faith would produce endurance (v. 3). He wanted them to be quick to hear, slow to speak, and slow to anger (v. 19).

Building on that thought, he told them to put aside all filthiness and other forms of wickedness as they humbly received the Word of God. Putting off wickedness isn't something you do in your flesh. The flesh cries out for wickedness. Instead, putting it off comes as you hear, read, meditate on, and submit to the Word of God. Receiving it in humility means not arguing with it or justifying your sin when the Word confronts it, but rather, recognizing the darkness of our hearts, confessing it, and repenting.

You will never fully escape the pull of wickedness in this world, but the degree to which you struggle with it equates to the amount of time you spend interacting with and submitting to the Word of God. If the world's pull is stronger than it should be in your life now, find more time to hide the Word in your heart so you won't sin against God (see Psalm 119:11).

FAMILY MANAGERS

If anyone does not know how to manage his own family,
how can he take care of God's church?
1 Timothy 3:5 niv

As Paul spelled out the qualifications for a bishop (or deacon) to Timothy, he included the qualification we find in today's verse. A man must be able to manage his own family before he can take care of God's church.

Note that in 1 Timothy 3:1, Paul sets all of this up by saying, "Whoever aspires to be an overseer." In other words, this office isn't a calling, but an aspiration. Think about the setting for a moment. Who would actually aspire to become a bishop/deacon in the hostile environment the first-century church existed in? Persecution and death would have hung around every corner—especially for leaders. Yet, wanting to shepherd young converts is a work of the Holy Spirit who dwells within believers.

As a man, you're called to be a priest in your home. If you don't desire to lovingly lead your family in devotions, prayer, spiritual discussions, and guidance—especially in a country that *allows* such religious freedom—then something is wrong. Yes, Paul's words refer to aspiring bishops in the context of a church, but in a broader context, this should be the call for every Christian man, no matter what his position.

GOD SHOWS NO PARTIALITY

Then Peter opened his mouth and said: "In truth I perceive that God shows no partiality. But in every nation whoever fears Him and works righteousness is accepted by Him."
ACTS 10:34–35 NKJV

On that fateful day in 1963 when the Reverend Martin Luther King Jr. spoke about his dream, he couched it in biblical language, knowing that God shows no partiality. As the Author of all human life, how could He?

"I have a dream that one day every valley shall be exalted, every hill and mountain shall be made low, the rough places will be made plain, and the crooked places will be made straight, and the glory of the Lord shall be revealed, and all flesh shall see it together," King said on that day, confident in the Lord's return and certain that every person would see it.

Racial tensions weren't much different in King's day than they were in Peter's. When the first disciples walked the earth, Jews believed God would never bring Gentiles into the fold. Peter himself believed this until the Lord sent him a vision (Acts 10:9–15) and it changed his perspective. Immediately, the Lord sent Peter to preach the Gospel to Cornelius the centurion and his household. While doing so, the Holy Spirit fell on the Gentiles (Acts 10:34–46).

The scriptures call us to share the Gospel with people who are different from us. How quick are you to do so?

ACCURATE WEIGHTS

The LORD detests the use of dishonest scales,
but he delights in accurate weights.

PROVERBS 11:1 NLT

One of the ancient practices in commerce that scripture refers to often is the use of stones to keep fair and accurate measures.

Deuteronomy 25:13–14 (NKJV) says, " 'You shall not have in your bag differing weights, a heavy and a light. You shall not have in your house differing measures, a large and a small.' " Hosea 12:7 (NKJV) says, " 'A cunning Canaanite! Deceitful scales are in his hand; he loves to oppress.' " And Proverbs 16:11, as well as Proverbs 20:10, addresses this issue of unbalanced scales and using unjust weights.

Today, it would be the equivalent of going to the supermarket and purchasing two pounds of roast beef. You watch the butcher put the meat on the scale, see that it's two pounds, and thank him. But when the person after you places the same order, the butcher switches the scales and places much more meat on the (clearly unjust) scale for the same price you paid.

You would be understandably upset over such a thing. The Lord also detests such business practices. He's just and therefore is on the side of those who are treated unjustly. As you head to your workplace today or slide into your home office chair, consider all *your* business practices. Are they fair and just?

PEACEFUL HOUSEHOLDS

"If the household is worthy, let your peace come upon it.
But if it is not worthy, let your peace return to you."
MATTHEW 10:13 NKJV

When Jesus sent out His twelve apostles, He told them to inquire about those who were worthy (receptive to the Gospel) and to stay with those households (Matthew 10:11–12). Then He told them to let their peace come upon those families.

The Greek word for *peace* here means "by implication prosperity, peace, quietness, rest." The disciples were to seek such peace as they entered a house (Luke 10:5), praying with the occupants, offering instruction, and when they left, leaving a spoken blessing behind. Ultimately, they were seeking to offer peace between those who were receptive and God Himself, through the death of Christ on the cross. But their hosts got a healthy dose of the practical implications of the faith by interacting with the disciples in their homes.

Offering a place for strangers to stay was the custom in the first century, but not so much today, so how can you apply this teaching? You can still inquire about people's receptivity to the Gospel by talking to them in supermarkets, baseball games, and over the backyard fence. And you can also meet receptive people in public places like coffee shops. You might even get invited into their homes to speak peace over their families.

BE COURAGEOUS AND OBEDIENT

*"Only be strong and very courageous; be careful to do
according to all the law which Moses My servant commanded
you; do not turn from it to the right or to the left,
so that you may have success wherever you go."*

Joshua 1:7 NASB

As Israel stood on the edge of the Promised Land, God spoke the words in today's verse to Joshua. Every place Joshua and the Israelites stepped inside the Promised Land would be theirs (v. 3), and no man would be able to stand before Israel because God was with them (v. 5). But His promise was conditional. They were to be strong and courageous, acting according to the Law, so that they'd find success.

Sadly, Israel didn't always follow this instruction, and it cost them dearly. They started off strong, conquering Jericho (Joshua 6). But they stumbled in Ai after Achan sinned against the Lord (Joshua 7), and it cost thirty-six men their lives (Joshua 7:5). They went on to have several more victories and then divided the land among the tribes. After the death of Joshua, the next generation didn't know God and began to serve false gods, forsaking the Lord. He then brought judgment on them (Judges 2:11–15) and let them suffer numerous defeats.

Courage must always be tied to obedience to God. Does this describe your walk with Christ? Have you ever exhibited courage without regard for obedience?

THIRSTING FOR GOD

You, God, are my God, earnestly I seek you; I thirst for you,
my whole being longs for you, in a dry and
parched land where there is no water.

PSALM 63:1 NIV

Physical thirst is tangible. Your throat is dry. Your muscles begin to cramp. In extreme cases, confusion or hallucinations will set in. No matter how severe the case, nobody needs to tell you that you're thirsty. You instinctively know all the signs.

You also know all the signs of thirst for the good things of this world. You know the longing to finally watch a movie you've been waiting to see. You know how it feels to thirst for the presence of a spouse. You know the thirst you feel to hit a physical fitness goal when you're getting close.

But do you know the signs of spiritual thirst? David did. His whole being longed for God. Bible commentator John Gill suggests that spiritual longing will include a deep desire for the Bible, for worship, for church ordinances, for communion, for greater knowledge of Him, and for more grace from Him.

If you aren't thirsty for such things, something is lacking. When David penned the words of today's verse, he was in the wilderness of Judah. Even in such extreme circumstances, he knew and experienced all of the signs of spiritual thirst. If you don't experience this, engage with God and He will slake your thirst today.

YOUR HELP

I look up to the mountains—does my help come from there?
My help comes from the LORD, who made heaven and earth!
PSALM 121:1–2 NLT

In the Old Testament, the Hebrews were accustomed to facing Jerusalem—which was built on a mountain—whenever they prayed (see Daniel 6:10). The temple had been built there on Mount Moriah. Judea itself was mountainous. The ark of the covenant once rested on the holy hill of Zion. So, it's understandable why the Israelites looked to the hills for spiritual help. Other nations believed, in fact, that "the LORD is God of the hills" (1 Kings 20:28 KJV).

But Jeremiah 3:23 (NLT) declared, "Our worship of idols on the hills and our religious orgies on the mountains are a delusion. Only in the LORD our God will Israel ever find salvation." Looking to the hills for help was useless.

Modern Christians turn to all sorts of things in search of spiritual help or deliverance: anointed artifacts, crucifixes, a word of knowledge, even statues. Some even elevate pastors, healers, and spiritual gurus. But your power and salvation don't come from any such activity. It comes from the Lord, who made heaven and earth.

Spend some time today taking spiritual inventory. Have you elevated anything or anyone above God? Maybe the better question to ask yourself is, if anything was removed from your life, would you lack spiritual power? If so, you're depending on that particular object or person too much.

REMEMBERING THEIR CHAINS

I, Paul, write this greeting in my own hand.
Remember my chains. Grace be with you.
COLOSSIANS 4:18 NIV

In April 2014, Boko Haram—an Islamic extremist group—abducted 276 girls in Nigeria, compelling them to convert to Islam and forcing many into marriage, according to Open Doors (an organization that serves persecuted Christians worldwide). Some of the girls escaped, and some have been released via negotiations, but as of 2016, nearly two hundred girls remain missing.

Open Doors advocacy director Kristin Wright met with the parents of the girls in 2015 to let them know that Christians around the world were praying for them. You can imagine the stress they're under. Wright reports that at least eighteen of the parents have died of stress-related diseases since the abduction.

She also made this observation on the organization's website: "However, the fathers we spent time with said they do not see the persecution they are facing as something extraordinary, but as a natural part of being a Christian and walking in the footsteps of Jesus."

In today's verse, the apostle Paul asked fellow believers to remember his chains. This very moment, captive girls need you to remember their chains. As you pray with your family today, remember these girls. Become their advocate. If, by God's grace, they're released, find another group of persecuted Christians and keep your family informed of their plight.

HOPE

*Now the God of hope fill you with all joy and peace
in believing, that ye may abound in hope,
through the power of the Holy Ghost.*
ROMANS 15:13 KJV

If you look around at the unbelievers in your life, all of them are lacking one thing: hope, in the eternal sense. Some have earthly hope, finding it in fulfilling work, wealth, or even family. Others have false hope in their good deeds. But most of the people you know outside of the church have no real assurance or peace about their standing before a holy God.

In Romans 15, Paul explains that Christ is the great hope for Jews and Gentiles alike. In fact, in today's verse, Paul calls Him the God of hope—a title no Gentile could have dared believe in days gone by. Jesus is the long-awaited Messiah. And belief in Him leads to joy and peace in the here and now, but it also settles eternity in the heart of the believer.

Notice, in fact, that Paul is talking to believers here in Romans 15. You know that it's possible for even Christians to fall into despair and to feel genuine sadness. Even Jesus, God's Son, felt sorrow on occasion. But beyond the tears and grief is the great hope of heaven. Not hope in the sense of a child wishing for ice cream, but rather an earnest expectation for deliverance from life's problems.

PLANT, NURTURE, AND WATER

He that gathereth in summer is a wise son: but he that
sleepeth in harvest is a son that causeth shame.
PROVERBS 10:5 KJV

A farmer who doesn't put in the necessary work in the summer shouldn't expect to see a harvest in the fall. Nor should he expect to simply put in the work during the summer and then sleep during the harvest. Planting, nurturing, and gathering all have natural seasons and rhythms. They are not changed by human whims or bouts of laziness.

When you think of a farmer, do you think of someone who avoids work? No. Farmers understand that avoiding work isn't an option. Often they don't even attend worship services during the fall because it's the time for harvesting and that window of time is very limited.

From the big-picture perspective, you're to be about the business of planting and nurturing during your prime income-earning years because a time is coming in the fall and winter of your life when you'll no longer be able to gather as much.

Today's verse is written with a family in mind. A son who gathers and harvests at the appropriate times is wise. He puts the needs of his family before his own wants. Does your work life resemble a farmer's? Are you consistent in your planting and nurturing, knowing that fall is on the way?

LET COOLER HEADS PREVAIL

Let all bitterness, wrath, anger, clamor, and evil speaking be put away from you, with all malice. And be kind to one another, tenderhearted, forgiving one another, even as God in Christ forgave you.

EPHESIANS 4:31–32 NKJV

A worship service in a church in Zimbabwe ended abruptly one Sunday morning in 2016 when some of the members accused the church's provincial secretary and his administration of embezzling funds. One newspaper account said women rushed the altar, crying and praying loudly, while others called for the pastor's blood. Yes, blood.

The chaos began after someone sent an anonymous letter to the church, leveling the accusations. The church did set up a five-member committee to look into the allegations, but tempers flared out of control before any decisions could be reached.

The situation the church found itself in was difficult, no doubt. If funds were used improperly, church members had a right to be upset and to call for action. But the message of today's verse is that cooler heads ought to prevail among believers—and Christians should be gracious and refrain from rushing to judge.

That doesn't mean this congregation shouldn't have looked into the allegations, and even have pressed charges if they were true, but this situation escalated far beyond that. And the church's witness was harmed as a result. If you have issues with somebody in your church, work it out through the proper channels for God's glory.

SLOW, STEADY PROGRESS

The end of a matter is better than its beginning;
patience of spirit is better than haughtiness of spirit.
ECCLESIASTES 7:8 NASB

If you've ever been to a rally—spiritual, sports, or business-related—then you know how a great message can fire up a crowd. Everybody plans to go home and implement what they learned, but as soon as they walk through the door, reality hits them.

The sink is backed up, the car needs repairs, their son needs a ride to soccer practice, and the baby is crying. So, they dive into their responsibilities, and the end of the matter (their new goal) fades as quickly as the emotion that swept through the auditorium hours earlier. They're like "the man who hears the word and immediately receives it with joy; yet he has no firm root in himself, but is only temporary" (Matthew 13:20–21 NASB).

In today's verse, Solomon calls you to be patient of spirit as you set your mind on something. If your goal is to read God's Word every day without fail, then tend to your responsibilities, but try getting up a little earlier. If your goal is to walk five miles a day, start with one mile and work your way up. If your goal is to set a new sales record, then study the current leader and carefully implement his strategies.

Slow, steady progress beats quick, emotional commitment every time. The end is better than the beginning.

A GOOD SOLDIER

Thou therefore endure hardness,
as a good soldier of Jesus Christ.
2 TIMOTHY 2:3 KJV

Because of God's grace, Paul wanted Timothy to understand that the Christian can and should endure much hardship as a good soldier of Jesus. Consider the hardship a soldier of your country endures for your sake.

He leaves family and friends behind. He leaves career advancement behind. He leaves his personal dreams behind. In their place, he endures hunger, sleep deprivation, and constant threats and danger. Why would someone put himself through something like that?

Partially because he loves his country—the country that granted him his freedom to have a family, to pursue a career, and to chase his dreams. Partially because he knows that if he doesn't go, someone else might *not* and his nation's borders might be insecure. And partially because he wants to keep his family, friends, and community safe. In all three instances, he's motivated by love and a sense of duty.

This is the life that every Christian man is called to—except that your calling is to advance and preach the Gospel of Christ so the next generation can know His grace. You sacrifice and endure hardship because He sacrificed and endured for you. If you haven't been living the life of a solider of Christ, reenlist in His army and pick up your spiritual weapons.

REORIENTATION

Let everyone see that you are considerate in all you do.
Remember, the Lord is coming soon.
PHILIPPIANS 4:5 NLT

At first glance, it's surprising to see Paul telling believers in Philippi to let everyone see that they're considerate in all they do. Aren't Christians supposed to avoid calling attention to themselves? Elsewhere, scripture says to not let your left hand know what your right hand is doing (Matthew 6:3). A few verses later, Jesus tells His disciples to pray in private (v. 6).

But a closer look at all these verses reveals no contradiction with today's verse. In verse 3, Jesus was talking to His disciples about giving in secret to avoid drawing attention to themselves for the sake of self-glorification. And in verse 6, He was talking about not praying for show. Paul, on the other hand, wants believers to live out loud for God's sake, not their own, because Jesus is coming back soon. Having that sense of urgency reorients the way a person lives and keeps him from becoming self-centered.

If you knew Jesus was coming back today, how would it change the way you lived your faith? You'd probably have a short account with God, making sure that each action you took glorified Him. You'd empty yourself of selfish ambitions and seek the good of those around you.

Wouldn't that be a refreshing way to live? Prayerfully commit yourself to such a vision.

WORDS LIKE MEDICINE

Gentle words are a tree of life;
a deceitful tongue crushes the spirit.
PROVERBS 15:4 NLT

What is the most hurtful thing anybody has ever said to you? Can you recall the circumstances? How long ago was it? Did you embrace it as truth—even if it wasn't true—and allow it to affect your life for more years than you care to admit?

Have you ever said something hurtful to somebody that you wished you could take back a second after it left your lips? You saw the reaction on the other person's face, and it confirmed the devastation you realized it might bring. You can say you're sorry later, and that helps, but you can't unsay those words.

Gentle words are a tree of life. That doesn't mean you can't be truthful, but it does mean you should be gentle. Even tough love can be gentle. Some translations (NIV, NASB) use the word *soothing* in place of *gentle*, and the KJV has *wholesome*. The Hebrew word actually means "medicine, cure, deliverance, and remedy," among other things.

Are your words like medicine? Do they offer deliverance and a cure? Or are they sometimes deceitful or crushing? Consider how the negative words you recalled so easily at the beginning of this devotion affected you and resolve to not weigh anybody down with such a tone going forward.

GOD STILL SPEAKS

We ourselves heard that voice from heaven
when we were with him on the holy mountain.
2 PETER 1:18 NLT

At the transfiguration, Peter saw something that changed him—giving him a message he wanted people to hear. He says James, John, and he himself saw Christ's majestic splendor with their own eyes as Christ received honor and glory from the Father. Can you imagine what that must have looked like? And if that wasn't enough, they heard the very voice of God say, "This is my dearly loved Son, who brings me great joy" (2 Peter 1:17 NLT).

The apostles went on to pass this truth along to the other disciples, and ultimately the Church throughout the ages via the scriptures. The three who climbed the mountain with Jesus had a firsthand account of Christ's majesty. You don't have to wonder about it in the abstract. Jesus is God's dearly loved Son, who brings Him great joy.

God has spoken to His people differently from one generation to the next. He talked from a burning bush, whispered on the wind, and even spoke through a donkey. But when Jesus arrived in the flesh, God spoke audibly.

If you've been seeking proof of God's existence before placing your faith in Christ, here you have it—an eyewitness account. If you have become more trusting because the Spirit bore witness with your spirit, then praise God that you can also experience that.

HEAVENLY THOUGHTS

*The mind governed by the flesh is death, but the mind
governed by the Spirit is life and peace.*

Romans 8:6 niv

If you've ever wondered how a Christian is supposed to set his mind
on what the Spirit desires, Paul's admonition to a Greek church
(Philippians 4:8 niv) is a great place to start: "Finally, brothers
and sisters, whatever is true, whatever is noble, whatever is right,
whatever is pure, whatever is lovely, whatever is admirable—if
anything is excellent or praiseworthy—think about such things."

While you'll never fully achieve success in doing so, when
you begin to steadfastly meditate on truth, things that are noble,
pure, lovely—and anything praiseworthy—you'll notice a decrease
in your fleshly desires. Your actions are in direct response to
your thoughts, and pure thoughts result in pure actions. Impure
thoughts become impure actions.

Practically speaking, you might begin to change your thinking
by finding and meditating on a different Bible verse every day;
or you might consider how to overhaul a system at work so
everything is aboveboard and transparent; or you could begin
discipling a man who needs someone to walk alongside him
(which means you'll be praying for him and always thinking
about your next meeting).

"Set your minds on things above, not on earthly things,"
Paul writes to the Christians at Colossae (Colossians 3:2–3 niv).
"For you died, and your life is now hidden with Christ in God."

FULL OF GOODNESS

*And concerning you, my brethren, I myself also am convinced
that you yourselves are full of goodness, filled with all
knowledge and able also to admonish one another.*

ROMANS 15:14 NASB

When a man is converted to Christ, a seismic shift takes place
in his soul. He begins the process of being transformed into a
new person as the Holy Spirit directs. The Christians in Rome
eventually reached a point in which Paul said he was convinced
that they were full of goodness, filled with all knowledge, and
able to admonish one another. The three go hand in hand.

As your new nature becomes more concerned with pleasing
God and helping others, you're filled with knowledge from on
high to the point that you're able to teach new converts about
putting off the old man. It's a lifelong pursuit, and you'll never
arrive. You might even take one step forward and two steps back
on occasion, but don't let that stop you.

If your pastor had to describe your level of spiritual maturity,
could he say the same thing about you that Paul said about these
believers in Rome? Would he be confident in your goodness? Has
your pastor witnessed you being filled with godly knowledge? Has
that led you to encourage fellow believers in your congregation?
You shouldn't merely try to please your pastor, but he's bound
to learn about your steady habits.

A HISTORY OF WISDOM

*The entirety of Your word is truth, and every one
of Your righteous judgments endures forever.*
PSALM 119:160 NKJV

On this day in 1790, Chief Justice John Jay presided over the first meeting of the highest judiciary body of history's most audacious experiment in democracy. Since then, the Supreme Court has made top-level decisions, for better and for worse, throughout America's history, its interpretations, resolutions, and judgments based on a single enduring document, the US Constitution— which has been amended and reinterpreted but never replaced.

God's Word is the only document with a better pedigree and record of reliability. But where the Constitution, for all its strengths, was created by fallible humans, the Bible was inspired by a perfect, good, and just God. His words will never pass away (Matthew 24:35), and they contain the riches of wisdom (Proverbs 2:4). A wise man makes no decisions without them. And God stands ready and willing to give you all the wisdom you need—if you'll just ask (James 1:5).

The US Supreme Court has made decisions with life and death impacts on the nation. The decisions you make each day also have impact, too, so make sure the Holy Spirit governs your words. Jesus promised that, as you seek and follow Him, He " 'will give you a mouth and wisdom which all your adversaries will not be able to contradict or resist' " (Luke 21:15 NKJV). Trust in the only wisdom that will outlast history.

BREAK THE CYCLE

As a dog returns to its vomit, so fools repeat their folly.
PROVERBS 26:11 NIV

Today is Groundhog Day, and in the movie *Groundhog Day*, Bill Murray plays Phil, an arrogant weatherman who relives the same day over and over until he learns to become a better person. Because it's a movie, the process has a sort of inevitability—you know Phil will learn his lesson, realize that other people have feelings, and get the girl in the end, snapping the time loop and moving forward.

Real life offers no such guarantees. The world promises liberty in the form of things that sound like the work of an accomplished man—a successful career, the ability to hold your liquor (and lots of it), and the attention of desirable women. But true freedom in Christ delivers you from the dark side of those same things—enslavement to the corporate ladder, hangovers and addiction, and empty affairs that leave you feeling less than you were meant to be.

It's even worse if you know Jesus and then return to those old-man habits. It's no different than when your dog eats his own upchuck. The only true freedom from a Groundhog Day cycle of sin is to give your life wholly and unreservedly to Jesus. The future He has for you won't be problem-free, but you'll be free of the pressure to conform to the world and its ways.

WONDERS OF A HIDDEN WORLD

O LORD, how manifold are Your works! . . .This great and
wide sea, in which are innumerable teeming
things, living things both small and great.
PSALM 104:24–25 NKJV

On this day in 1953, Jacques Cousteau published his most famous work, *The Silent World*. The film of the book revealed previously unseen vistas of the world beneath the waves—tropical fish and whales and coral reefs.

Some of God's best gifts are found in the great outdoors—and you don't have to be a world-class kayaker or hardcore rock climber to appreciate them. Simple pleasures like sunsets and constellations aren't just indulgences for guys with extra time on their hands. They're an essential part of the way that God speaks. "Day unto day utters speech, and night unto night reveals knowledge" (Psalm 19:2 NKJV). Are you listening?

If you can, carve out some time to get out in the natural world and look for God's hand at work. If you're thinking, *Rocks and trees just don't do it for me*, you can still look for God's handiwork in your daily life. Of all the marvels of creation, humans are at the top of the list. Everyone you see, though damaged by sin and life experiences, is a beloved son or daughter of the Creator. Each is fearfully and wonderfully made, and there's nothing better than being a part of God's purposes in your interactions with them.

EXCEED YOUR GRASP

But now they desire a better, that is, a heavenly country.
Therefore God is not ashamed to be called their
God, for He has prepared a city for them.
HEBREWS 11:16 NKJV

Some Christians have been accused of being so heavenly minded that they're no earthly good. While that may be so, without the promise of heaven's peace, justice, and reward to inspire you, putting all your hope in this world does you no eternal good. The poet Robert Browning was onto something when he wrote, "A man's reach should exceed his grasp, or what's a heaven for?"

When Joseph and Mary found their twelve-year-old son in the temple, He told them, "Why did you seek Me? Did you not know that I must be about My Father's business?" (Luke 2:49 NKJV). Through the parable of the minas, Jesus told His followers, "Do business till I come" (Luke 19:13 NKJV). The challenge is clear: do whatever you do with the ultimate goal of building God's kingdom.

The full impact of your work on earth is measured not in material wealth but spiritual. How have you used what God has given you to see souls saved? That effort starts at home, extends through the church, and goes out into the world, always with the objective of seeing as many as possible arrive at the wonderful home God has for them. If you look beyond the cares of this world, you can just see it.

FAITHFUL IS SUCCESSFUL

*Make it your ambition to lead a quiet life and attend
to your own business and work with your hands.*
1 THESSALONIANS 4:11 NASB

In the parable of the talents (Matthew 25:14–30), Jesus told of three men, each of whom was given a different amount of money, "each according to his ability" (Matthew 25:15 NIV). The first two doubled their investment but the third held onto his money and was condemned for doing nothing with it. That tells you a few things about God's definition of success.

First, success comes when you've done the work in front of you—the work God has "prepared in advance" for you to do (Ephesians 2:10 NIV). It also means that God hasn't assigned everyone the same type of work, or given everyone the same resources, but it *does* mean that whatever He has given you is enough for you to do your job. So, no matter what you do for a living, do it to honor God.

No amount of money can increase God's kingdom, but one man, whether he's digging ditches or investing stocks, can make the difference for the people he's working with, one at a time, to build the eternal nation. When you're focused on living the life God has for you, "attending to your own business" takes on a fresh attitude—you're minding God's business. In His view, to be faithful is to be successful.

REALITY-CHECK THE PECKING ORDER

But if you show favoritism, you sin.
JAMES 2:9 NIV

It's natural for men to establish a pecking order. Whether it's at work, playing softball, or raking leaves—if other guys are involved, you want to know where you stand. Which guys are stronger, smarter, faster, and which aren't? But while it's fine to get the lay of the land, it can also provide a false standard of a person's worth. What better shows a man's worth—a sports car and a fat stock portfolio, or the way he treats those from whom he has nothing to gain?

The message of the Gospel is not about getting in good with the Guy who can get you in the pearly gates—you can't. It's not about impressing heaven with earthly success—you won't. The cross reveals an unsettling truth: we're all on the same footing before God and the earth is shaking. But Jesus offers a hand up to rich and poor alike; the guy in the penthouse and the one in the gutter matter equally to Him.

That's why James spoke against saving seats up front at church for the wealthy contingent; if anything, Jesus wants you to save a seat for the guy who's lost it all, whose sin has messed up his life and hurt others to boot. Save a special place in your heart for the man with the greatest need. It's what Jesus did for you.

WHAT'S REALLY POSSIBLE?

Behold, I am the LORD, the God of all flesh:
is there any thing too hard for me?
JEREMIAH 32:27 KJV

You've met the man who considers it a mark of his intelligence to try to outsmart the Bible. He's the one who knows you're a Christian and makes it a priority to let you know that there's no way Jonah could've survived three days in a whale's belly, or that there must have been some mass hallucination when Joshua and his army fought under a sun that stood still in the sky.

He conveniently ignores the real miracles—that a resistant prophet's message caused the biggest, most wicked city of his day to repent, from the king down to the kids. Or that God actually let a man call the shots for a day and obliged him with a meteorological wonder. Really, though, if you can believe the first line of the Bible—that God created the heavens and the earth—the rest is easy.

And a God who can speak everything you can see and know into existence—and a whole bunch of things you can't—is a God who can take care of your needs. Take your cares to Him, even the one about the guy at the office who thinks he knows better than his Creator. Maybe he's closer to faith than either of you could ever imagine; after all, God's done bigger miracles than that.

REAL POWER

"My grace is all you need. My power works best in weakness."
2 CORINTHIANS 12:9 NLT

When Anthony "Spud" Webb bounced the ball off the glass and threw down a tomahawk slam to win the NBA Slam Dunk Contest on February 8, 1986, the entire crowd had forgotten he was only five feet seven inches tall—the shortest player ever to win.

Webb's triumph reflects God's favorite method of accomplishing His work in the world: using the least likely people to do the most amazing things. Look at the men He put to work: Moses stuttered, Gideon hid in a hole, David was a kid herding sheep, and Paul was as hard-boiled a Pharisee as ever hunted a Christian. Each of them resisted God's call on their life; each one He told, "Don't worry. I'm with you." After they accepted that key truth, they accomplished great things.

If you think you're the least likely person God could ever use, you might be right. But have you realized that your inability opens the door for His ability? And if you think you've got a lot going for you, God can still use you. He might have to trip you up a bit to remind you that you need Him, but when He does, be receptive to your weakness. When you're open to God's guidance, that's when you'll really make a difference in the world.

FINISHING STRONG

"I wholly followed the LORD my God. . . . As yet I am
as strong this day as on the day Moses sent me."
JOSHUA 14:8, 11 NKJV

Following a five-decade career as a pitcher, Leroy "Satchel" Paige became the first Negro Leagues veteran to be nominated for the Hall of Fame on February 9, 1971. Paige broke into the majors in 1948 as a forty-two-year-old rookie, and later pitched three innings at fifty-nine. Asked about his accomplishments at such an experienced age, Satchel famously quoted Mark Twain, "Age is a question of mind over matter. If you don't mind, it doesn't matter."

That's a statement Caleb, son of Jephunneh, would have fully embraced. As one of the advance spies Moses sent to scout the promised land, he brought back a report detailing the challenges but undergirded by his belief that God could handle whatever giants and walled cities awaited. Because of Israel's unbelief, he didn't get his chance to make good on God's promise until he was eighty-five years old.

But when the call to move into the land came, there he was, ready to take the battle to the enemy. Caleb knew that if God was with him, nothing could stop him, not fortified cities nor huge armies nor trick knees, cataracts, and high cholesterol. There are few things more inspiring than a godly man finishing strong, and it starts with the belief that God isn't done with you till He's done with you.

LET GOD AVENGE YOU

*"Is there not still someone of the house of Saul,
to whom I may show the kindness of God?"*
2 SAMUEL 9:3 NKJV

When God's Spirit departed from Israel's first king, Saul hunted his replacement, the young shepherd who had killed a giant and played peaceful harmonies to lull his troubled soul. David lived on the run for years, refusing to fight back against God's anointed, even when presented with two ideal opportunities to end Saul's life.

David not only passed up taking revenge, but after Saul died in battle, he sought out his remaining descendants, not to kill them and consolidate his power but to see if he could do them any good.

In David's day, mercy was seen as weakness. To refuse to retaliate or return a slight to your honor tainted you in most eyes as unreliable. The whole turning-the-other-cheek thing would have been as ridiculous to them as wearing a clown nose to meet your future in-laws would be to you.

But, as David demonstrated, the higher virtue is in being able to avenge yourself but refusing to do so. It takes faith to refrain—a belief that when God said vengeance belonged to Him (Proverbs 25:21–22; Romans 12:19), He meant it. Not only will He hold you accountable for all you've said and done, He'll do the same for everyone else. Have the faith to let Him.

SET YOUR EYES ON GOD

Be sure you know the condition of your flocks,
give careful attention to your herds.
PROVERBS 27:23 NIV

What's your vision for your family? Through all the challenges He faced, Jesus had a single vision: to do the will of the Father. God's will is often clear in scripture: men are the spiritual leaders of their families, kids are supposed to obey parents, dads aren't supposed to wear kids out with constant criticism, and we are to respect authorities because God put them in charge.

But more than a list of *dos* and *don'ts*, doing God's will means recognizing that you're a part of His greater story, not the other way around. The best thing you can do for your family is be the man He asks you to be—a husband and father committed to following Him. One of the ways you do that is by becoming an expert on each member of your family—their strengths, weaknesses, love languages, and daily challenges. Through it all, listen before you speak, stay calm, pray tons, and do it all with love.

That will move you out of your comfort zone at times, and you will make mistakes. Worry less about goofing up than developing the overall vision. Jesus knows you—all your ups and downs—and still thinks you were worth dying for. How's that for a model of the kind of love you should show your family?

LOVE'S HONEST WORK

Let us not love with word or with tongue,
but in deed and truth.
1 JOHN 3:18 NASB

On this, Abraham Lincoln's birthday, tales of his legendary honesty spring to mind—how he walked miles to repay a woman a few pennies, or how even his two-time political opponent Stephen Douglas called him an honest man. Of course, Lincoln had his enemies, but, friend or foe, no one questioned where they stood with him. Because of that degree of sincerity in his words and conduct, he was able to set his mind to solving problems with all his cards on the table.

One of the few direct commands Jesus gave His followers was to love others (John 13:34–35). It was a clear way for them to identify with Him, and to identify themselves as His followers to nonbelievers. But the kind of love Jesus was talking about has less to do with warm feelings or pulled heartstrings than it does with hard, honest effort. Jesus loved sacrificially, giving up divine privilege to come be whipped, beaten, and executed painfully and shamefully.

Given that kind of commitment, you can see how real love is not for wimps. It demands a burning drive to seek someone else's best and highest good, even if you do so imperfectly. But the occasional wrong note played in an honest attempt to love someone beats the "clanging cymbal" of a life lived without it (1 Corinthians 13:1).

ON THE BLEEDING EDGE

Have we not all one Father? Has not one God created us?
Why do we deal treacherously with one another. . . ?
MALACHI 2:10 NKJV

On this day in 1905, Teddy Roosevelt gave a stirring speech on race relations. The wounds of the Civil War and Reconstruction lingered between North and South, as did the question, *When will every citizen be treated equally, regardless of color?* Though Roosevelt addressed primarily whites, exhorting compassion to all, his words did little to advance the conversation. To his credit, though, he nailed the issue at the end of his speech, quoting the wisdom of Solomon: "Righteousness exalts a nation, but sin condemns any people" (Proverbs 14:34 NIV).

Jesus died because God loved the whole world, and His blood unifies all believers in a family where no man-made distinctions apply (Galatians 3:28). When it comes to salvation, we all stand on the same ground: "For there is one God and one mediator between God and mankind, the man Christ Jesus, who gave himself as a ransom for all people" (1 Timothy 2:5–6 NIV).

Living that out, however, is much more complicated. That's the best reason for the church—and you as a Christian man—to take the lead in the discussion, modeling God's vision of equality, grace, and forgiveness. Start with prayer, and remember: the blood of Christ can unite us in ways that are beyond race and ethnicity. They're genuine connections of spirit that will last into eternity.

CHAMPIONING LOVE

"We must obey God rather than men."
ACTS 5:29 NASB

Some people write off Valentine's Day (perhaps correctly) as a holiday manufactured by greeting card companies. That's a far cry from its far less trite, far bloodier origins. Way before Hallmark entered the scene, Rome ruled the world through a series of rather unstable emperors. One of the more dangerous and sociopathic ones, Claudius II, outlawed engagements and marriage because he thought that men were failing to enlist in the army due to their strong connections with their wives and families.

In AD 278, a Christian priest named Valentine defied the emperor and began to perform secret weddings. When Claudius the Cruel found out, he had Valentine arrested, beaten, and beheaded. Later, Pope Gelasius declared in AD 496 that February 14 would be celebrated as Saint Valentine's Day, in honor of the martyred priest's championing of love and obedience to God's call.

You live in a time when honoring God by observing His guidelines for love is increasingly unpopular. To commit to one woman for life takes a different degree of courage than it used to—though, done right, it's never been a cakewalk. So, even if you're staging a principled boycott from buying your sweetheart a card today, make sure she knows that you're willing to lose your head for her.

ALONE BUT NOT ALONE

How can a young man cleanse his way?
By taking heed according to Your word.
PSALM 119:9 NKJV

Somehow, it's fitting that the day after Valentine's Day has been claimed as Singles Awareness Day. You know—*Go hug a single; they're lonely—no! Not you; you're single!* That caught-in-betweenness can be confusing and painful when you're an unwed Christian.

Being single carries its own joys and challenges. When you're single, you make all kinds of good decisions. Cereal for dinner? Good call! Jeans standing upright in the corner? Still got two wears in 'em! When it comes to where you go and what you'll do, it's just you and God—a stripped-down, efficient operation.

Of course, singleness isn't always a gift. Sometimes, it's downright lonely, never more so than when you're in a crowded room, feeling a lack of connection to a special someone. And then there's porn—the devil's most effective workshop for idleness. That's when you lean hard into God's Word and plans, knowing that they don't include feeding your lust or pouring your heart into fantasies (Romans 13:14).

If you can trust God and commit to following Him when it's just you and Him, you're on track for the life God wants you to have, whether you stay single or not. And if you end up abandoning the ranks of singledom, you'll be on track to being the husband your wife needs and deserves.

OLD GUNSLINGERS DIE HARD

" 'These people honor me with their lips,
but their hearts are far from me.' "
MATTHEW 15:8 NLT

The notorious gunslinger John Wesley Hardin was pardoned on this day in 1894. After spending the previous fifteen years in jail for murder, he got on the right side of the law after his release, becoming an attorney. His past came back to haunt him, however, and an ugly exchange over a man's wife, coupled with Hardin's violent reputation, heavy drinking, and gambling, ended with him being shot in the back in an El Paso saloon.

Hardin had behaved himself in prison, even becoming a Sunday school leader. It sounds like the kind of thing God does, getting ahold of a man at his lowest point and changing his heart. But foxhole conversions carry an inherent risk: when the moment of desperation is past, will a man continue to seek and follow Christ, or will he fall back into old, sinful habits?

Whichever it was with Hardin, what seems clear is that there was enough of his old ways about him that his enemies couldn't see the evidence of a changed heart.

In that sense, it didn't matter whether or not he was in an actual jail cell; John Wesley Hardin was imprisoned by his own pride and vices. He may have ended up on the right side of man's law, but he lost the battle of the Spirit versus the flesh (Galatians 5:16–18).

REASON TO REJOICE

We can rejoice, too, when we run into problems and trials,
for we know that they help us develop endurance.
ROMANS 5:3 NLT

At various points in your life, you'll sit on the other side of the table from bad news. Sometimes, you'll see it coming, but more often than not, it'll ambush you, a single shot from a stun gun: *downsizing, accident, cancer*. Somehow, you press on, working through the immediate details as if from a distance, and it's only later when you have a moment to breathe that the grief comes on. You wrestle with the *whys* and the *what nexts*, and begin to find out what you're made of.

Like a cup that's been filled to the brim with whatever you've poured into your heart over the course of your life, when a hard trial strikes, what's inside spills over. If you've habitually sown to the flesh, bitterness gushes out, blended with hopelessness. All your self-sufficiency comes to nothing, and you let God know how He has disappointed you.

But if you've habitually sown to the Spirit, it's different. Previous trials forced you to your knees, but that's where you found God waiting to comfort and strengthen you. You know that Paul wasn't just spouting some holy-sounding advice about tribulation, because you've seen the truth behind it: God uses trials to produce endurance, building character and producing hope. When hope spills over, you have reason to rejoice: God is with you.

DO JUSTICE

*Don't let anyone look down on you because you are young,
but set an example for the believers in speech,
in conduct, in love, in faith and in purity.*
1 TIMOTHY 4:12 NIV

On this day in 1943, German college students and siblings Hans and Sophie Scholl, leaders of the resistance group The White Rose, were arrested by the Gestapo for distributing pamphlets criticizing Hitler and the Nazi regime. They were tried in a kangaroo court reserved for political dissidents and beheaded five days later, their young lives cut short because of their willingness to stand against tyranny.

Inspired by their parents' outspoken criticism of the Nazis, Hans and Sophie chose nonviolent resistance, even though they knew it could lead to their deaths. They looked at the world around them, saw injustice, rallied their Lutheran principles and their courage, and acted.

A key marker of a man of God, whether young or old, is a love of justice. Over and over, the Bible calls God's people "to do right; seek justice. Defend the oppressed. Take up the cause of the fatherless; plead the case of the widow" (Isaiah 1:17 NIV).

Along these lines, the apostle John asked a probing question: "Whoever has this world's goods, and sees his brother in need, and shuts up his heart from him, how does the love of God abide in him?" (1 John 3:17 NKJV). No matter your age, what will you do with what God has given you?

A GREATER VISION

He made himself nothing by taking the very nature
of a servant, being made in human likeness.
Philippians 2:7 NIV

Today is Presidents' Day, and though George Washington was elected America's first president in 1789, the most remarkable thing he ever did was *give up* his power. So potent were Washington's popularity and leadership that there was a public outcry that he remain president as long as he would.

His guidance of the nation in its infancy, however, was matched only by his desire to see it thrive beyond his life, and to do so, there needed to be a safe, stable transfer of power. It was unheard of to give up power—still true today!—especially when victory had been so hard fought for and won, but Washington had a bigger vision.

God had an even more impressive vision for all of mankind—a way to buy His people back from sin and its deprivations—and He had just the Man for the job. Where Washington gave up his office so that he could enjoy the fruits of his accomplishments (and justifiably so!), Jesus gave up His place in heaven at God's right hand to be bound by the frailty of flesh and blood, to have needs and urges, to face temptation and opposition and betrayal firsthand (unheard of!).

He fought your biggest foes—sin, death, and hell—to be able to adopt you as a son and brother.

PUT OUT FIRES BEFORE THEY START

He that covereth his sins shall not prosper:
but whoso confesseth and forsaketh them shall have mercy.
PROVERBS 28:13 KJV

Tragedy struck a Rhode Island nightclub on this day in 2003, when pyrotechnics from a rock concert ignited a fire that killed one hundred people. The band Great White insisted in their contract that a certain type of fireworks be used, but the club's safety standards weren't up to the task, and people died as a result.

Van Halen had a contract rider requiring that no brown M&Ms be found among their green room snacks. Rather than a diva move, it was actually a safeguard: the band knew that if they found brown M&Ms, the venue hadn't reviewed or abided by the contract. They would then go through the hall with a fine-toothed comb, almost inevitably finding potential safety hazards that would have caused disaster had they gone unaddressed.

Sin works like that in your life, a hidden livewire behind the walls of your life, just waiting to set it aflame and burn you down. Sin progresses like a burning fuse: desire tempts you, then drags you away to do its bidding. Once it has conceived, it gives birth to sin, which grows up and gives birth to death (James 1:13–15).

Whatever temptation beckons you—whether women, status, or wealth—root it out at the point of contact, like a brown M&M you know isn't supposed to be there.

EVERYDAY DOUBLE AGENTS

A double minded man is unstable in all his ways.
JAMES 1:8 KJV

Aldrich Ames, a CIA operative, was arrested on this day in 1994 and charged with selling secrets to the Soviet Union. The information he sold had led to the exposure, arrest, and deaths of dozens of CIA operatives in the East Bloc. His careless spending on pricey homes and cars led to *his* arrest, and he eventually received a life sentence.

Ames is one of history's most infamous double agents, but a far greater number of men have, in similar ways, sabotaged themselves spiritually. While they haven't sold state secrets to enemy nations, they have secretly tried to have it both their way and God's way. These nominal Christians put on all the airs of discipleship, shaking hands and offering prayers on Sunday morning but carrying on with affairs, shady business deals, and self-serving behavior the rest of the week.

James called this behavior being "double minded." A man like that will fool a lot of people a lot of the time, but never God. As Paul wrote, "Don't be misled—you cannot mock the justice of God. You will always harvest what you plant" (Galatians 6:7 NLT). When you know about God and His ways but try to play both sides rather than giving *all* you are over to Him, you'll destabilize your whole life. Better to trust Him all the way or not at all.

BETWEEN THE HIGHS AND LOWS

When pride comes, then comes disgrace,
but with humility comes wisdom.
PROVERBS 11:2 NIV

On this date in 1980, the upstart United States upset the mighty Soviet Union in Olympic hockey. The "Miracle on Ice" became the slapshot heard 'round the world, as a bunch of plucky college kids beat a Russian Army machine made of men paid to destroy their opponents. Even decades later, Soviet team members lived in a state of general denial about that day. It was simply unimaginable—reminiscent of another historical upset, when a shepherd boy laid low a giant warrior in the valley of Elah.

If Goliath had survived, he would never have lived his defeat down. As his people's champion, the thought of losing to an enemy runt just wouldn't have registered on any level but that of a fading nightmare. The blame wouldn't have been a matter of pure vanity as much as bone-deep complacency. What had no doubt begun as a military career of overwhelming might and success had become a legacy of laziness—susceptible to being shattered by a Hebrew "stick" and his deadly stone.

The lesson is simple: don't let yourself get too comfortable. Life is both mountains and valleys because God knows that's what you need to become the man He wants you to be. God won't abandon you in the lows, but don't forget Him during the highs. Being faithful in between is what defines you as His.

AS IF THROUGH FIRE

If anyone's work which he has built. . .endures, he will receive
a reward. If anyone's work is burned, he will suffer loss;
but he himself will be saved, yet so as through fire.
1 Corinthians 3:14–15 NKJV

When Prussian military officer Friedrich von Steuben arrived at Valley Forge on this day in 1778, he had his work cut out for him. Washington had hired him to whip the worn-down and disorderly Continental Army into shape. All through that brutal winter, von Steuben did just that, instilling exacting discipline and basic hygiene with outstanding efficiency. His methods helped turn the tide not only of that miserable season but the entire war.

Just as the dream of a free nation wasn't enough by itself to bring about victory for Washington's men, so faith isn't an automatic ticket to success in life. Once the foundation of Christ is laid, you still have to build on it—and the materials you use are crucial.

Just like with the Three Little Pigs, it's easier to build with straw than with bricks, but only one will withstand the wolf. Each choice you make—praying in the morning instead of sleeping in that extra fifteen, unplugging the laptop rather than watching porn, talking with your wife before you make a big decision instead of afterward—places a brick on your foundation instead of straw. Discipline wins the internal battles that help win the external war.

ANSWER THE CALL

He saw a large crowd, and He felt compassion for them
because they were like sheep without a shepherd;
and He began to teach them many things.
MARK 6:34 NASB

When Colonel William Travis sent out a desperate plea for help to defend the Alamo on February 24, 1836, he knew things were headed south in a hurry. Only thirty-two men from a nearby town responded to his call, and while it's likely that even a turnout of hundreds wouldn't have been enough to hold off the Mexican army, no one will ever know because so few came to the aid of their brothers-in-arms.

When Jesus told us to pray for God to send workers out into the ripe harvest fields, the next thing He said was, "Go! I am sending you out like lambs among wolves" (Luke 10:3 NIV). Even if you leave the work of conviction to its rightful handler, the Holy Spirit, it still takes courage to go out and share about Jesus.

If you don't feel equipped, get equipped. Seek an experienced, trustworthy believer to guide you through walking with God. If you already know how, equip others. The battle is right there, not just in the world, but in your home, at work, and in the church. Keep your knees bent and your eyes peeled; ask God to break your heart with what breaks His. The call has been sent to get involved. How will you answer Him today?

THE BIGGER PICTURE

*Do you despise the riches of His goodness, forbearance,
and longsuffering, not knowing that the goodness
of God leads you to repentance?*

ROMANS 2:4 NKJV

Why is patience a virtue? Sometimes, people just need to be corrected—like your kids when they're headed for the wall socket with a fork, or the server when she brings your steak well done instead of medium rare. That guy at work who keeps taking your lunch out of the fridge needs to be stopped, and the committee you're on at church is about to make a bad decision about buying a piano. You sitting back and being "patient" isn't going to help anyone.

In those situations, quick action and uncompromising conversations are needed. You're right to act; there are matters of safety, courtesy, professionalism, and stewardship at stake. But *how* will you do it? There's the rub.

Think of all the times Jesus' disciples messed up—Peter with his ongoing foot-in-mouth disease, or John and James arguing over who should be top dog or calling down fire on entire villages. Sometimes you bluntly share your mind, only to succeed in offending people. So frustrating!

While Jesus did correct His followers' failures, He was gentle, courteous, and polite. He saw a bigger picture—their overarching needs rather than their momentary misdeeds. Patience, then, seems to be made up of other virtues—love, mercy, and humility among them. Consider God's patience when others test yours.

BROKEN BUT BEAUTIFUL

The earth suffers for the sins of its people, for they have
twisted God's instructions, violated his laws,
and broken his everlasting covenant.

ISAIAH 24:5 NLT

Two national parks were established on February 26, ten years apart: the Grand Canyon (1919) and the Grand Tetons (1929). The idea was to conserve and protect America's stunning natural vistas, ecosystems, and wildlife. The implication, however, was that they needed protecting. Sin's effects include the breaking of nature.

What many Jews call *tikkun olam*—"repairing the world"— includes morally righteous behavior as a way of fixing hearts, which would then act rightly toward other people, as well as the environment. Messianic Jews see that work as ongoing, but only completely possible—and possible to complete—in the person and work of Jesus Christ.

The wounds that Jesus came to heal include those our sin has wrought on the world (Isaiah 53:4–5). The peace that His blood purchased for mankind will be extended toward healing the earth during the kingdom age (Isaiah 11:6–9).

There's a middle path between rampant industrial greed and radical environmentalism: biblical stewardship. Nothing you can know, see, or hear has been spared sin's impact—not a mountain range or a whale or a redwood. However, God's beautiful creation, though broken, is still worth preserving. Even knowing the earth will get an extreme makeover when Jesus returns doesn't excuse you from doing what you can to take care of it now.

START STRAIGHT

*"Which one of you, when he wants to build a tower,
does not first sit down and calculate the cost
to see if he has enough to complete it?"*
LUKE 14:28 NASB

On February 27, 1964, the Italian government decided to take suggestions for how to extend the life of the leaning tower of Pisa. The tower has been tilting almost since its construction began in 1173, because engineers either weren't aware of or didn't consider that it was being built over an ancient river estuary, which made the ground watery and silty.

Because of the grandiose efforts over the centuries to keep the tower from crumbling, it's been esteemed as an architectural marvel. However, it also serves as an object lesson in the value of counting the cost before undertaking a project.

If something starts out off-center or crooked, it's harder to repair later. There are obvious parallels for raising kids here. As Frederick Douglass noted, "It is easier to build strong children than to repair broken men."

Don't worry about being a perfect husband, father, or son; you won't be. What matters more is that you let your Father in heaven, who is perfect, guide you as you follow Him. When you count the cost of being the man God wants you to be, you're deciding that the cost of trying to go it alone or in half measures isn't worth it. There's too much at stake.

PLUG INTO THE POWER

When I am afraid, I put my trust in you.
PSALM 56:3 NIV

The big choices you make—the woman you marry, the job you take, the place you live—should be guided by your trust in and understanding of God, but the main mark of a son of God is his battle against sin. "For if you live according to the flesh you will die; but if by the Spirit you put to death the deeds of the body, you will live" (Romans 8:13 NKJV).

Fear is a red flag that alerts you to oncoming danger. God's Spirit helps you move past that fear, giving you the strength and will to do what is right. "For as many as are led by the Spirit of God, these are sons of God" (Romans 8:14 NKJV). As an adopted son, you don't have God at your beck and call; rather, you're a tool in His hands. His role isn't limited to responding to your needs; you're being led and moved and shaped by Him.

If your sin doesn't scare you as much as those big decisions you face, you're poised on a precipice. But when you confess your sins to God, you're grabbing a live wire and plugging into hopeful expectation. The results will be initially painful but ultimately empowering. That ruthless approach to being more like Jesus is what conquers fear and confirms you as His son.

REASON TO CELEBRATE

Mordecai. . .sent letters to the Jews. . .calling on them to celebrate an annual festival on these two days. He told them to celebrate these days with feasting and gladness and by giving gifts of food to each other and presents to the poor.
ESTHER 9:20–22 NLT

Today is Purim in the Hebrew calendar, a commemoration of the Jewish people's deliverance from a Persian attempt to utterly exterminate them. Only in the Nazi death camps some 2,400 years later would the Jews face such a concerted threat to their very existence. Small wonder that to this day they celebrate Purim with joy.

One of the ways they demonstrate their thankfulness to God for delivering them is to give to the needy, just as Mordecai instructed. They give away food baskets and other gifts of food, so that everyone will be able to celebrate the Lord's goodness.

Are you in trouble, on the verge of disaster? Trust in God! When David was in danger of being killed, he prayed, "Be merciful to me, O God, for man would swallow me up; fighting all day he oppresses me." Then he confidently declared, "Whenever I am afraid, I will trust in You" (Psalm 56:1, 3 NKJV).

Has God ever delivered *you* from great trouble? Take a few moments to think back on times God has mightily helped you, and pause to give thanks. He's *still* all-powerful and able to deliver you from *new* troubles.

EMPLOYEE APPRECIATION DAY

"His lord said to him, 'Well done, good and faithful servant. . . .Enter into the joy of your lord.'"
Matthew 25:21 NKJV

Today is Employee Appreciation Day, so if you run a business, make sure to show the people working for you that you're thankful for them. You may not be able to give them the day off, but you can order in pizza or Chinese food and spend time socializing with them. Or you can send out an e-mail thanking them for the job they do. Show that you value people. It will improve company morale and loyalty.

Good people are hard to find, and without them you wouldn't be able to run your business and provide customer service. If your staff feel unappreciated, they might look for another job. Some businesses have a high employee turnover rate, and as a result, employers are constantly losing staff and having to train new people. So it makes dollars and sense to show appreciation to people, not just today, but every day.

If you're an employee and your boss doesn't observe this day, be thankful for your employment anyway. Peter advised, "Servants, be submissive to your masters with all respect, not only to those who are good and gentle, but also to those who are unreasonable" (1 Peter 2:18 NASB).

Christians are constantly advised to be thankful, including being grateful to others for what they do, so the idea behind Employee Appreciation Day is very scriptural.

STRONG AND SILENT

*Don't make rash promises, and don't be hasty in bringing
matters before God. After all, God is in heaven,
and you are here on earth. So let your words be few.*
ECCLESIASTES 5:2 NLT

Many men need to be encouraged to speak up more—to
communicate better and speak words of encouragement and
endearment to their loved ones. But on other occasions there's
a great deal to be said for being a man of few words.

You need to be especially careful when trying to resolve
difficult problems. You're a limited mortal, and it's frequently
impossible for you to be aware of all the bits of information that
need to be factored into a decision. So tread carefully.

God "inhabits eternity" and says, "I dwell in the high and
holy place" (Isaiah 57:15 NKJV). He is high above the earth and
able to see all the pieces of the puzzle from His lofty vantage
point, so cry out to Him to help you. Don't waste time trying to
persuade God to go with *your* plan. Your plan might be doomed
to failure from the onset.

When confusing events swirl around you and deadlines loom,
it will be very tempting to try to make a snap decision or to
force a solution, but refrain from being impetuous. Don't commit
yourself to a course of action until you're sure that *God* is in it.

STRIVING VERSUS CONTENTMENT

I saw that all toil and all achievement spring from one person's
envy of another. This too is meaningless, a chasing after the wind.
ECCLESIASTES 4:4 NIV

People were trying to keep up with the Joneses and Jonahs even
back in Bible times. Solomon took a long, hard look at the agrarian
society of his own Middle Eastern kingdom and realized that all
toil and all achievement spring from one person's envy of another.
Most Israelites weren't wealthy and usually had just enough to
make ends meet. Yet even they prided themselves in what few
comforts, objects of beauty, and amenities they could afford.

People are always comparing themselves to those around them,
even though the Bible says that they, "measuring themselves by
themselves, and comparing themselves among themselves, are
not wise" (2 Corinthians 10:12 KJV). This was such a persistent
problem that right from the beginning God commanded, "You
shall not covet. . .anything that is your neighbor's" (Exodus 20:17
NKJV). When you covet their belongings, you're likely to scheme
to *take* those things.

In fact, even trying to accumulate material possessions
through your own hard work can be misguided. The Bible
says that any "pursuit of happiness" that expresses itself in the
accumulation of things is bound to fail. It's "meaningless, a
chasing after the wind." Jesus emphasized that "one's life does
not consist in the abundance of the things he possesses" (Luke
12:15 NKJV). So learn to be content.

THE SHIELD OF FAITH

In addition to all, taking up the shield of faith with which you will be able to extinguish all the flaming arrows of the evil one.
EPHESIANS 6:16 NASB

The shield of faith is a very important part of your spiritual battle gear. It's primarily a defensive piece of weaponry. The KJV mentions "fiery darts," what we now refer to as flaming arrows. In ancient days, archers would unleash a vast barrage of arrows at one time against an enemy army. The best thing that the attackers could do was to hold up their shields to protect themselves from the deadly hail.

At times, the archers would cover their arrowheads in pitch and set them aflame, to start fires in the opposition's camp. But if the arrows were stopped by shields, they went out harmlessly, causing no damage.

These flaming arrows are the lies of the devil, and in this passage God is promising that if you have faith in His Word, it will render Satan's onslaught of lies harmless. This is very important, because the devil continually seeks to wound you or take you out of commission with his discouragement, condemnation, and lies.

Don't become a casualty. Keep your shield of faith up to prevent his mental and spiritual attacks from taking you out. Your faith in God's love and mercy will "extinguish *all* the flaming arrows of the evil one."

TOWN MEETING DAY

If the Son therefore shall make you free,
ye shall be free indeed.
JOHN 8:36 KJV

Every year, the state of Vermont holds Town Meeting Day in some forty towns on the first Tuesday of every March. This holiday is also the anniversary of Vermont's admission to the Union in 1791, but it's better known as gatherings where direct democracy is freely practiced. This is because all citizens of a town can discuss and vote on community issues, and any issue is open to debate. They discuss the town business, elect local officials, approve the coming year's budget, and debate other issues.

This is the most basic example of democracy, where neighbors gather to discuss pressing matters that affect their local community, as well as the state and nation. You may take such liberties for granted, but the fact is, many people in the world don't enjoy such things.

Even if you don't live in Vermont, take some time today to ponder this nation's unique Christian heritage, history, and unrivaled freedoms. It's a good time also to be thankful for the freedom you enjoy in Christ, and to determine to guard it. Avoid slipping back into slavery to sin or into the bondage of legalism.

Remember, you live by the love and grace of God! Paul wrote, "Stand fast therefore in the liberty by which Christ has made us free, and do not be entangled again with a yoke of bondage" (Galatians 5:1 NKJV).

REST IN THE LORD

The LORD replied, "My Presence will go with you,
and I will give you rest."
EXODUS 33:14 NIV

This is a tremendously encouraging promise. Moses apparently had a pretty clear idea of the hardships that awaited them in the barren Sinai Desert and of the enemies that they'd face in Canaan, which is why he pleaded with the Lord, "If your Presence does not go with us, do not send us up from here" (v. 15). Moses knew that they didn't dare face such challenges unless God was with them.

However, as it turned out, even though God upheld His end of the bargain and did mighty miracles to bless them and protect them, the Israelites constantly doubted and disobeyed Him. The result? God vowed, "So I swore in My wrath, 'They shall not enter My rest' " (Psalm 95:11 NKJV).

God still promises to give His people perfect peace and rest, and this can only be found by dwelling in His presence. The Bible promises that "he who dwells in the secret place of the Most High shall abide under the shadow of the Almighty," and "under His wings you shall take refuge" (Psalm 91:1, 4 NKJV). That's where you want to be—under His wings and close to His heart.

Have you found rest by spending time in the presence of God? Spend some time in prayer today, meditating on Him and His Word.

LIVING LIKE JESUS

Those who say they live in God
should live their lives as Jesus did.
1 JOHN 2:6 NLT

This short verse is packed with a powerful message to those who call themselves followers of Jesus Christ. If you say that you live in God then it's beholden to you to prove it by living your life as Jesus lived—and that means sincerely loving others.

But what does it mean to "live in God"? The Bible tells you that God sent the Spirit of Christ to live in your heart (Galatians 4:6), but Jesus also said, "Remain in me, and I will remain in you" (John 15:4 NLT). His Spirit dwells in your heart, but you in turn must seek to walk so close to Him that you're dwelling in His presence, bathed by His Spirit. This is truly living in God.

In the book of Revelation, John described some devoted disciples, saying, "These are the ones who follow the Lamb *wherever* He goes" (Revelation 14:4 NKJV, emphasis added). His slightest wish was their command. May this be true of you. When you read in your Bible that you are to love others and have patience with them, may you strive to do exactly that. When you read that you are to love your enemies, may you do that.

Being a true follower of Jesus Christ isn't always easy, but it's what God calls you to.

IMMEASURABLE FORGIVENESS

*"Through this Man is preached to you the forgiveness of sins;
and by Him everyone who believes is justified from all things
from which you could not be justified by the law of Moses."*

ACTS 13:38–39 NKJV

The new covenant in Jesus' blood is so much better than the old covenant. Under Moses' law, the Jews could make a sacrifice and be forgiven for minor offenses and "sins committed in ignorance" (Hebrews 9:7 NKJV) and escape a death penalty. But for sins like murder and adultery, there was *no* reprieve. The guilty party was to be executed. Period. "Anyone who has rejected Moses' law dies without mercy" (Hebrews 10:28 NKJV).

But Jesus bore God's wrath in our place, enabling John to say, "If we confess our sins, He is faithful and just to forgive us our sins and to cleanse us from *all* unrighteousness" (1 John 1:9 NKJV). No matter what sin you are guilty of, God can and will forgive you—even the worst sins.

Notice that it says that God is *faithful* and *just* to forgive you. God will not only be invariably true to His promise (faithful) to forgive, but He is *just* in so doing. You might have expected this to say that He's merciful to forgive you, but it states that He's *just*. Why? Because His requirement for justice has been fulfilled by Christ's sacrifice on the cross.

Rejoice! You have been forgiven!

NOTHING TO PROVE

Don't try to impress others. Be humble,
thinking of others as better than yourselves.
PHILIPPIANS 2:3 NLT

When you feel threatened by others in any way, your natural reaction is to puff yourself up to appear bigger than them, in an effort to impress or intimidate them. Bushmen have found this technique effective with hyenas: they simply hold a piece of wood on their heads to make themselves appear taller.

It's one thing to strike a defensive posture when physically threatened. That's often a necessity. It's usually *not* necessary, however, to allow yourself to feel threatened by someone socially or personally. If you're confident about your identity, who you are in Christ, you won't let their words and actions get to you.

In fact, rather than trying to give others the impression that you're more powerful or better than them, or of a higher social standing, you can sit back and let them play their "I'm-better-than-you" game all by themselves. When you have the Spirit of Christ in you, you don't need to be concerned for your self-esteem, but can focus on the needs of others. . .including show-offs.

This is the secret of the attitude Jesus wanted you to have when He said, "Whoever desires to become great among you, let him be your servant" (Matthew 20:26 NKJV).

DAYLIGHT SAVINGS TIME

*The sun ariseth. . . Man goeth forth unto his work
and to his labour until the evening.*
Psalm 104:22–23 kjv

Daylight savings time is the practice of setting clocks forward one hour so that daylight lasts an hour longer in the evening during summer months. This new schedule means, however, that sunrise comes an hour later than it used to, so you get an hour's less sunlight in the morning. But overall the idea behind this annual change is to give people extra sunlight during their workday.

On this date in spring, you need to adjust your clocks forward one hour, whereas in autumn (fall), you adjust them backward one hour. People use the expressions "Spring forward" and "Fall back" to remind them of which way to set their clocks—but still manage to get mixed up much of the time.

When this change was first introduced, some Christians were convinced that it was of the devil because Daniel 7:25 (kjv) says that the Antichrist will "think to change times and laws." Humorous assumptions aside, there is still a great deal of argument as to whether daylight savings time is worth the trouble and confusion that it sometimes causes.

You may not *feel* like setting your clocks forward and backward, but you need to do it to be in step with the rest of society. The Bible says, "Submit yourselves for the Lord's sake to every human institution" (1 Peter 2:13 nasb).

LONGSUFFERING LOVE

Love. . . . is not irritable,
and it keeps no record of being wronged.
1 CORINTHIANS 13:4–5 NLT

Some men are just plain grouchy. They're easily irritated and quick to respond negatively. Far from "keeping no record of being wronged," they keep detailed mental tabs of the times people step on their toes. They may overlook an offense once or twice, but keep repeating it and they write you off.

If *you* do this to others, you may feel justified in having such an attitude, arguing that you can't go through life being a doormat. Or you may reason, "This is just the way I am, rough and unvarnished—like it or leave it." What then did God *intend* when He inspired the apostle Paul to pen the above verse?

Paul was no pushover. When he needed to speak out for what was right, he stood up boldly and refused to back down. He opposed the Judaizers in Antioch and engaged in a heated argument with them. He even publicly rebuked Peter, leader of the Jerusalem church (Acts 15:1–2; Galatians 2:11–14). But Paul wasn't defending his personal rights in such cases, much less a wounded ego. When it came to offenses against himself, Paul was longsuffering.

Longsuffering love means precisely that: love that suffers (puts up with someone) for a long time. May God give you such love.

GETTING GOOD NUTRITION

*Bless the LORD, O my soul, and forget not all His
benefits. . .Who satisfies your mouth with good things,
so that your youth is renewed like the eagle's.*

PSALM 103:2, 5 NKJV

Most men—unless they have some food allergy—eat pretty much whatever they want in their youth. And in this fast-paced society, this frequently means lots of fast food, processed foods, and unhealthy meals. But often when they reach middle age, decades of a decadent diet catch up in the form of blocked arteries, diseases, and other body ailments.

Most men frankly know better. They often read snatches about good nutrition in the media or meet others who preach the values of eating healthy and cutting junk food from their diet. Yet they ignore the warnings, assuring themselves that they have an "iron gut" and will be exempt from the maladies that strike so many in their later years.

The Bible says, "Why do you spend money for what is not bread, and your wages for what does not satisfy? Listen carefully to Me, and eat what is good" (Isaiah 55:2 NKJV). Too many men spend money on food that *doesn't* satisfy their body's basic nutritional needs, but all the while, the Bible is pleading for them to listen carefully and eat what is *good*.

The happy news is, unless you're too far gone, you can start eating healthy today and reap the benefits; your youth will be renewed like the eagle's.

GOD'S MIGHTY PROTECTION

*The Lord is faithful, and he will strengthen you
and protect you from the evil one.*
2 THESSALONIANS 3:3 NIV

This verse can be a tremendous source of comfort to you in times when the devil, the enemy of your soul, is attacking you. The Lord wants you to know in no uncertain terms that He won't leave you to face the enemy on your own, but is *certain* to be with you and empower you, so that you'll have the strength to resist the devil. And God will protect you from him.

Elsewhere in the Bible, God promises, "Resist the devil, and he will flee from you" (James 4:7 KJV). He won't always flee the instant you first stand up to him. You may have to steadfastly resist the enemy for some time, but eventually he will buckle under the pressure of the unrelenting power of God, turn, and flee.

The Bible assures you: "God is faithful, who will not allow you to be tempted beyond what you are able, but with the temptation will provide the way of escape also, so that you will be able to endure it" (1 Corinthians 10:13 NASB). The enemy is always seeking to tempt you to do evil, to choose the selfish path, but God has promised to be faithful to strengthen you to help you resist him. And He is more than able to help you emerge victorious.

THE SPIRIT AND OBEDIENCE

"And we are witnesses of these things; and so is the Holy Spirit,
whom God has given to those who obey Him."
ACTS 5:32 NASB

As today's verse brings out, God gives the Spirit to those who *obey* Him. Acts 1:8 (NIV) says, " 'You will receive power when the Holy Spirit comes on you,' " so you know it's the Spirit who gives you the power to live for God. But it's a partnership: you must *respond* to Him. And the more you yield to Him, the stronger His presence becomes.

Obedience brings on the Spirit's power, enabling you to obey Him even more. Jesus described this principle when He said, "To everyone who has, more will be given" (Luke 19:26 NIV). This makes perfect sense: the closer you are to His presence, the more you're able to receive of His power.

What saves you is having the Spirit of Christ in your heart (Galatians 4:6). He marks you with God's seal of ownership, making you His (2 Corinthians 1:22), and "if any man have not the Spirit of Christ, he is none of his" (Romans 8:9 KJV). So every true Christian has a *measure* of the Spirit. But to walk in the fullness of His anointing, you must obey Him.

Many believers think that being filled with the Spirit is a one-time event, but while such initial encounters are important, you must seek to be full of His Spirit every day.

YOUR IDENTITY IN CHRIST

By the grace of God I am what I am.
1 CORINTHIANS 15:10 NIV

When you were born again of the Spirit (John 3:7–8) you gained a new identity in Christ. "If anyone is in Christ, he is a new creation; old things have passed away; behold, all things have become new" (2 Corinthians 5:17 NKJV). You are now attached to Christ the true Vine and get your life and power from Him. That's why Jesus said, "Apart from me you can do nothing" (John 15:5 NIV).

God has made each believer different and has a unique plan for your life. By the power of His Spirit, He enables you to fulfill your part in His great plan. It's good to remember that whatever your gifts and talents, God is the one who is empowering you to do what you do. "Not that we are competent in ourselves to claim anything for ourselves, but our competence comes from God" (2 Corinthians 3:5 NIV).

You still have to work hard and do your best, but ultimately, it's up to God to bring about the desired results. Knowing that He's working through you allows you to trust Him and not worry about accomplishing things. Paul said that he "worked harder than all of them" (the other apostles), "yet not I, but the grace of God that was with me" (1 Corinthians 15:10 NIV).

May you find your identity and fulfillment in Christ!

ST. PATRICK'S DAY

How beautiful on the mountains are the feet of those who bring good news, who proclaim peace, who bring good tidings, who proclaim salvation.

ISAIAH 52:7 NIV

St. Patrick's Day began as a Catholic feast day to honor the life of St. Patrick who brought Christianity to Ireland in the AD 400s. It's chiefly celebrated by the Irish and Irish immigrants, but has become very popular with the general populace of many countries. It's widely known for its parades, festivals, the wearing of green, the display of shamrocks, and the drinking of alcohol.

These days, many criticize St. Patrick's Day celebrations for their commercialism, for promoting negative stereotypes of Irish culture, and for encouraging drunkenness. Almost forgotten amongst the endless greenery, leprechaun costumes, and mugs of frothy beer is the fact that this day was intended to commemorate an outstanding missionary.

Jesus commanded His disciples, "Go ye into all the world, and preach the gospel to every creature" (Mark 16:15 KJV). Elsewhere He said, "Go therefore and make disciples of all the nations. . . teaching them to observe all things that I have commanded you" (Matthew 28:19 NKJV).

There is still a great deal of missionary work to be done in the world today—often right in your own neighborhood. People from all over the world—who have never heard the Gospel—have immigrated to North America. Help bring them eternal hope.

DONE WITH SIN

Therefore, since Christ suffered in his body, arm yourselves also
with the same attitude, because whoever suffers
in the body is done with sin.

1 PETER 4:1 NIV

When you're very sick for a prolonged period of time, your suffering strips you down to the bare basics of existence. You no longer care to indulge in pleasurable activity—whether it's sex, parties, delicious food, or amusing pastimes. Your pain and suffering loom so large in your mind that you can think of little else. The Bible talks of this when it describes people who "loathed all food and drew near the gates of death" (Psalm 107:18 NIV).

When you lose your tight grip even on a desire for life, and all your ambitions and dreams are no longer important to you, you're approaching the state God wants you to be in. Now, finally, you begin to grasp what Jesus was talking about when He said, "Whosoever will save his life shall lose it: and whosoever will lose his life for my sake shall find it" (Matthew 16:25 KJV). As you approach the gates of death, you understand eternal truths and values much better.

The Psalms say, "It was good for me to be afflicted so that I might learn your decrees" (Psalm 119:71 NIV), and difficult as it is to go through prolonged suffering, it can be a very enriching and eye-opening experience.

MIND YOUR OWN BUSINESS

Make it your goal to live a quiet life, minding your own business and working with your hands.
1 THESSALONIANS 4:11 NLT

When Paul said, "Make it your goal," he meant that *this* is what you as a Christian are to focus on, *this* is what you are to strive for: to live an uneventful life, to keep busy with gainful employment, and stay out of trouble.

This sounds a lot like what many Christians are *already* doing—working unobtrusively at a nine-to-five job. It might not seem like a goal worth striving for. Wouldn't it be much more exciting to travel from city to city like Paul, preaching the Gospel full-time, stirring up the crowds, causing citywide riots in the amphitheater, getting beaten up, and so on?

Exciting? Yes. But remember, Paul never went *looking* for such thrills and spills. He was happier to quietly stick to a schedule, teaching disciples day after day at Tyrannus's school in Ephesus, faithfully instructing church leaders, and working in silence for long hours, sewing tents.

There is much to be said in favor of holding down a steady job, year after year, humdrum and unexciting as it might seem. God is in just such faithful obscurity.

This is an ideal state for Christians to live in: "Then the church throughout Judea, Galilee and Samaria enjoyed a time of peace and was strengthened. . . . Encouraged by the Holy Spirit, it increased in numbers" (Acts 9:31 NIV).

FIRST DAY OF SPRING

See! The winter is past; the rains are over and gone.
Flowers appear on the earth; the season of singing has
come, the cooing of doves is heard in our land.
SONG OF SONGS 2:11–12 NIV

Spring was a welcome season in ancient Israel. They rarely had snow in winter, but they had heavy winter rains, and they were often chilly. But the cold rains brought great blessings in their wake: from Dan in the north to Beersheba in the south, the entire land came alive with blossoms, flowers, and greenery. Jesus said, "Notice the fig tree, or any other tree. When the leaves come out, you know. . .that summer is near" (Luke 21:29–30 NLT).

Also, "the cooing of doves" indicated that the mating season had arrived. In ancient times, spring was known as the season of love (see Song of Songs 6:11–12; 7:12).

Winter was when the Israelites sowed their grain, and harvest was in late spring/early summer. It's in this context of seasons that the Psalms say, "He that goeth forth and weepeth, bearing precious seed, shall doubtless come again with rejoicing, bringing his sheaves with him" (Psalm 126:6 KJV).

You may be going through a cold, dark winter season, the land may seem dead and dreary, and your eyes may be moist with tears, but take cheer! Spring is coming!

KNOWING JESUS

Whatever were gains to me I now consider loss for the sake of Christ. What is more, I consider everything a loss because of the surpassing worth of knowing Christ Jesus my Lord.

PHILIPPIANS 3:7–8 NIV

Paul had an exceptional education in two worlds. He was born a Roman citizen, and from reading his epistles, it's clear that he had a wide knowledge of Greek literature. He quoted Greek writers such as the Cretan poet Epimenides in Titus 1:12 and both Epimenides and the Cilician poet Aratus in Acts 17:28. And in 1 Corinthians 15:33, he quoted from *Thais*, a popular comedy written by the Greek playwright Menander.

On the other hand, Paul "conformed to the strictest sect of [his] religion, living as a Pharisee" (Acts 26:5 NIV). He moved to Jerusalem where, as he said, "I studied under Gamaliel and was thoroughly trained in the law of our ancestors" (Acts 22:3 NIV). Even the Roman governor Festus recognized Paul's great learning (Acts 26:24).

Paul had once been self-assured and cocky because of his vast studies, but when he became a Christian, he "resolved to know nothing. . .except Jesus Christ" (1 Corinthians 2:2 NIV). He pared his focus way back and concentrated wholly on knowing the Son of God, and "the depth of the riches both of the wisdom and knowledge of God" (Romans 11:33 KJV).

Knowledge is good, but don't forget life's main focus.

SHINING LIKE THE SUN

Let them that love him be as the sun
when he goeth forth in his might.
JUDGES 5:31 KJV

This is very appealing imagery, and you're probably glad to envision yourself ardently loving God, proceeding triumphantly through your day. This is also a scene of great joy. God states that the sun "bursts forth like a radiant bridegroom after his wedding" (Psalm 19:5 NLT). And Jesus said that the righteous shall "shine forth as the sun in the kingdom of their Father" (Matthew 13:43 KJV).

But there's a price tag for acquiring such power and glory, and it's often passing through deep, fiery trials. John described a glorious heavenly being, saying that his feet were shimmering "like unto fine brass, as if they burned in a furnace" (Revelation 1:15 KJV). Precious metals are purified in a furnace, and the process is similar for believers. God says, "I have refined you. . .in the furnace of affliction" (Isaiah 48:10 NKJV).

You may be going through a difficult phase in your life—a time of seemingly endless testing and frustration—and wonder what good can possibly come of it. Hang on a little longer! God is purifying you. "These trials will show that your faith is genuine. It is being tested as fire tests and purifies gold. . . .So when your faith remains strong through many trials, it will bring you much praise and glory and honor" (1 Peter 1:7 NLT).

THE COST OF DISCIPLESHIP

"Whoever of you does not forsake all that
he has cannot be My disciple."
LUKE 14:33 NKJV

Large crowds were traveling with Jesus, and multitudes of them liked to think that they were His disciples but weren't really committed to Him. So He informed them, "If anyone comes to me and does not hate father and mother, wife and children, brothers and sisters—yes, even their own life—such a person cannot be my disciple" (Luke 14:26 NIV). These are some of Jesus' most difficult words, and they shook a lot of people off His coattails.

Then He added, "And whoever does not carry their cross and follow me cannot be my disciple" (v. 27 NIV). He was telling them that they had to be like condemned criminals, carrying their crosses to the place where they'd be publicly executed. But some people still didn't get the picture, so that's when Jesus bluntly told them in verse 33 that they had to forsake *everything* they held dear—loved ones, possessions, and reputations.

Like the people in that crowd, you may simply not "get" the message that Jesus is trying to get across, that it's very serious business, following Him. It can cost you literally everything. Be prepared to lose earthly possessions and relationships as you steadfastly follow Him. Expect setbacks and losses.

That's part of the process of God stripping the outer layers away from you. But in return you'll gain great spiritual riches.

MISJUDGING JACOB

Esau became a skillful hunter, a man of the open country,
while Jacob was content to stay at home among the tents.
GENESIS 25:27 NIV

Jacob and Esau were twins, but not identical twins. Esau's "whole body was like a hairy garment" (Genesis 25:25 NIV) whereas Jacob was smooth skinned (27:11). Their temperaments were also different: Esau was loud, emotional, and impetuous; Jacob was quiet, thoughtful, and restrained.

Some men however, note that Esau was, as the NLT puts it, "an outdoorsman" (Genesis 25:27), while Jacob, his mother's favorite, hung around the tents and learned to cook. They therefore get the idea that Esau was a muscular he-man, and Jacob a slender wimp, a mama's boy. But there's more to the picture.

According to the Bible, Jacob was *also* a powerfully muscled man: "When Jacob saw Rachel. . .and Laban's sheep, he went over and rolled the stone away from the mouth of the well and watered his uncle's sheep" (Genesis 29:10 NIV). This required exceptional strength, because "the stone over the mouth of the well was *large*" (v. 2, emphasis added).

Too often, men have set opinions about people before they've even met them, simply because of what others say about them. And, as we have seen with Jacob, if they leave out key pieces of information, you can get a skewed picture. Don't be quick to form an opinion or pass judgment on someone. "Judge nothing before the appointed time" (1 Corinthians 4:5 NIV).

PALM SUNDAY

They took palm branches and went out to meet him,
shouting, "Hosanna!" "Blessed is he who comes in the
name of the Lord!" "Blessed is the king of Israel!"

John 12:13 NIV

The temple complex, a sprawling architectural wonder, crowned the western edge of Jerusalem. The temple was Herod's greatest masterpiece, and its massive stones of white marble, gleaming with gold and gems, dazzled eyes in the morning sunlight (see Luke 21:5).

Meanwhile, thousands of Jewish pilgrims swarmed across the flanks of the Mount of Olives, congregating around a man riding down the slope and into the Eastern Gate. It was Jesus, a carpenter from Nazareth, and He was fulfilling an ancient prophecy: "Rejoice greatly, O daughter of Zion! . . . Behold, your king is coming to you; He is. . .humble, and mounted on a donkey" (Zechariah 9:9 NASB).

The temple appeared to be blazing with glory while the Messiah, by contrast, looked quite ordinary. Isaiah said of Him: "He has no stately form or majesty" (Isaiah 53:2 NASB). But in the spiritual realm, the reverse was true. David declared: "Lift up your heads, O gates, and be lifted up, O ancient doors, that the King of glory may come in! Who is the King of glory? The Lord strong and mighty, the Lord mighty in battle" (Psalm 24:7–8 NASB).

God still cries out for the gates of your heart to be opened so that Jesus, the King of Glory, may enter in.

RENEWED DAILY

*Therefore we do not lose heart. Though outwardly we are
wasting away, yet inwardly we are being renewed day by day.*
2 CORINTHIANS 4:16 NIV

It's easy to become discouraged as the years go by and you start
to age, wrinkles begin to mark your face, and your strength
eventually fails. You look at your reflection and wonder who
hung a photo of your grandfather where the mirror used to be.
You feel like—in the words of the Bible—you're "wasting away."

An unknown psalmist lamented, "My days are like a shadow
that declineth; and I am withered like grass. But thou, O LORD,
shall endure for ever; and thy remembrance unto all generations"
(Psalm 102:11–12 KJV). It seems unfair. Mortals are like flowers of
the field: they live a few decades, rapidly bloom, then quickly
reach old age and wither, while the immortal God remains eternal
and awesome throughout all generations.

But take heart! Even though you're fading outwardly, within
you're growing in increasing glory. David prayed, "Let the beauty
of the LORD our God be upon us" (Psalm 90:17 KJV). And it will
be. "My flesh and my heart faileth: but God is the strength of my
heart, and my portion for ever" (Psalm 73:26 KJV).

God will keep your heart and your faith strong, and He
is already renewing your spirit. One day He will renew your
physical body, too, and give you an immortal, powerful, eternally
young body.

FIVE THINGS TO HATE

To fear the LORD is to hate evil; I hate pride and arrogance,
evil behavior and perverse speech.
PROVERBS 8:13 NIV

It might surprise you to learn that it's not only kosher to hate certain things, but that, if you love God, it's actually *required*.

First of all, if you fear God, you are to hate evil. No surprises there. The Bible clearly states, "You who love the LORD, hate evil!" (Psalm 97:10 NKJV). And in case you think *hating evil* is just an Old Testament concept, note that this command is repeated practically word for word in the New Testament, where Paul writes, "Hate what is evil" (Romans 12:9 NIV). You're not to hate people, but you should definitely hate evil whenever you see it.

You are also to hate proud and arrogant attitudes, evil behavior, and evil speech. Where this goes quickly sour, however, is if you make a point of hating these things in *others*, first and foremost. This can cause you to have a critical and smug attitude. The big question is: Do you hate these sins when you find them lurking in your *own* heart? Do you ruthlessly root them out?

A psalmist prayed, "Search *me*, O God, and know my heart: try *me*, and know *my* thoughts: and see if there be any wicked way in *me*" (Psalm 139:23–24 KJV, emphasis added).

DON'T GIVE UP

*Let us not be weary in well doing: for in due
season we shall reap, if we faint not.*
GALATIANS 6:9 KJV

An old saying goes: "Well begun is half-done." But even in cases
when this overly cheerful maxim is true, well begun is still only
half-done. It's not finished. You don't win the prize until you
actually cross the finish line.

You can be temporarily "weary in well doing" because you're
going through a lazy spell or you're overwhelmed by a new task
or responsibility. But it's more serious when you're weary and
giving up on doing good because you're simply worn out by a hard
life or discouraged from years of setbacks and disillusionments.

In both cases, however, Jesus offers hope and can breathe new
life into you. "Anxiety in the heart of man causes depression, but
a good word makes it glad" (Proverbs 12:25 NKJV). The difference
is that when you're temporarily weary, you can be cheered up
quickly by one well-timed piece of encouragement—but when
you've been worn down over a period of years, getting a positive
attitude back takes time.

You may have to deliberately *focus* on positive, uplifting
things—and *stay* focused on them and refuse to fall back into
a negative mental rut. This is what David did when he faced
great discouragement. "David encouraged himself in the LORD
his God" (1 Samuel 30:6 KJV).

LIVING AN EMPOWERED LIFE

Put on the Lord Jesus Christ, and make
no provision for the flesh, to fulfill its lusts.
ROMANS 13:14 NKJV

You're told to "put on" the Lord Jesus Christ, which sounds similar to putting on a change of clothing—and that's exactly what the scripture means. In Luke 24:49 (NIV), Jesus told His disciples, "I am going to send you what my Father has promised [the Holy Spirit]; but stay in the city until you have been clothed with power from on high."

The Spirit of Christ is like a force field that clothes you; you step into Him and He envelops and surrounds you. Paul explained, "You have taken off your old self with its practices and have put on the new self, which is being renewed in. . .the image of its Creator" (Colossians 3:9–10 NIV).

Your "new self" is empowered by God's Spirit, enabling you to live victoriously in this fallen world. That's why scripture warns not to look for ways to indulge your fleshly appetites. You're a new person, so yield to God's Spirit dwelling inside you, not your old sinful habits.

The Bible commands, "As you therefore have received Christ Jesus the Lord, so walk in Him" (Colossians 2:6 NKJV). When you first became a Christian, you knew that living as a believer would entail resisting old temptations and living according to Jesus' teachings. And this is still true.

GOOD FRIDAY

*And he said to them, "I have eagerly desired to eat
this Passover with you before I suffer."*
LUKE 22:15 NIV

On this day, some two thousand years ago, under cover of darkness, Jesus and His disciples gathered in an upper room in the city of Jerusalem. There, in the light of flickering oil lamps, they ate their final meal together. The Passover lamb had been killed and cooked earlier that afternoon, and now after sundown they were celebrating a traditional Jewish seder.

Jesus told them, "I have eagerly desired to eat this Passover with you before I suffer." He had not only looked forward to a time of food and fellowship, but *earnestly desired* it. It meant a great deal to Him. Even today He says, "Here I am! I stand at the door and knock. If anyone hears my voice and opens the door, I will come in and eat with that person, and they with me" (Revelation 3:20 NIV).

Jesus earnestly desires intimate, heart-to-heart fellowship with you every day—not just at Easter. Be sure to spend quiet time with Him daily, whether in the morning or evening, feasting on His Word and meditating on Him. "Thy words were found, and I did eat them; and thy word was unto me the joy and rejoicing of mine heart" (Jeremiah 15:16 KJV). As you speak to Him, He in turn will respond in "a still small voice" (1 Kings 19:12 KJV).

GOD REMEMBERS YOU

*God. . .will not forget your work and the love you have
shown him as you have helped his people.*
HEBREWS 6:10 NIV

Sometimes, despite God's promise to never leave or forsake
you (Hebrews 13:5), you may feel like He has forgotten you.
Isaiah urged, "The Lord has comforted His people and will have
compassion on His afflicted. But Zion said, 'The LORD has forsaken
me, and the LORD has forgotten me.' " To which God responded,
"Can a woman forget her nursing child and have no compassion
on the son of her womb? Even these *may* forget, but I will *not*
forget you" (Isaiah 49:13–15 NASB, emphasis added).

It's difficult to imagine a nursing mother—the very epitome
of tender love—having no compassion on her newborn child, but
God assures you that His love for you is even deeper and stronger.

Perhaps you sometimes feel like God doesn't notice your
faithful service for Him. One time, Isaiah—echoing the Jews'
cry—lamented, "I have toiled in vain, I have spent My strength
for nothing and vanity." Then, refusing to remain discouraged,
he declared, "Yet surely the justice due to Me is with the LORD,
and My reward with My God" (Isaiah 49:4 NASB).

God's love for you is eternal, and He notices every tiny thing
you do. One day soon He will proclaim His love for you before
all heaven and lavishly reward you.

A PERFECT RESCUE

The gift of God is eternal life in Christ Jesus our Lord.
ROMANS 6:23 NIV

Before mankind drew a first breath Jesus knew that *He* would need to take His last. Before the creation of the world there was a plan to save humanity from its own foolish decision-making. Salvation was never an afterthought. God had the answer for your rescue before you knew to ask for help.

On this Easter Sunday you might attend a church service, spend time with family, and have a traditional meal, but the commemoration of this day is more important than any single event in the history of mankind. When Jesus rose from the dead He offered forgiveness, relief from guilt, unconditional love, and a future beyond our last breath.

This is the best news available today, and its impact can extend to future generations when you believe and then share this truth about Jesus: " 'Salvation is found in no one else, for there is no other name under heaven given to mankind by which we must be saved' " (Acts 4:12 NIV).

Easter is the remembrance of a rescue plan that brought mankind to a place of an unlikely friendship with God. The plan was impeccable. The sacrifice was flawless. The new connection between God and man is perfect. Humanity has been offered rescue. They must recognize the Rescuer, accept rescue, and discover gratitude knowing that God loves them and has provided a way home.

WORKING FOR GOD

Whatever you do in word or deed, do all in the name of the
Lord Jesus, giving thanks through Him to God the Father.
COLOSSIANS 3:17 NASB

You're an employee of the Most High God. Your work matters to Him. He gave you skills that can be used to serve Him well. No matter where you work, you really work for God. He's paying attention. And He wants your best.

If you want to have the opportunity to share your faith with coworkers, begin by being a dependable, faithful, and exceptional employee. Your work ethic has a strong bearing on the believability of your statement of faith.

Your words should reflect God's heart. Your work should bring honor to His name. Be wise. Bring Jesus to work and let Him instill joy, responsibility, and willingness to work in even toxic environments. You can bring light to a spiritually dark workplace. You can bring your *Life* CEO with you and let Him provide the life coaching you need to do your work well. He can change your attitude and impact others who struggle with their own workplace issues.

Office politics, workplace dramas, and bad attitudes are all small issues to the God who created you and who accepts your work as a gift of gratitude and praise. Work was never meant just to be a way to make a living, but to bring *life* to one more area of influence.

ABSOLUTELY TRUSTWORTHY

*Do not be anxious about anything, but in every situation,
by prayer and petition, with thanksgiving,
present your requests to God.*

PHILIPPIANS 4:6 NIV

This is the age of superheroes. They fill comic books, television series, and big-budget movies. They have distinct personalities and impressive abilities. Have you ever wondered why they're so popular?

Confidence is hard to find when life seems uncertain. The result is high anxiety. Superheroes become substitutes for diminished personal confidence. God has always had a better idea. In every circumstance you can pray and ask a loving God for help. He is looking out for you. Be grateful. Above all, refuse every delivery of anxiety. Be confident in the God who rescues and delights in taking care of His family.

You don't need to wear a cape, have a secret cave filled with expensive super toys, or look for help from super-powered friends. Psalm 20:7 (NIV) says, "Some trust in chariots and some in horses, but we trust in the name of the LORD our God."

Anxiety diminishes your ability to trust, fills your mind with scenarios that aren't acquainted with reality, and has an odd way of diminishing your ability to hear others speak truth. Anxiety tells God that you're not convinced He's strong enough to handle your deepest struggles.

Find your greatest confidence in the One who has always been *super* trustworthy.

PERSONAL WORSHIP

How long will they speak with arrogance?
How long will these evil people boast?
PSALM 94:4 NLT

The Bible has its fair share of leading characters who let arrogance bring them to personal ruin. Moses killed a man, David committed adultery, and Paul sought to harm the very people Jesus came to rescue. Each man acted as if God's law didn't apply to him. They justified each decision because it was intended to lead to a desired outcome.

Pride and false humility are two sides of the same coin. One side wants to be noticed and the other wants to be noticed by saying they *don't* want to be noticed. Both shine a light on self. When Jesus points you toward true life, you should expect Him to do two things. The first is to teach you that who you are is all about who *He* is and what *He's* done. Nothing you can do changes who you are to God (see Ephesians 2:9). The second is that when you take credit for something God has done through you, it will be the only credit you receive (see Matthew 6:5).

Arrogance is the source of the downfall of men because it replaces God's perfection with man's misguided intentions, and the resulting self-worship is something others don't want to observe. God led Moses, David, and Paul through arrogance to a humble acceptance of the true source of their success. He can do the same for you.

SET FREE FROM SIN

"If the Son sets you free, you will be free indeed."
JOHN 8:36 NIV

It's tough to argue with the truth that you sin (see Romans 3:23). God wants you to admit your sin so He can forgive you (1 John 1:9). You can't undo what you've done. You can't justify your actions in God's courtroom. You come to Him burdened with sin debt and leave as His adopted and forgiven son.

Unlike those who dredge up your old sin to use as a club against you, God takes an entirely unexpected course. He forgives. He forgets (Psalm 103:12). God offers freedom, but Christians often remain incarcerated by choice. You may not feel ready to forgive yourself, but you can't ignore the truth that God can, and does, forgive you. You can accept His forgiveness and discover the freedom your soul has always craved.

Of course, you need to understand the depth of your sin before you can accept and appreciate the freedom found in Christ. But accepting God's forgiveness is important because He's got an incredible future awaiting you, and you won't experience it by living in the past while clutching the *sin rags* that God has already forgiven.

Jesus shared His plan for your life in John 10:10 (NIV): "I have come that they may have life, and have it to the full." Jesus sets you free. Believe and accept His freedom.

GODLY MEN

How blessed is the man who does not walk in the counsel of the
wicked, nor stand in the path of sinners, nor sit in the seat
of scoffers! But his delight is in the law of the Lord,
and in His law he meditates day and night.

Psalm 1:1–2 nasb

Godly men—men who follow God and whose lives are blessed by Him—pay no heed to wicked advice. They don't identify themselves with those who mock God. Rather, they draw their inspiration from God's instruction book. They learn what it says and their actions reflect what they learn. They take the time to meditate on it. They want to make sure God's Word gets into their minds, filters down deep into the core of their being, and changes their motivations.

Godly men recognize there's a battle for their minds. They refuse to rent head space to their adversary. Second Corinthians 10:5 (nasb) tells them to take "every thought captive to the obedience of Christ." The world's opinions fluctuate and mean little if they're not aligned with God's truth. The actions of godly men are always tied to what they believe.

Godly men recognize that dining at the Lord's Table of Truth doesn't allow for picky consumerism. There's much to taste, and spending time completely engaged with God's Word is the best way to be fully fed and entirely convinced that He has a personal plan for every new sunrise.

LIFE IS SHORT—CHOOSE GOD

Your life is like the morning fog—
it's here a little while, then it's gone.
JAMES 4:14 NLT

At the end of your life you don't get a mulligan, do-over, or a divine reset in an attempt to get it right. You have one life to make the decisions you need to make to determine your place in eternity. Your time on earth isn't an end game, it's a potent beginning. If you only live for what you can get here, you're missing out on the preparation for what's to come.

Life is like grass—here for a season and gone. Life is like fog—visible and impacting for a short period of time. Life is shorter than you realize, yet long enough that you're sometimes convinced to put off making the kind of decisions that must be made *today*.

You can choose to do things your own way or you can find out what God wants you to do. You can determine your own truth or you can consult the God of *all* truth. You can live as though this life is all there is or you can discover this life is a small step into forever.

The only redeemable promises and guarantees you have in life are *God-made*. He promised to be with you. He guarantees Christians an eternal home with Him. There's no good reason to intentionally separate yourself from God. Life is short, so choose Him.

WISDOM SPEECH

Sin is not ended by multiplying words,
but the prudent hold their tongues.
Proverbs 10:19 niv

God used words to bring the world into existence (Genesis 1). When He describes His Son, He calls Him the Word (John 1:1). What God has to say with His words must have meaning because God is perfect. God has freely given us the words of spirit and life (John 6:63).

Men fall into a different category. You can't call a world into being by your words. You aren't the one who originated language. You aren't perfect. Your words can bring a sense of life to those who hear you, but they often leave scars on hearts, impaired thinking due to a lack of truth, and may even encourage the hearer to follow a bad example. But you can follow God's lead and speak words that heal, share truths that alter thinking, and send out a trust invitation.

If you can't seem to say things that help, you can at least be prudent by holding your tongue, as today's verse states. Some men aren't able to do this and unnecessarily bring trouble upon themselves.

Some men struggle with speaking important words that positively impact others because positive words weren't spoken to them. That's why your best example is the God who created words. Hold your tongue when you have to, speak when you need to, and gain the wisdom to know the difference.

WHITE-WASHED REBELLION

"I want to see a mighty flood of justice,
an endless river of righteous living."
AMOS 5:24 NLT

The people of Israel said the right things, sang great songs, and got together to celebrate their national religion. The prophet Amos wasn't impressed. God showed him where the people were at. He told them in verse 12 (NLT), "I know the vast number of your sins and the depth of your rebellions." So God invited the people to come back to Him and seek His heart once more. He told them to hate evil and love what was good, stop the show and pretense, and cease the meaningless offerings (Amos 5:14–15, 22–23).

Hadn't they done the right things publicly, attended the expected religious services, and sought to show evidence of faithfulness? Yes, but God also saw every moment *out* of the public eye. He saw their divided heart. He was aware that they were engaged in white-washed living, and it was time to confront their rebellion.

He wasn't interested in their diligent spiritual *to-do* list. God wanted the hearts of His people to line up with the desires of His heart. Righteous living and compassion were rarely practiced.

Today, God continues to look for righteous living among His people. He desires to see compassion poured out on behalf of those who need love more than a hearty "Serves you right." God still desires a people whose outer life lines up with His truth.

THE ENCOURAGEMENT SPUR

*If someone is caught in a sin, you who live by the Spirit
should restore that person gently. But watch
yourselves, or you also may be tempted.*

GALATIANS 6:1 NIV

There's a reason the Bible says, "Let us not neglect our meeting
together, as some people do, but encourage one another" (Hebrews
10:25 NLT). Call it a gathering, assembly, fellowship, or church,
but each word carries the idea that the Christian life should be
lived in community. A church is filled with the battle-scarred,
the newly trusting, and those who struggle to follow truth.

A church should be a place where you can experience mercy,
expect grace, and from time to time deal with the darkness in
the heart of all mankind.

God's people are never asked to accept sin, but to lovingly hold
a spiritual mirror to the bad behavior of believers who are caught
up in sin. This isn't an *"I'm better than you"* moment. It's a *"God
is better than all"* revelation. God can use you to restore someone
to righteous living, but you can't treat this lightly because you're
also told these situations can bring personal temptation to follow
the poor choices of those you're called to restore.

God didn't call believers to meet together so they could find
out how much others thought they could get away with, but
to "consider how we may spur one another on toward love and
good deeds" (Hebrews 10:24 NIV).

JUSTIFYING FAVORITISM?

*If you show favoritism, you sin and are
convicted by the law as lawbreakers.*
JAMES 2:9 NIV

Favoritism is a plague and can lead to idol worship. If that seems like a stretch, consider this: God says you're not to show favoritism. You sin when you do. By showing favoritism you may be saying you believe that individuals are more important than God. More honorable than His commands. Anything placed above God becomes an idol.

To make this a little clearer, God instructed His people in Exodus 20:3 (NIV), "You shall have no other gods before me." If God gives a command, you shouldn't redefine His instruction. Favoritism, prejudice, discrimination, and racism are examples of lawbreaking—and they grieve God. Most people rarely consider this sin, but instead consider ways to justify their favoritism.

God sent His Son for the lost. He didn't exclude people with certain addresses, bank statements, ethnic backgrounds, or a large sum total of personal sins. Second Corinthians 5:15 (NIV) adds, "[Jesus] died for all, that those who live should no longer live for themselves but for him who died for them and was raised again."

Any time you shrink the community of God by excluding someone, you tell the world you don't need more friends, that only some should have access to God, and that relatively few people really matter. That message doesn't stand up to God's love letter to *all* mankind.

PUT ON MERCY

*Judgment is without mercy to the one who has shown
no mercy. Mercy triumphs over judgment.*
JAMES 2:13 NKJV

Be harsh with other people and you can expect a substantial return
on your investment. Mercy gives birth to mercy, and justice to
justice. God offers you mercy and forgiveness, and His desire is for
mercy to be your go-to response with others. Colossians 3:12–13
(NKJV) says, "As the elect of God, holy and beloved, put on tender
mercies, kindness, humility, meekness, longsuffering; bearing with
one another, and forgiving one another, if anyone has a complaint
against another; even as Christ forgave you, so you also must do."

God blesses those who show mercy (Matthew 5:7). God wants
mercy even more than sacrifice (Matthew 9:13). An understanding
of mercy can help you draw close to God (Hebrews 4:16).

Identify sin and keep your distance. Don't ever start to invite
sin to spend time with your thinking. Make no mistake, you
will sometimes entertain sin, but that's when the God of mercy
invites you to come home. You don't have the right or even the
ability to excuse sin, but. . .you can meet people in Mercy Place
just beyond Justice Junction.

Why? Justice is always closer, but mercy takes the extra
steps when the offender can't. Personal justice always accuses
and demands payment while mercy understands that restoring
relationship is the greater priority. God says mercy triumphs
over judgment.

PRAY ON

You don't have what you want because you don't ask God for it. And even when you ask, you don't get it because your motives are all wrong—you want only what will give you pleasure.

James 4:2–3 NLT

Many say prayers under pressure. These are spontaneously uttered during the worst possible life moments. They're not often part of regular conversations with God, and—for many people—may not even be sent with an understanding of who God is or what He wants.

You can look at the first part of today's verses and conclude that all you have to do is ask and God *has* to give you what you want. However, this passage was actually a response to the way early Christians had been dealing with selfishness: "You want what you don't have, so you scheme and kill to get it. You are jealous of what others have, but you can't get it, so you fight and wage war to take it away from them" (vv. 1–2 NLT).

Prayer can be proof that you're following God's lead. As you draw closer to God you begin to speak prayers that reflect what you're learning. As you grow, you're less likely to ask for something you already know He couldn't answer with a yes.

Your prayer life always reflects your relationship with God. When you know God wants the best for you, you'll begin to ask for His best because you will *want* His best.

THE TRANSFORMED DIFFERENCE

Do not be conformed to this world, but be transformed by
the renewing of your mind, so that you may prove what the will
of God is, that which is good and acceptable and perfect.
ROMANS 12:2 NASB

Society is pretty good at churning out cookie-cutter characters. If you follow the pattern, you'll want what others have, wear clothing approved by society's elite, and be discontent when nothing you want satisfies.

Society says only some people are special and if you want to be special you need to do what *those* people do. This may explain why there are so many websites and television shows dedicated to telling you who's *in* today and why you need to change everything about you to be like them.

God wants you to stop looking, acting, and sounding like society's special people, but it will mean changing your perspective. God wants to change that old way of dealing with life and transform everything about you into someone who agrees to pursue God's good, acceptable, and perfect will. You see, God has always had a plan for your life, but when you take your eyes off Him and pursue the approval of others who seem to have more of something you like, you lose connection with the God who understands your personal life map.

Keeping up with the Joneses could keep you from following the life plan God created just for you.

WISDOM'S ROADMAP

*Be careful how you live. Don't live like fools, but like those
who are wise. Make the most of every opportunity in these
evil days. Don't act thoughtlessly, but understand
what the Lord wants you to do.*
EPHESIANS 5:15–17 NLT

The pursuit of wisdom requires intentional decision-making. The choices you make impact personal wisdom. God's Word says it's better to follow the wise than lament your own poor choices. You've probably heard, "You'll learn from your mistakes." While that may be true, God places a great emphasis on obedience.

Because God wants you to have a good reputation He says, "Be careful how you live." Because you're to reflect God's character He says, "Don't act like fools." Because He built you for positive relationships He says, "Make the most of every opportunity." Because He wants you to love others He says, "Don't act thoughtlessly."

So, what is godly wisdom? Making an intentional choice to follow, knowing God will help you "understand what [He] wants you to do." Wisdom isn't available in any store, can't be inherited, and is nontransferable. God can make you wise as you learn what He's said and do what He's asked.

You'll make mistakes. Sin will inevitably be part of your life experience. Wisdom understands that God gave you a choice and the help you'd need to keep your distance from decisions that keep you at arm's length from the One who loves you most (see 1 Corinthians 10:13).

WISDOM, COUNSEL, AND UNDERSTANDING

"Is not wisdom found among the aged? Does not long life bring understanding? To God belong wisdom and power; counsel and understanding are his."

JOB 12:12–13 NIV

Who do you listen to when you need advice? Is it someone who doesn't have a fully formed picture of life? Or is it someone who's spent time in life's trenches and has lived to gain understanding? There's a reason you might seek the advice of your father or other mature men. Their life experience may help you learn what to avoid and what to pursue.

This idea is linked to finding a mentor or becoming a disciple. You'll need to admit you don't know everything in order to learn something. If it's true that you'll likely seek those older men with more life experience to draw from, then shouldn't it be true that you become doggedly determined to follow the God who possesses *complete* wisdom, power, counsel, and understanding?

God wants you to pay attention and make choices as to whose voice you allow into your thinking. If you're careful whom you listen to among your sphere of friendships, shouldn't the voice of God and the wisdom He's given in His Word take first place as your source of counsel for today's tough choices? And tomorrow's?

"Come near to God and he will come near to you" (James 4:8 NIV).

THE COMPANION

[Jesus said] "The Helper, the Holy Spirit, whom the Father
will send in My name, He will teach you all things,
and bring to your remembrance all things that I said to you."
JOHN 14:26 NKJV

Friends are important. It can be lonely without them. Proverbs 27:17 (NLT) says, "As iron sharpens iron, so a friend sharpens a friend." Your best friends help keep you focused, honest, and inspired. These traits are also found in the Holy Spirit, the least-discussed member of the Trinity. He takes up residence in the core of who you are.

Every temptation you face can be endured with the help of this friend. Jesus sent the Spirit as a personal companion to help you when you need help. Listen closely and learn what God wants from you. The Spirit can speak to your inner man and remind you of things God has already said. He's the Companion, the One sent to walk beside you, the One who teaches, and the One who helps God's character grow in your heart, mind, and soul.

Saying that the Holy Spirit and your conscience are the same thing doesn't take into account all the things God's Holy Spirit can do. He can and does remind you when you're heading in the wrong direction. He can point you in the right direction. And, if allowed, He can teach, train, and transform you into the man God wants you to be.

CROP FAILURE

All Scripture is inspired by God and is useful to teach us
what is true and to make us realize what is wrong in
our lives. It corrects us when we are wrong and
teaches us to do what is right.

2 TIMOTHY 3:16 NLT

God inspired the writing of scripture, but how *much* of the Bible did He actually inspire? *Every word.* Why is this important? Well, if you think some of the Bible is from God but other parts aren't, then you'll be confused as to what can be trusted.

If only part of the Bible is true, how can you believe *any* of it? If it's not all true, you're left to pick and choose what you believe. If you're like most, you'll end up picking what seems easiest to believe and follow. You might believe in God's grace, but not His command to obey Him. You'd accept His love without acknowledging God is the final authority. You'd accept forgiveness while refusing to forgive others.

You should realign your thinking and actions with God's truth. He never said you could simply accept the parts of His Word that make you feel good. In fact, Galatians 6:7 (NLT) puts this in farming terms: "Don't be misled—you cannot mock the justice of God. You will always harvest what you plant."

Determine to believe and obey God's Word, starting with His *simplest* (but hardest to obey) commands—to love others and forgive those who offend you.

YOU JUST KEEP STRANDING

Put on the full armor of God, so that when the day of
evil comes, you may be able to stand your ground,
and after you have done everything, to stand.

EPHESIANS 6:13 NIV

He'd been homeless, but his life changed when he met two men who joined him around a fifty-five-gallon oil drum warming their hands in a barrel fire in the inner city. One began to sing, and he eventually joined in. Quiet and a bit reluctantly at first, the song's beauty began to be filled with brushstrokes of harmony and soul that provided an authentic polish to the rusty voices that rarely spoke.

This trio was discovered by someone passing by, and they recorded a CD. One of the songs was written on the foundation of standing firm by using God's full armor. This man said in a raspy voice, "Evil days are bound to come, so stand your ground. And when you've done everything you can, why, you just keep standing."

This man and the impromptu musical group soon faded back into obscurity, and even their names were eventually forgotten, but their lesson endures forever.

This man's faith was tested on streets paved with disappointments and hide-and-seek opportunities. His hope came in spurts. His future seemed bleak. And in the midst of much personal opposition, he said what Christian men should always say when facing opposition: "When you've done everything you can, why, you just keep standing."

SPIRITUAL INVESTMENTS

*Godliness actually is a means of great gain
when accompanied by contentment.*
1 TIMOTHY 6:6 NASB

Godliness always begins with identifying yourself as a man willing to follow God. This decision can include a profound sense of gratitude to the One you're certain holds the answers to living life well, has a plan for your life, and customized it specifically for you. Godliness seeks to line up personal decision-making within the framework of God's Word.

Instead of being fixated on what you don't own, godly living suggests that being content with what you have is a better option. The reason is simple. This current life is extremely short when compared with the eternal life God has prepared for His children, and some things people invest in have extremely short shelf lives.

Matthew 6:19–20 (NASB) says, " 'Do not store up for yourselves treasures on earth, where moth and rust destroy, and where thieves break in and steal. But store up for yourselves treasures in heaven, where neither moth nor rust destroys, and where thieves do not break in or steal.' "

Spending time chasing things you can never take to heaven is a poor use of time and resources. The three greatest investments you'll ever make in life are relationships with God, family, and friends. People are the only investments you have any chance of seeing again in heaven.

Godliness + contentment = God's approved life investment strategy.

MORE THAN AN "ATTA BOY!"

Praise the LORD, all you nations. Praise him, all you people
of the earth. For his unfailing love for us is powerful;
the LORD's faithfulness endures forever. Praise the LORD!
PSALM 117:1–2 NLT

Christian men demonstrate wisdom every time they praise God. Nations who honor God make the right choices. Every bit of praise and every word of honor should be a response to the God who never fails to love and who demonstrates His faithfulness every moment of each new day.

Some translations say God's love is *steadfast.* This word suggests something immovable—like a mountain or a house-sized boulder in the middle of a stream. God's love is unfailing, powerful, and guaranteed to last forever. It's not going anywhere.

You can't earn it, make Him love you more, or make Him love you less. You're one of His creations, and His love extends to every human ever born—even the ones you don't like.

This is where the praise should be lavished on a magnificent God. He's good. He's mighty. He loves you. Praise and honor isn't simply an "Atta boy!" shouted out to God. Your praise should take the time to think of the many blessings you've discovered in your walk with God that brought you to this moment. By remembering the past you're able to see more clearly that God's unfailing love has always been enough to get you to, through, and beyond life's toughest moments.

DEAL WITH IT

Create in me a pure heart, O God,
and renew a steadfast spirit within me.
PSALM 51:10 NIV

The Bible is clear; you are to bear with other people who struggle with sin (Galatians 6:2). It requires patience, sacrifice, and love. At some point you've likely received the kindness of strangers and friends. Bearing with others helps you maintain positive relationships. Remember, God puts up with you, too.

When *you* sin by disobeying God's commands, you aren't supposed to give yourself a free pass. Grace is God's gift and your example. You're not to bear (put up) with your *own* sin. God wants you to deal with it, and His example is ruthless (see Matthew 5:29–30). There are sins that catch the attention of law enforcement like murder and theft, but there are other sins that are equally offensive to God. A short list of these sins includes gossip, envy, and dishonesty.

The only way you can really deal with sin is with help. Men show the greatest wisdom when they allow God's Holy Spirit to create a new heart and a steadfast spirit in a heart born sinful (Psalm 51:5, 10).

God does what you can't. He helps when you ask for help. You can't defeat sin on your own. Wise men understand the best answer to the problem of sin is new life offered by a good God and accepted by fallen men (see Colossians 3).

AUTHENTIC GRATITUDE

In everything give thanks; for this is the will
of God in Christ Jesus for you.
1 THESSALONIANS 5:18 NKJV

Sometimes knowing God's will for your life is as simple as reading His Word. For example, it's always His will for you to express gratitude. Wisdom proclaims thankfulness as a daily exercise matching actions with God's will, but at the end of the day you might discover some gratitude you still need to express.

You might be standing in the way of God's will. Every time you choose self-pity over gratitude, God's plans are set aside and delayed. The same is true whenever you entertain greed, envy, lust, covetousness, hatred, bitterness, selfishness, and cynicism.

The list is longer, but the common reason for setting aside God's will is. . .*self*. When you pay too much attention to what you don't have, what you want, and how others have hurt you, then there's no room for authentic gratitude.

God is good, and He supplies everything you need to live. He sends bonus moments like beautiful sunsets, impressive scenery, and the love of family and friends. Yet it's possible to develop a blindness to the good things because difficulties frequently demand your attention. . .and God's will is set aside for another day.

You can't be thankful when you think you deserve more than you have. When you're grateful for what you have, you not only position yourself to follow God's will, but you also give yourself the greatest chance to enjoy contentment.

FOR EACH NEXT STEP

Let my cry come before You, O LORD;
give me understanding according to Your word.
PSALM 119:169 NASB

The Psalms are more than source material for praise songs. They also express human struggle and personal questioning. Take today's verse, for example. There are three takeaways.

"Let my cry come before You." Even the psalmist wanted to be heard. In moments of anger, frustration, and even joy, men need to believe that when they pray, God listens.

"Give me understanding." God's ways, plans, and truth don't always line up with common thinking. Men need direction and shouldn't be afraid to ask God to make things clear.

"According to Your word." God's answers often come in the form of words on the pages of His book, the Bible.

God explains in Isaiah 55:10–11 (NLT) how His Word does something remarkable in helping you understand what He wants. It also lets you know He's heard you. "The rain and snow come down from the heavens and stay on the ground to water the earth. They cause the grain to grow, producing seed for the farmer and bread for the hungry. It is the same with my word. I send it out, and it always produces fruit. It will accomplish all I want it to, and it will prosper everywhere I send it."

His Word nourishes and causes you to grow, and it can produce something productive in the soil of receptive hearts. Read it for wisdom, life, and for each next step.

HELP APPRECIATED

Two are better than one, because they have a good return for their labor: if either of them falls down, one can help the other up.
ECCLESIASTES 4:9–10 NIV

Elizabeth got her first job in 1936. More than eighty years later she was still on the job. The telegraph was in use when she gained employment, Franklin Roosevelt was president, and computers may have been a dream, but not one she entertained. A typewriter was her companion, and her boss regularly scoured the newspaper ads to find replacement parts, but there was a willingness to do that for the living history book of the school.

Today is Administrative Professionals Day, a time to salute and appreciate those who help you. That probably goes beyond the intent of the day, but there's a more universal reminder in this celebration. You, too, have people who help you do your job.

God designed you to work. You gain satisfaction from working, earning a living, and using some of what you earn to help others. God also designed you to need help. Every moment of your workday is an opportunity to demonstrate teamwork.

When you allow God to influence your work life, you might actually have an opportunity to share why your work ethic is unique. Colossians 3:23–24 (NIV) reminds you, "Whatever you do, work at it with all your heart, as working for the Lord, not for human masters. . . . It is the Lord Christ you are serving."

Work together.

FOLLOWING YOUR STEPS

*"You must commit yourselves wholeheartedly to these commands
that I am giving you today. Repeat them again and again to
your children. Talk about them when you are at home
and when you are on the road, when you are
going to bed and when you are getting up."*
DEUTERONOMY 6:6–7 NLT

Teach your children. God wants you to. Sometimes that means verbally reinforcing your lessons. Other times it means showing them.

Today, many will celebrate Take Your Daughters and Sons to Work Day. It can be a time to show what integrity in the workplace looks like. You could celebrate by demonstrating a great work ethic. Your children might learn by seeing you complete something in a team environment. First Corinthians 10:31 (NLT) says, "Whatever you do, do it all for the glory of God." Your children could benefit from knowing that the work you do is important for the well-being of your family, and that work represents purpose and responsibility.

Celebrate the day even if you're self-employed. Show your children it takes hard work to provide for your family, but you work because you love your family and care for their needs.

Your children pay attention to what you do even more than what you say. They follow your footsteps, making your example important. You shouldn't be surprised when they want to be just like you. Perhaps that's why God made your "daddy footprint" so visible.

INSPIRED VIEWS

All things have been created through Him and for Him.
COLOSSIANS 1:16 NASB

Today is Arbor Day. Take a look at the trees, the sky, and the stars. God made it all for you to enjoy, but He also made it for Himself. He made things He likes—streams, geysers, tulips, and you. And God takes care of His creation.

Everything in nature has its origin in God. Sometimes in the face of nature's grandeur this truth is forgotten. Romans 1:25 (NIV) says, "They exchanged the truth about God for a lie, and worshiped and served created things rather than the Creator." Enjoy creation, take care of what you can, learn new ways to appreciate what God has made—and then praise Him for taking care of creation. That care extends to you.

If you find yourself overwhelmed by the beauty of God's creation, then let it serve as a reminder that friendship with God is deep, rewarding, and surpasses the beauty of this earth.

As inspired as creation may be here, it can be hard to imagine the heaven God has prepared for His family. It's not just the beauty of what you see, but the beauty of God's perfect home where " 'He will wipe every tear from their eyes. There will be no more death' or mourning or crying or pain, for the old order of things has passed away" (Revelation 21:4 NIV).

The greatest beauty on earth is a reflection of God's best future.

NO BARRIER EQUALITY

There is no longer Jew or Gentile, slave or free,
male and female. For you are all one in Christ Jesus.
GALATIANS 3:28 NLT

Jesus came with a radical and unexpected message: God loved all mankind, He didn't discriminate; women had equal standing in His plan, and the sick were never considered unacceptable.

A person's social status meant nothing to Jesus. Each person had a gift to share and a role in His plan. Where women and children were once treated as property to be discarded at will, men were told, "Love your wives and never treat them harshly" (Colossians 3:19 NLT). God also taught in Ephesians 6:4 (NLT), "Fathers, do not provoke your children to anger by the way you treat them. Rather, bring them up with the discipline and instruction that comes from the Lord."

Part of Jesus' plan was to equalize humanity. No one was less important to Him than another. He didn't come to save a few. His rescue plan was for all. His love was accessible to everyone.

Jesus introduced a new pledge, and He didn't change His mind. This generous pledge challenged thinking and created new opportunities. God doesn't erect barriers when it comes to a relationship with Him. Christian men should remove every barrier that makes it hard for others to meet Jesus or love people the way Jesus loves.

Jesus brought exceptionally good news. Share it. Live it.

ASK

*Wise words bring approval,
but fools are destroyed by their own words.*
ECCLESIASTES 10:12 NLT

Wisdom recognizes the importance of every decision. Wisdom understands time should be used well. It seeks advice, makes a house a home, and softens the hardest disposition.

Wisdom knows that personal opinion is less important than God's truth. Wisdom is simply knowledge until it's filtered through God's truth. Get wisdom and find that it guards you. Seek wisdom and discover it in the pages of God's Word. Follow wisdom and meet the Lord. Wisdom has rewards that exceed the possession of gold or silver. The greatest wisdom of man is foolishness when compared to the wisdom of God.

Everything you just read was paraphrased from God's Word. If you want to become a man dedicated to wisdom, you will need to return often to wise words in the book that God wrote. It's an instruction manual and book of encouragement, filled with words of grace, and it's offered to enhance life, improve marriage, and deliver wisdom.

The wisdom you'll discover will bring light to dark places, hope to desperate situations, and a way forward when the way seems blocked.

Make wisdom your pursuit; know and stop guessing; seek God's heart and find that doing His will is the pinnacle of your life's purpose. God promised to give wisdom to all who ask, so if what you've read sounds good, ask.

WAVER NO MORE

Let us hold fast the confession of our hope without
wavering, for He who promised is faithful.
HEBREWS 10:23 NKJV

Buy a product, and you might waver in your opinion of the purchase. It's possible the product never actually delivered on its promise, or it might have failed along the way. Watch a movie and discover your opinion wavering between a waste of time and something more memorable.

Your opinions can waver about almost everything. You like a certain restaurant, but struggle when it comes time to decide if that's where you really want to eat. When it comes to your relationship with God, you shouldn't waver. Your trust in Him doesn't need to change, and your hope in God will never disappoint.

Wavering means "being prone to a divided opinion." Either God is good or He isn't. He loves or He doesn't. He can rescue or He can't. If God has proven faithful, then wavering in your opinion of Him doesn't make sense. Chances are you've felt some doubt. Perhaps you've wavered. You're not alone. Jesus told a man who came to Him for help that he should believe. The man's reply? "Lord, I believe; help my unbelief!" (Mark 9:24 NKJV).

God doesn't want you to waver in your belief, but He knew this would be an issue for all mankind. Spend time remembering the faithfulness of God, and discover a harmony between what you believe and the God you believe in.

KNOWING YOUR SOURCE

*Every good and perfect gift is from above,
coming down from the Father of the heavenly lights.*
JAMES 1:17 NIV

In a 2016 interview featured on the ESPN feature show E:60, interviewer Jeremy Schaap asked retiring sports broadcasting legend Vin Scully, "What are the moments that give you the most pride?"

Scully, a man of faith who began his broadcasting career in 1949, replied, "I don't know about pride. I try to keep that word out of my life. I really mean that when I say it. I'm not prideful. Because what has happened to me, I believe in all honesty, it was a gift that was given to me. I can lose that gift as soon as I get out of this chair. . .so there's really no pride."

The Bible has a lot to say about pride, and none of it is good. God tells us in His Word that He hates human pride and that He will actively oppose those with pride-filled hearts and minds (James 4:6).

But today's verse gives believers a great antidote for human pride, and it's this: Keep in mind that every good thing we have and every good thing we accomplish in this life is a gift from God. So when the devil whispers in your ear that you should feel pride over something you've done, you do well to simply answer, "It's all a gift from my Father in heaven."

A TRUE PRAYER WARRIOR

*Epaphras, who is one of you and a servant of Christ Jesus,
sends greetings. He is always wrestling in prayer for you,
that you may stand firm in all the will of
God, mature and fully assured.*

COLOSSIANS 4:12 NIV

If you've ever watched a *real* wrestling match (as opposed to the spectacle that's called professional wrestling), you see two highly trained, well-conditioned athletes trying to impose their wills on each other. You see two opponents applying the techniques they've learned from practice and from prior experience to achieve their goals.

In today's verse, the word *wrestling* implies contending passionately and continuously for something. It means coming to God again and again and requesting that which you're convinced in your heart He wants to do for you. Epaphras engaged in that kind of prayer on behalf of the Colossians. Jacob prayed like that during his encounter with God, too (Genesis 32:22–31). And the good news is that God invites you to pray the very same way.

Can you think of someone you know who could benefit from your prayers? Maybe a pastor or other full-time minister who is doing battle with the forces of evil? Or a married man who is working to save his marriage? Or how about a friend whom you know needs Jesus? If so, learn from Epaphras and from Jacob, and don't stop asking until God gives you what you know He wants to give you.

PRAY DAILY

*And pray in the Spirit on all occasions with all kinds of
prayers and requests. With this in mind, be alert and
always keep on praying for all the Lord's people.*
EPHESIANS 6:18 NIV

On the first Thursday of May every year, the United States observes
a National Day of Prayer. In 1952, the United States Congress
passed a resolution encouraging Americans to "turn to God in
prayer and meditation." Since that resolution, every president
every year has signed a proclamation encouraging Americans to
pray on this day.

While you, as a follower of Jesus, should be grateful that your
nation has set aside a day to focus on prayer and meditation, and
while you should do everything you can to encourage others to
pray, you should also make *every* day a personal day of prayer.

There are certainly occasions and life situations that call
for a more focused, more fervent time of prayer. But you should
always remember that God wants to hear from you—and speak
to you—as you spend time every day in prayer.

So pray every day. Pray and give thanks and praise to God.
Pray for your nation and its leaders and representatives, pray
for your family and friends, pray for those you know who need
Jesus, and pray for your church. The list is endless. So are the
opportunities.

HANDLING ANGER PROPERLY

Fools vent their anger,
but the wise quietly hold it back.
PROVERBS 29:11 NLT

This may come as a surprise to some Christian men, but the Bible teaches that the emotion of anger isn't necessarily a sin. God Himself expressed His anger in scripture (see Psalm 7:11; Mark 3:5). And the apostle Paul made a distinction between anger and *sinful* anger when he wrote, " 'In your anger do not sin': do not let the sun go down while you are still angry" (Ephesians 4:26 NIV).

Godly anger—also known as righteous indignation—can motivate men to act in ways that glorify God and further His kingdom. It moves you to defend those who are being wronged or mistreated, or to stand up for a biblical principle you see being violated.

But sinful anger, the kind of anger that moves you to contend for your own selfish desires, can damage relationships, cause unneeded pain to those you love, and hurt your witness for Christ.

Life will afford you many opportunities to feel anger. But when you feel that emotion rising up within you, stop and ask yourself if the way you're considering expressing that anger will hurt others or displease your Father in heaven. If the answer to that question is yes, then patiently hold your words in check, and choose to find a godly, healthy way to express how you feel.

THE IMPORTANCE OF "ONE ANOTHER"

*"A new command I give you: Love one another. As I have
loved you, so you must love one another. By this everyone
will know that you are my disciples, if you love one another."*
JOHN 13:34–35 NIV

During His earthly ministry, Jesus brought to His followers some
radical new (*new* to them) teachings about the Law, about the
nature of their relationship with God, and about love. He taught
that by-the-letter "obedience" to the Law of Moses wasn't nearly as
important as obedience to the spirit of the Law. He gave them a
glimpse of the loving nature of their heavenly Father, and taught
them the vital importance of loving one another.

The New Testament is filled with references to "one another,"
starting with Jesus' commandment that His followers love one
another in the same way He loved them—selflessly, sacrificially,
and compassionately. Here are just are a few examples from the
pen of the apostle Paul:

- "Be devoted to one another in love. Honor one another
  above yourselves" (Romans 12:10 NIV).
- "Live in harmony with one another" (Romans 12:16 NIV).
- "Serve one another humbly in love" (Galatians 5:13 NIV).
- "Be kind and compassionate to one another" (Ephesians
  4:32 NIV).

Clearly, God never intended for followers of Jesus Christ to
live self-focused lives. On the contrary, He has commanded you
to be lovingly devoted to your brothers and sisters in the faith.

FIRST IMPRESSIONS

Just then Boaz arrived from Bethlehem and greeted the harvesters,
"The LORD be with you!" "The LORD bless you!" they answered.
RUTH 2:4 NIV

When you're first introduced to Boaz, a key character in the beautiful story of redemption that is the book of Ruth, you get a pretty good idea of what kind of man he is. After he greets his workers with a hearty "The LORD be with you!" they respond with an equally enthusiastic "The LORD bless you!"

These words give you a great first impression of Boaz, don't they? Right away, you know that Boaz is a godly man who apparently treats his servants with kindness and compassion, and you know they know him as a man who loves God and others.

As you make your way through Ruth's story, you find that your first impressions of Boaz are well-founded. He indeed is a man who loves God and cares for the well-being of those who enter his sphere of influence.

Someone has rightly observed that you have only one chance to make a first impression. What kind of first impression do your words and actions make on those you meet? Do you think people who encounter you know right away that you're a man who loves God and loves other people—no matter their position in life—and wants to bless them?

That's a first impression any follower of Jesus should want to make on everyone he meets.

KIND WORDS SPOKEN

*Kind words are like honey—sweet to the
soul and healthy for the body.*
PROVERBS 16:24 NLT

In recent years, leaders in the modern corporate or business world have made an interesting discovery: many, if not most, workers tend to perform better when the boss or supervisor gives them verbal pats on the back for their good work. This may be old news to you, but it was apparently a revelation to many hard-boiled business leaders.

This should challenge you as a Christian to consider something: Would the same principle work on your wife and children, your friends, and your coworkers, or the people you lead in the workplace? Well, if you take today's verse to its logical conclusion. . . yes, it would!

People are just naturally *wired*—or should we say *created*—to need affirming, kind words. And while there is certainly a place for correction and discipline, never forget that everyone needs to hear some kind words coming from those they love and those whom God has placed in authority over them.

Do you want to see the best in your wife and children, in your friends, and in those you work with? Try speaking kind words to them. Verbalize your observations of something they're doing well. Let them know you appreciate them for the things they do and for who they are. Let them know they're valued. The results just might pleasantly surprise you.

GUILT: A USELESS EMOTION

*Where is another God like you, who pardons the guilt
of the remnant, overlooking the sins of his special people?
You will not stay angry with your people forever,
because you delight in showing unfailing love.*

Micah 7:18 nlt

A big part of the fallen human condition is negative, destructive emotions, one of the worst being guilt. You've probably felt guilty over things you've done, or failed to do, in the past. But guilt can be an anchor in your life that can hold you down and keep you from living the abundant life Jesus promised those who follow Him.

As a follower of Jesus Christ, you needn't dwell on guilt over your past mistakes and sins. If you find yourself feeling guilt, you should spend some time dwelling on *these* words directly from the mouth of God: "I—yes, I alone—will blot out your sins for my own sake and will never think of them again" (Isaiah 43:25 nlt).

God didn't save you, forgive you, and set you on a new path in life so that you can spend the rest of your days being eaten alive by guilt over your past sins. Yes, learn from your past mistakes and sins and become a better man of God through what you learn, but don't ever let yourself believe, for even a moment, that God holds that which He has forgotten against you.

A PICTURE OF DEPENDABILITY

*As Scripture says, "Anyone who believes
in him will never be put to shame."*
ROMANS 10:11 NIV

In modern psychology, those who have a difficult time trusting in or depending upon another person are said to have "trust issues." Sometimes those trust issues come as a result of a father who repeatedly proved himself to be undependable.

While some earthly fathers weren't as dependable as they should have been, you never have to worry about this with your Father in heaven. He always keeps His promises, and is always there for you if you simply call out to Him.

Jesus, who knew your heavenly Father better than anyone, said this of Him: "Which of you, if your son asks for bread, will give him a stone? Or if he asks for a fish, will give him a snake? If you, then, though you are evil, know how to give good gifts to your children, how much more will your Father in heaven give good gifts to those who ask him!" (Matthew 7:9–11 NIV).

When you come to God in faith for something—your salvation or some other pressing need—you can trust in Him to generously give you what you ask for. When you place that kind of trust in your heavenly Father, He will never let you down or leave you wondering where He is. Even when it seems He's *not* there, He's still there.

A LIVING FAITH

What good is it, my brothers and sisters, if someone claims
to have faith but has no deeds? Can such faith save them?. . .
faith by itself, if it is not accompanied by action, is dead.
JAMES 2:14, 17 NIV

Do you find today's verse a little troubling or, at the very least, confusing? If so, you're not alone. Taken in isolation, these words seem to say that without good works, you can't be saved.

However, this passage is a clear example of how context means everything. When you take these words as part of the bigger picture of New Testament teaching about your salvation, you understand that your good works are not a *means to an end* for your salvation, they are a *result* of that salvation.

The New Testament is clear that you're not saved through your own works, no matter how good they are. But when you have God's Spirit dwelling inside you as a result of coming to Jesus Christ for salvation, your Spirit-inspired attitude will always result in good works.

Are you looking for ways to put your faith into action? Then ask God what good works He'd like you to take part in today. But never forget that your good works here on earth can't save you for eternity, and they can't earn you additional favor with God. What they *can* do, however, is make your faith more real to you and others.

AS YOU MAKE YOUR PLANS. . .

Commit your works to the LORD
and your plans will be established.
PROVERBS 16:3 NASB

If you've ever been involved in planning for a new project or a new direction at work, you know that there's one all-important step you need to take before those plans can become a reality: your managers or bosses need to sign off on it. Without their approval, you're likely to run into serious problems.

The same thing can be said for the Christian who wants to launch out into some kind of new ministry, professional, or personal endeavor. In today's verse, Solomon offers a great bit of wisdom when it comes to planning. The best kind of planning, he tells you, starts with committing your vision for something to your ultimate Boss, your heavenly Father, and continues as you allow Him to give ongoing direction.

Many seemingly great plans—even plans for what looked like a God-appointed ministry—have failed because those with the vision didn't first submit their work to God.

Planning is an important part, a bedrock, in fact, of all great and important things you do. It's simply not a good idea to launch out on some new endeavor without it. So by all means plan, but as you make your plans, don't forget to submit what you're thinking about doing to God for His approval and His direction.

THE IMPORTANCE OF ACCOUNTABILITY

*Confess your sins to each other and pray for each other
so that you may be healed. The earnest prayer of a righteous
person has great power and produces wonderful results.*

JAMES 5:16 NLT

Making yourself accountable to others isn't easy a lot of the time, is it? Most men seem to have a touch of "rugged individualism" in them, and they'd rather handle their struggles on their own. Besides being rugged, if they're honest, most of them have some hidden, personal sins they'd rather not reveal to even their best friends.

Today's verse, however, shows that this is exactly the wrong approach to living an overcoming life for Christ. The apostle James challenges all men to come clean with one another and confess their sins—even those sins they might not be comfortable divulging. This is a great piece of wisdom for Christian men. First of all, life experience can teach you that most men won't be shocked when you confess a sin you feel is holding you back in your walk with Jesus. On the contrary, you just might find that your brothers are struggling with a similar sin.

Even more important, however, is that confessing your sins to your brothers allows them to know how to pray for and with you so that you can find lasting freedom. And it also helps you to become accountable to those who love you and want you to overcome.

PRAISE FOR YOUR WIFE

*A wife of noble character who can find? She is worth far
more than rubies. . . . Her children arise and call her blessed;
her husband also, and he praises her: "Many women
do noble things, but you surpass them all."*
PROVERBS 31:10, 28–29 NIV

In Proverbs 31:10–30, King Lemuel relays to his son the wise words
his own mother had given him concerning what an incredible
blessing a wife of noble character is. He lists her many character
qualities and the many things she does for her household and
other people, and as he concludes, he tells his son how a blessed
husband speaks words of praise directly to his wife.

Family life is busy, and sometimes it can be easy to neglect
the basics of marriage such as speaking uplifting, encouraging
words to your spouse. But making it a point to compliment
your wife for who she is and what she does—especially today,
on Mother's Day—can move your marriage from good to great,
or from great to amazing.

If you're married, thank God for this special day to remind
you to be thankful for your wife. But you should tell her every
day how much you love her, value her, and appreciate everything
she does for you, for your children, and for others. And just to
make those words even more special now and then, make sure
to say them within earshot of your children.

THE PRIVILEGE OF PAIN

For you have been given not only the privilege of trusting
in Christ but also the privilege of suffering for him.
PHILIPPIANS 1:29 NLT

When the apostle Paul wrote of suffering, he did so with authority. He had suffered threats of death and more severe beatings than he could count. He had suffered through sleeplessness, hunger, thirst, and cold. His life as a servant of Jesus Christ was one of constant danger and great personal suffering (see 2 Corinthians 11:23–28).

But this same man not only wrote of suffering for Christ as a privilege, he also wrote of suffering as a means to grow in his faith: "We also glory in our sufferings, because we know that suffering produces perseverance; perseverance, character; and character, hope. And hope does not put us to shame, because God's love has been poured out into our hearts through the Holy Spirit, who has been given to us" (Romans 5:3–5 NIV).

In America these days, Christians don't suffer the way Paul did. This is a time and a place of peace and prosperity. But when you suffer—be it from a personal loss, an illness, a disability, or other difficulties—you can look at it as a privilege and a blessing. And you can live in the assurance that your joy is not based on your suffering or on your *lack* of suffering, but in knowing God intimately and walking with Him every day.

LIVING IN THE PAST

Do not say, "Why were the old days better than these?"
For it is not wise to ask such questions.
ECCLESIASTES 7:10 NIV

Have you ever gotten together with a group of old friends—maybe at some reunion—to catch up with one another and reminisce about your times together many years back? Those kinds of gatherings can be enjoyable because you get to see people you haven't seen in a long time and share laughter and memories.

But they can also be frustrating if they cause you to look at your current experiences through the lenses of days gone by. As many have found out, that's not a good thing.

It can be easy sometimes to find yourself living in the past and longing for what you remember as "better times." That can be especially true when you feel dissatisfaction with the present or when you're going through difficult circumstances. In times like these, you may find yourself feeling a sense of ingratitude for what God is doing in your life at present.

There's nothing wrong with reminiscing, with thinking and talking about great times you've enjoyed in the past. You can remember those days fondly and even thank God for them. But you should never let your great memories of days gone by get in the way of living in what God has for you in the here and now.

HONESTY WITH GOD

"I do believe; help my unbelief."
MARK 9:24 NASB

The words spoken in today's verse came from the mouth of a man who was out of options. He wanted Jesus to heal his demon-possessed son, and he had no doubt heard of this Man who had healed many sick, lame, and demoniacs. But still, he doubted.

At first glance, you may wonder how a man who had heard so much about Jesus could possibly doubt Him. And you may even look at his words as a contradiction. But maybe you shouldn't see his words as a contradiction at all. And maybe you shouldn't assume that he had a hard time believing Jesus could heal people. Maybe you should look at his words as an admission that he wondered if Jesus could and would help *him*.

The thought of speaking to God with this kind of honesty scares many men. There are things, after all, you wish you could hide from Him, things you don't even want to admit to yourself. But when you come to the end of yourself and still need God to do something great *for* you and *within* you, it's just the kind of honesty He wants from you.

Do you sometimes find yourself doubting that God wants to do a miracle for *you*? If so, then confess your doubt to Him. He can handle it, and He can also open your heart and mind to what He has planned for you.

GOD NOTICES

*By faith Enoch was taken from this life, so that he
did not experience death: "He could not be found,
because God had taken him away." For before he was
taken, he was commended as one who pleased God.*

HEBREWS 11:5 NIV

If you've ever read the Bible cover to cover, starting with the first verse of Genesis and ending with the last words of Revelation, and you still don't know much about a man named Enoch, don't feel bad.

Enoch is mentioned, seemingly in passing, in only four verses in Genesis 5 (vv. 21–24), in one verse in Hebrews 11, and from a quote in Jude 1:14–15. Nothing else is written of anything he did or said, and yet this man—whom we know little about other than that he "walked faithfully with God" (Genesis 5:24)—rated a mention alongside some of the Bible's greatest people of faith.

Maybe Enoch never did anything of note other than walk faithfully with his God during his 365 years here on earth. Or maybe, just maybe, Enoch's short mention in scripture is there to teach you that your God is concerned not with what you *do* but with the fact that your life is an example of choosing to walk faithfully with Him.

Either way, while you may read the Bible and barely notice Enoch, God most certainly noticed this man, and He counted him worthy to take him to heaven without experiencing physical death.

RECEIVING WISDOM

Listen to counsel and accept discipline,
that you may be wise the rest of your days.
PROVERBS 19:20 NASB

One of the many amazing things about God is that as long as you're committed to walking with Him, He never allows an experience to go to waste. That is especially true of the difficulties and suffering you're sure to encounter as you make your way through this journey called life.

The apostle James understood this well, so as he closed out a section of his epistle dealing with suffering, he wrote, "If any of you lacks wisdom, you should ask God, who gives generously to all without finding fault, and it will be given to you" (James 1:5 NIV).

James had no doubt observed what many Christian leaders since the first century have seen: that people don't always know how to respond wisely during difficult times. That is why he instructed the first-century believers, who lived during very perilous times, to seek God for wisdom—and to be assured that He would give them what they asked for.

God has promised to give wisdom to anyone who asks for it. And like many of His gifts, He uses many means to provide you with the wisdom you ask for—His written Word, His Holy Spirit, life experiences, and other people. So ask God for wisdom, but be open to the many different ways He can give you what you've asked for.

WHO'S YOUR ENEMY?

Be alert and of sober mind. Your enemy the devil prowls around
like a roaring lion looking for someone to devour.
1 PETER 5:8 NIV

If someone were to ask you who or what is the greatest enemy of
the church today, how would you answer? Some would answer
that the biggest enemy is government institutions, which in
many ways are becoming more hostile toward the Christian faith.
Others might say that other human institutions seem to work
tirelessly to oppose the preaching of the Gospel.

While there's no doubt that some worldly and human
institutions want to keep Christianity in a corner, Christian
men need to understand that they're in a spiritual battle, not a
political or physical one. The apostle Paul put it like this: "Our
struggle is not against flesh and blood, but against the rulers,
against the authorities, against the powers of this dark world
and against the spiritual forces of evil in the heavenly realms"
(Ephesians 6:12 NIV).

Yes, you should stand against evil in the secular world today
and contend for what is right in God's eyes. But you should
never forget that your ultimate enemy is the devil, not the lost
and misguided people who oppose God.

And above all, you need to remember to put on the full
armor of God (Ephesians 6:10–18) as you do battle against the
devil and his minions.

WHAT ARE YOUR CREDENTIALS?

Amos answered Amaziah, "I was neither a prophet
nor the son of a prophet, but I was a shepherd,
and I also took care of sycamore-fig trees."

AMOS 7:14 NIV

You may have felt challenged to get more involved in outreach or some other ministry at some point, but thought, *I don't know how much help I can be. I don't have any kind of education or credentials.*

Men tend to put a lot of stock in credentials, don't they? They see those with high levels of education or impressive accomplishments as somehow more qualified or trustworthy. But God doesn't necessarily see it that way. As someone once wisely said, "God doesn't call the qualified; He qualifies the called."

God doesn't look first at your credentials, and He doesn't focus first on your training and natural abilities. He's concerned, first and foremost, with your willingness to obediently step out and be used by Him to influence your part of the world for His kingdom. When He finds you willing, He enables you to do what He's called you to do.

You don't need a doctorate in theology or a PhD in biblical studies for God to use you in your own sphere of influence. You need just one thing: willingness. So if you'd like to know what you can do to expand the kingdom of God, just ask Him! He'll never answer by first asking about your credentials.

WALKING WITH GOD

The LORD has told you what is good, and this is what
he requires of you: to do what is right, to love mercy,
and to walk humbly with your God.
MICAH 6:8 NLT

Sometime during the course of human history, going for walks with one another became an occasion not just to get some exercise (as beneficial as that was), but also to enjoy one another's company. Many a friendship has been enhanced and many a marriage has been strengthened just through going for walks—or for hikes in the case of the more athletic, more motivated crowd.

The Bible contains two examples of people it says "walked with God," using those exact words: Enoch (Genesis 5:21–24) and Noah (Genesis 6:9). Of course, many other men "walked with God" in the sense that they remained in close relationship with Him and obeyed His commands.

But it's probably not much of a stretch to see the use of that exact phrase in reference to Enoch and Noah as word pictures of men who walked with God in the sense that they could fellowship with Him as closely as if they literally went for a stroll with Him, sharing their hearts with Him and allowing Him to share His heart with them.

What about you today? Maybe going for a walk and taking God with you through prayer—talking and listening to Him—could enhance and strengthen your relationship with Him.

REPULSED BY PRIDE

Human pride will be brought down, and human
arrogance will be humbled. Only the LORD will be
exalted on that day of judgment.

Isaiah 2:11 nlt

Have you ever been forced, through a set of circumstances beyond
your control, to spend time around a proud, boastful person?
You know, the kind of person who never seems to have anything
to say unless it's about himself and his accomplishments?

Being around that kind of man for any length of time can
be draining, can't it? Pride is a sin each man struggles with in
one way or another. But most men find those who seem ruled by
pride and arrogance difficult to handle. In a very real way, most
of us find excessive pride. . .well, kind of repulsive.

Think about it, though. If you find pride repulsive, then how
much more so is it for a God who lists humility as a high virtue
and pride as a detestable sin? So much so that He tells you, " 'God
opposes the proud but gives grace to the humble' " (James 4:6 nlt).

James's use of the word *opposes* in this verse carries with it
an ominous meaning. It connotes a God who doesn't just let the
prideful man go about his way, but who actually works against
him in every way.

Pride is a serious sin that leads you nowhere good. On the
other hand, God gives this promise to those who choose humility:
"Humble yourselves, therefore, under God's mighty hand, that
he may lift you up in due time" (1 Peter 5:6 niv).

A BIBLICAL ANATOMY LESSON

Just as a body, though one, has many parts, but all its many parts form one body, so it is with Christ.
1 CORINTHIANS 12:12 NIV

In 1 Corinthians 12, the apostle Paul likens the church (not the building but the believers who gather there to worship God and fellowship with one another) to the human body, which consists of many individual parts that work wonderfully together for one purpose: to keep you alive and moving.

Paul wanted the believers in Corinth to understand that they all had a role to play within the local church—some bigger and others smaller, some more up front and others more behind the scenes—but all important to the church as a whole. "Now you are the body of Christ, and each one of you is a part of it," he wrote (v. 27).

If Paul were writing to the different church bodies today, he'd tell them the same thing. Each member has a part to play for the greater good of the church.

God doesn't intend for you to attend church services every week just to warm a pew. On the contrary, He has given you special gifts and abilities so that you can serve this wonderful organism called the Body of Christ. Your part in this bargain is to seek out and discover your gifts so that you can begin serving.

A LEGACY OF FAITH

All these people earned a good reputation because of their
faith, yet none of them received all that God had promised.
For God had something better in mind for us, so that
they would not reach perfection without us.
HEBREWS 11:39–40 NLT

The eleventh chapter of Hebrews is an amazing New Testament passage that gives you a pretty good idea of what kind of legacy God calls you to leave behind when your days on this earth are over.

As you read through this chapter, you may recall that the people listed by the writer of this epistle weren't perfect. Far from it! Noah got drunk, Abraham lied because he was afraid, Jacob was a deceiver, Moses doubted God, and David. . .well, his many failings as a man, as a king, and as a father are well chronicled in the Bible.

Yet the writer of Hebrews goes out of his way to tell you that all the people listed in this chapter played their own important parts in making God's plan of redemption a reality for men today—not because they were perfect, but simply because they believed God when He spoke.

As you read Hebrews 11, let it challenge you. Let it bring you to a place of asking yourself what kind of legacy you'll leave behind—for your friends, for your family, and for people whose lives you may touch without even knowing it.

OVERCOMING YOUR SIN

I have hidden your word in my heart
that I might not sin against you.
PSALM 119:11 NIV

The great nineteenth-century American evangelist Dwight L. Moody is credited with many profound and inspiring quotations, one of them being: "The Bible will keep you from sin, or sin will keep you from the Bible."

The writer of Psalm 119 would heartily agree with this. In today's verse, he declared that he kept his heart and mind focused on the Word of God so that he could avoid falling into sin against his God. The same thing can be true for you today.

The writer of the epistle to the Hebrews wrote this of the Bible's power: "For the word of God is alive and active. Sharper than any double-edged sword, it penetrates even to dividing soul and spirit, joints and marrow; it judges the thoughts and attitudes of the heart" (Hebrews 4:12 NIV).

Sadly, too many Christians don't make sufficient use of what the apostle Paul called "the sword of the Spirit" (Ephesians 6:17)—and that results in weak, powerless lives. But if you can learn to walk in the tremendous power the Bible gives you to live an overcoming life, you find it possible to say yes to the things that please God and no to the things that displease Him.

Make it your goal to learn to wield this mighty sword by reading God's Word, memorizing it, and meditating on it.

SHOWING RESPECT

*Show proper respect to everyone, love the family
of believers, fear God, honor the emperor.*
1 PETER 2:17 NIV

Today's culture puts great value on respect. But while not everyone practices respect for their fellow human beings, nearly everyone feels entitled to it.

It may come as a surprise to many Christian men, but all people feel an innate need for respect. Even more surprising to some is that God calls each of His people to show respect for others, no matter their beliefs or lifestyles. It's not always easy to show proper respect to others, and it's especially difficult with people whose attitudes and actions show disregard for the truths revealed in God's Word. But the actions and words of others who don't know God don't relieve you who *do* know Him of the responsibility to treat them with respect.

Respect doesn't mean giving approval or acceptance to lifestyles and actions you know God disapproves of. It means simply seeing and treating those you meet—no matter how much you disagree with their views and lifestyle choices—as valued creations made in the image of God.

Your role as a Christian living in a fallen world full of imperfect people is to be an example of God's love and grace. You move yourself closer to that goal when you show love and respect for others, both in how you speak to them and how you treat them.

TELLING YOUR OWN STORY

Give praise to the LORD, proclaim his name;
make known among the nations what he has done.
PSALM 105:1 NIV

Each Christian has his own story about how he came to know Jesus. Not all of these stories may seem like a bona fide water-turned-to-wine miracle—at least not to the people hearing them—but they're all amazing in that they give an account of how Jesus came onto the scene, took what was once dead, and made it alive.

That's just the nature of salvation, isn't it?

The Bible tells you that you're to always be ready "to give an answer to everyone who asks you to give the reason for the hope that you have" (1 Peter 3:15 NIV). Among other things, that can mean being ready to tell others about how Jesus, through the Holy Spirit, brought you to a point of responding to God's love and receiving forgiveness and eternal life. It can also include your story of healing and deliverance from what you once were.

When you begin talking to a friend or family member who needs Jesus, very often the best place to start is not by talking about how that *person* needs Him but instead by telling your *own* story of what He has done for you and how He has impacted your life.

Always remember, your story of salvation is an amazing story people around you need to hear.

THE ULTIMATE SACRIFICE

"Greater love has no one than this:
to lay down one's life for one's friends."
JOHN 15:13 NIV

Once a year, near the beginning of summer, Americans celebrate a day set aside to honor the brave men and women who gave their lives in service to this nation on different fields of battle. When you properly recognize the true meaning of Memorial Day (and it's not about another day off from work, picnics, or big sales), you communicate to the friends and family of the fallen this simple message: "I remember. . .and I'm grateful."

The sacrifices this nation's fallen warriors have made to protect your freedom is a picture, albeit an imperfect one, of the sacrifice God made when He sent His Son to die for a humanity that was a slave to its own sinfulness. The apostle Paul put it beautifully when he wrote, "God demonstrates his own love for us in this: while we were still sinners, Christ died for us" (Romans 5:8 NIV).

On Memorial Day, take a few moments to think about those who made the ultimate sacrifice to protect the freedoms of people they didn't even know. And never forget the sacrifice of the God who knows everything about you but still chose to give you the very best He had.

LONE RANGER CHRISTIANITY

All the believers devoted themselves to the apostles'
teaching, and to fellowship, and to sharing in meals
(including the Lord's Supper), and to prayer.
ACTS 2:42 NLT

In several polls in recent years, more and more people—including many professing Christians—say they don't go to church services regularly, if at all.

One of the most common alibis for consistently skipping church is, "I don't have to go to church to be a Christian." While it may technically be true that you don't have to attend church to be a believer, it's also true that in order to *grow* in your faith, you need the teaching and fellowship you receive when you gather for worship and Bible study.

You receive these things when you attend services at church. That's why the writer of Hebrews admonishes followers of Jesus Christ to not neglect "our own assembling together, as is the habit of some" (Hebrews 10:25 NASB).

Today's verse gives a list of great reasons to attend church regularly, starting with receiving sound biblical teaching. It's also at church that you fellowship with other Christians, which the Bible teaches is important for your spiritual growth.

God never intended for you to be a Lone Ranger Christian. He established the church to provide believers a means to receive teaching and fellowship. That's why it's a good plan for you to find a church that provides sound teaching and then commit yourself to going there on a regular basis.

PRAYING THROUGH THE PAIN

*He touched the socket of his hip; and the socket of Jacob's
hip was out of joint as He wrestled with him. And He
said, "Let Me go, for the day breaks." But he said,
"I will not let You go unless You bless me!"*

GENESIS 32:25–26 NKJV

Today's passage is part of an account in which the patriarch Jacob became involved in an extended wrestling match with. . .God! It sounds odd to think of a mere man wrestling with the Almighty. Certainly, the Creator of the universe could not only have ended such an encounter in an instant, but with a thought. However, your Father in heaven had a lesson to teach Jacob—and you, too.

God wanted to bless Jacob, but He also wanted him to understand that prayer isn't always easy, that it means persistent, sometimes painful, times of pleading with God until he receives an answer.

If you've ever suffered through a dislocated joint, then you have some understanding of what Jacob went through in that hour before dawn. A dislocated toe or finger can be agonizing enough, but just think of the pain Jacob felt when God dislocated his *hip!*

When a nearly incapacitated Jacob still refused to let his God go that night, he set an example for believers to follow. Prayer hurts sometimes, but in the midst of your pain, you should keep praying and cling to your God with everything you have.

GODLY PAYBACK

Do not repay evil with evil or insult with insult.
On the contrary, repay evil with blessing, because to this
you were called so that you may inherit a blessing.

1 PETER 3:9 NIV

How do you respond when someone, intentionally or unintentionally, does you wrong or insults you? It's a rare man who doesn't feel anger and a desire for some payback when someone has done or said something that insults him. But while the anger may sometimes be justified, God tells you that your response to those who do you wrong is to. . .well, *bless* that person.

Your fallen human nature being what it is, you're prone to think that you're entitled to a little vengeance when you've been wronged or to a few sharp, biting comebacks when someone speaks unkind words to you. But God tells you that your responses to evil should be compassionate, kind, and understanding.

On a purely practical level, you need to remember that you can't know what's going on inside the mind of the person who does unkind things and speaks unkind words to you. But God does, and that's one of the reasons He tells you to repay evil and insults with blessings.

No one likes being hurt or insulted. But as a Christian, you must see those unpleasant moments not as negatives but as opportunities to bless those who need God's touch in their lives and to receive God's blessings on yourself.

WHAT GOD CAN'T DO

*Why do you look the other way? Why do you ignore our
suffering and oppression? We collapse in the dust,
lying face down in the dirt. Rise up! Help us!
Ransom us because of your unfailing love.*
PSALM 44:24–26 NLT

Can God truly hide from you or turn away from His own people?
Could God actually ignore what is happening in the world?

Your perceptions of God and reality can appear difficult to
reconcile when life begins to fall apart. Whether you're going
through a tragedy, a struggle, or a season of spiritual darkness,
God isn't hiding, ignoring you, or looking away from you. But
God's presence doesn't always mean your problems will be solved,
life will go smoothly, or that all of your doubts and uncertainties
will disappear.

This tension of suffering or doubt of God's presence goes
back centuries, and there's no reason to expect that you'll be
part of the generation that finally figures it out. The psalmist
leads you to the only place where you can find rest. Even as you
feel beaten down by life and struggle to rise up from where you
have fallen, place your hope in God's unfailing love.

Even if you have your doubts and come to the end of your
faith, because of His unfailing love God can't turn away from you
or ignore you. Even at your lowest point, you are always loved.

IS TRUSTING GOD A "RISK"?

Those who live in the shelter of the Most High will find rest
in the shadow of the Almighty. This I declare about the LORD:
He alone is my refuge, my place of safety;
he is my God, and I trust him.

PSALM 91:1–2 NLT

What would make you feel secure? For some it's a particular place. For others it may mean a certain amount of money in the bank or a particular position at work. Everyone craves security and assurances that they'll be safe from the storms of life that are sure to come.

What does it look like to dwell in God's shelter today and to have God's shadow over you? Perhaps it means releasing control over a specific life circumstance. For others, it may be a step of faith that feels more like a risk than a place of safety or security under God. The irony of living by faith and trusting God as your sole refuge and stronghold can feel risky and even a little chaotic as you perfect your faith in God.

As you grapple with your desires for security and safety, the words of this psalm challenge you to rethink your place under the protection of God. How does it feel to have God as your refuge and stronghold? Does it feel like a risk right now? Are there ways you can learn to grow deeper in your trust in God today?

WHY JESUS IS MERCIFUL

This High Priest of ours understands our weaknesses,
for he faced all of the same testings we do, yet he did
not sin. So let us come boldly to the throne of our
gracious God. There we will receive his mercy,
and we will find grace to help us
when we need it most.

HEBREWS 4:15–16 NLT

Sometimes it's hard to acknowledge your weaknesses or your need for help. You live in a self-sufficient culture, and so it may come as a shock to read that Jesus spent time on earth in order to feel your weaknesses and to show mercy to you.

If you struggle with sin or don't think you can set your life right, know this: Jesus felt your fears, inadequacies, and even weakness. He knows that you're tempted, that you struggle, and that you won't always make the best choices.

Jesus was tested in all of the ways you have been tested, and while that may be hard to believe, it's even harder to believe that He then is merciful to you. But He is. And He wants you to come to Him in your weakness and failure.

Do you need to know today that Jesus is merciful and ready to help you? He desires that you have no fear when you approach His throne of grace. And take note that this throne is one of grace, not judgment. Acknowledging your weaknesses and failures is the key to restoration.

HOW YOU'RE SAVED FROM SHAME

*For I fully expect and hope that I will never be ashamed,
but that I will continue to be bold for Christ, as I have
been in the past. And I trust that my life will
bring honor to Christ, whether I live or die.*

PHILIPPIANS 1:20 NLT

What do you fear?

Paul speaks of his fear of being put to shame, and shame is different for each person. Shame could come from the rejection of your peers or community. It could also result from a personal failure or the revelation that you've been inauthentic or fraudulent in some way. However, by identifying what you fear, you can begin to move toward the freedom that prompted Paul to speak with boldness.

If you fear what will become of you and your reputation, then you're in need of the freedom that comes through union with Christ. Your hope and glory are united with Him as you aim to bring God glory with your life.

This approach to glorifying God isn't always high profile or may not appear to be successful. Just as Jesus glorified God through His suffering and death, Paul reminds you that glorifying God looks like faithfulness amid the highs and lows of life. Whether in life or death, you need not fear the potential of shame and failure so long as you've drawn near to Christ and His glory becomes your own.

GOD IS YOUR STRENGTH

Though we are overwhelmed by our sins,
you forgive them all.
PSALM 65:3 NLT

How often do you mistake being strong in the Lord with simply being strong on your own?

There are no caveats in this psalm about being stronger than your sins. There are no special exceptions for people who are especially determined when it comes to their weaknesses and imperfections. Sin may overpower you, no matter how much you may want to choose obedience. This is not to excuse sinning. The Bible says, after all, that one of the fruits of the Spirit is self-control (Galatians 5:22–23). So God does expect you to resist sin.

But you can't make yourself more determined or more focused on your own. Your one and only recourse is the mercy and grace of a loving God. If you want to find your strength each day, you must find God, even if that requires beginning with a confession of your failures and weaknesses.

Whether you feel overwhelmed and powerless or you're gritting your teeth in determination, you'll never advance to a point that you'll be able to blot out your own sins. If you rely on your strength and willpower, you'll most assuredly lose eventually. But God's mercy and strength will be there to meet you and deliver you. So cry out to God for His strength.

Once you rest in God, your strength will be endless.

HOW WE GROW

So get rid of all evil behavior. Be done with all deceit,
hypocrisy, jealousy, and all unkind speech. Like newborn babies,
you must crave pure spiritual milk so that you will grow
into a full experience of salvation. Cry out for this
nourishment, now that you have had a taste
of the Lord's kindness.

1 PETER 2:1–3 NLT

Jesus told His followers to become like children in order to enter the kingdom of God (Matthew 18:3), but Peter seems to take things a step further, telling his readers to become like infants.

Imagining infants who have a simple, single-minded dependence on their mothers for milk, you can catch a glimpse of what Peter has in mind. Perhaps his readers struggled with many serious sins such as envy, hypocrisy, criticism, and deceit because they had turned their faith into something complex. They wondered if they could work harder in order to overcome these many spiritual struggles.

Peter assured them that trying harder wouldn't cut it. They had to become all the *more* dependent on God's nurturing care for them. There's no hope outside of God's spiritual provision for His children.

You may long to stop envying or to become more spiritual, but these are merely dead ends. Your longing should be for the presence of the Lord instead. When you have tasted the goodness of the Lord, you'll find deliverance from your greatest struggles.

WHERE DOES DESPERATION LEAD YOU?

As the deer longs for streams of water, so I long for
you, O God. I thirst for God, the living God.
When can I go and stand before him?
PSALM 42:1–2 NLT

Streams can be few and far between in the land of Israel. That's why so many stories of the Old Testament include details about wells and major problems stemming from droughts that drained cisterns. A reliance on wells in the time of Jesus meant He had conversations with people around wells quite often.

With limited water sources, the deer of the land could be hard-pressed sometimes to find water. Perhaps in a season of drought it may have seemed nearly impossible to find a stream.

This intense thirst for a scarce water supply captures the spirit of desperation and longing that the writer of this psalm shares while waiting on God's deliverance. Although you have the assurance that God is alive and well, a season of doubt or isolation can leave you desperate.

Then again, you could just as well become distracted by something else, spending your days longing for things other than God. Perhaps the question you could ask yourself is: *What am I desperate for today?* Your seasons of searching and thirsting for God won't last forever, but that doesn't mean you won't have your times of trial, uncertainty, and longing for God's presence.

WISDOM PUTS YOU IN YOUR PLACE

*Fear of the LORD is the foundation of true wisdom. All who obey
his commandments will grow in wisdom. Praise him forever!*
PSALM 111:10 NLT

Everyone wants to be wise, but fear is rarely valued as a positive
virtue. Fear is typically associated with running away, living in
paranoia, or lacking any kind of stability. Jesus repeatedly told
His disciples to *not* be afraid, so why would the writer of this
psalm note that "fear of the Lord" is the foundation of wisdom?
Isn't fear the opposite of faith?

What if this "fear" isn't quaking at the thought of God but
is a humbling, unsettling grasp of God's holiness and power?
The accounts of God showing up among the people in the Old
Testament are truly fear-inspiring, but God was also very careful
to avoid terrifying people. Even when Moses reflected the glory
of God, he veiled his face. God doesn't use His glory and power
in order to terrify you into submission. Jesus reaches out to you
in love, saying, "Do not fear" (Luke 12:32 NKJV).

However, if you begin to imagine that you're wiser than God,
capable of controlling your life, or free to do as you please, the
fear of God's power and holiness can offer a helpful correction.
Should God choose to show up, you'll have a fearful reminder
of how unwise your life choices have been.

YOU SHARE FROM GOD'S GENEROSITY

"But when you give to someone in need, don't let your left hand know what your right hand is doing. Give your gifts in private, and your Father, who sees everything, will reward you."
Matthew 6:3–4 nlt

Everything you have is a gift from God, and so Jesus challenges your desire to gain the praise of fellow men and church leaders when you give generously from your possessions. Giving as freely as you have received without the hope of recognition saves you from the illusion of self-sufficiency and pride in your own abilities. If you're depending on God for your provision, then your generosity to others is between you and God as you give as freely as you have received.

Think about it: the more attached you become to your money and possessions, the less likely you are to see God as your provider and sustainer. Most importantly, the less you live by faith, the more dependent you will become on the opinions of others. Without seeking God's praise first and foremost, you run the risk of building your life on the unstable foundations of what others think and say.

Giving from your possessions also ensures that you won't become dependent on them for your security. Privately giving to others may be one of the purest acts of faith possible.

LETTING GO OF GRUDGES

"So if you are presenting a sacrifice at the altar in the Temple and you suddenly remember that someone has something against you, leave your sacrifice there at the altar. Go and be reconciled to that person. Then come and offer your sacrifice to God."
MATTHEW 5:23–24 NLT

Your worship and your treatment of others are linked. Broken fellowship with a neighbor or colleague can get in the way of your worship of God, and your only path to freedom is through confession and forgiveness.

Perhaps your own pride has offended someone or a grudge has poisoned your relationship. If you give in to anger, you then demand your rights and this can cause divisions or alienate you from others. Whatever you are holding on to, your ability to pray and to worship freely will be damaged by the same things that damage your relationships.

Pride is always destructive, whether before God or before others. A grudge could point to a self-righteousness that keeps you from receiving God's mercy, let alone showing mercy to others. Anger counteracts the humility that keeps you in your place before God.

If you want to know where you stand before God, one of the first places to look should be in your relationships with others. Do your interactions or relationships indicate that you think too highly of yourself? What steps can you take to remedy that?

WHAT MOTIVATES YOU TO PRAY?

Enter his gates with thanksgiving; go into his courts with praise. Give thanks to him and praise his name. For the LORD is good. His unfailing love continues forever, and his faithfulness continues to each generation.

PSALM 100:4–5 NLT

You may be most likely to pray in a time of need, but your own circumstances shouldn't be the first thing on your mind when you enter a time of worship or prayer. In fact, you may struggle to pray if you don't approach God with thanksgiving and praise. Thanksgiving and praise keep your circumstances in proper perspective.

Why do you turn to God in prayer? Is it because of something you want? Or are you moved toward God because of His goodness, unfailing love, and faithfulness throughout the generations? Without a reality check into the love, goodness, and faithfulness of God, who knows which direction your prayers will go?

You come to God because you're His beloved child. You come to God in prayer because He could never forget His own or leave His children behind. You come to God in prayer because you can trust His goodness, even if you can't understand His place in your circumstances.

You have every reason to praise God as you enter into prayer. Skipping the praise that He is due could result in some very self-centered prayers that miss an understanding of how deeply God cares for you.

GOD BUILDS YOU UP FROM THE DUST

The LORD is like a father to his children, tender and compassionate
to those who fear him. For he knows how weak we are;
he remembers we are only dust.

PSALM 103:13–14 NLT

Do you feel pressure to appear capable, strong, or holy? Have you ever feared being "found out" as a fraud because you struggle either privately or publicly?

Your masks always fall off in God's presence, and while that may be devastating or humiliating for you, God knows full well that it is for your benefit. You will only find freedom from your weaknesses and the false sense of self that you fight to maintain when you see with clarity that although you're little more than dust, God still cares for you like a father cares for his children. You are His child. This is the only identity you have to claim.

When you wish to appear strong or capable, your admission of weakness and dependence opens you to God's strength. You will finally tap into God's greater compassion and mercy for you, and you will then be able to share the same with those around you. God is rebuilding you from the dust of the ground on up.

THE ULTIMATE PAYBACK

Don't repay evil for evil. Don't retaliate with insults when people insult you. Instead, pay them back with a blessing. That is what God has called you to do, and he will grant you his blessing.

1 Peter 3:9 NLT

In the heat of an argument or as you encounter a frustrating situation, it's hard to resist trading insults or giving someone a piece of your mind. As social media and e-mail make it possible to argue without seeing someone face-to-face, you often experience the worst parts of your anger and discord without the filter of empathy or understanding.

Peter challenges you to bless those who insult you and to avoid any kind of retaliation. While he was writing to Christians who were being actively marginalized and persecuted for their faith, his message remains powerful as you seek to infuse your world with God's hope.

You gain very little from insulting others, and even the act of receiving an insult can be good for you. Perhaps you need reminders that you define yourself as part of God's people and His beloved child. Although an insult may tend to undermine your fragile ego, as you release hurt or anger and hand over a blessing, you bring the other person one step closer to God while reminding yourself of where you find your identity.

WHEN GOD'S MERCY INCREASES

Our ancestors in Egypt were not impressed by the LORD's
miraculous deeds. They soon forgot his many acts of kindness
to them. Instead, they rebelled against him at the Red Sea.
Even so, he saved them—to defend the honor of his
name and to demonstrate his mighty power.

PSALM 106:7–8 NLT

Unfaithfulness toward God often begins when you forget how God has acted in the past. As the people of Israel lost sight of God's miracles and kindness, they began to seek other gods and even openly rebelled against God.

The stories in scripture about unfaithfulness, worshipping other gods, or failing to trust God could just as easily be your own stories. It's possible that the fantastic details of these historical accounts cause you to forget that the daily worries of life, the threats of political turmoil, and selfish desires or ambition caused God's own people to forget even the wonder of seeing the sea split before them.

The sins of those who went before you are most likely part of your story as well. If those who witnessed the greatest miracles could forget them, how much more should you be aware of your own weaknesses?

Even during these repeated acts of unfaithfulness and forgetfulness, God's mercy didn't cease. In fact, God's mercy increased in order to save His people. God didn't stop revealing His power.

SEEING GOD BY LOOKING BACK

The godly will see these things and be glad, while the wicked are struck silent. Those who are wise will take all this to heart; they will see in our history the faithful love of the LORD.

PSALM 107:42–43 NLT

What is filling your mind today? What have you pondered so far?

You're probably surrounded by entertainment, news reports, and commercials that can easily fill your thoughts. Your work and family surely occupy important spots in your mind as well. But how often do you pause to remember the ways that God has been at work in the past week, month, or even year? It's possible that His love may appear far off simply because you need to spend a little time today considering His faithful love.

Whether you're entertaining doubts or uncertain about the future, your faith can be bolstered by taking a moment to notice the ways that God has offered comfort, reassurance, guidance, or the peace of His presence. Just as God's people are expected to learn from their mistakes, there's also great benefit in remembering His provision.

As you consider your next steps, whether at home, work, or in your church community, you can take comfort in remembering God's past actions on your behalf. Sometimes you don't need Him to perform another miracle. You just need to notice what He has already done for you.

FINDING GOD EACH DAY

*Praise the LORD! I will thank the LORD with all my heart as
I meet with his godly people. How amazing are the deeds
of the LORD! All who delight in him should ponder them.*
PSALM 111:1–2 NLT

Today's psalm should encourage you to pause and to ponder the works of God around you. How is He present with you today? Can you see how the good and perfect gifts around you are from the Lord? You can see this moment today as an invitation to draw near to God and to become aware of His presence.

It's easy to run from one task to another, and by evening you may wonder where God was throughout the day. Perhaps you even feel abandoned by Him at the end of a busy day. While scripture assures you that He's always with you, you can surely overlook His presence and gifts for you. Unless you take time to see the Lord's works around you, you'll miss out on the delight and joy that belong to you.

You'll also see more of God's works if you spend time with His people. As you see the ways that He has blessed your friends and family, you'll become more aware of Him.

It's also likely that just as you hit a place of stability, someone in your circle will need a reminder of God's care. Your enjoyment of God isn't just for your own benefit, after all.

THE FATHER DELIGHTS IN CARING FOR YOU

"Seek the Kingdom of God above all else, and he will give you everything you need. So don't be afraid, little flock. For it gives your Father great happiness to give you the Kingdom."

LUKE 12:31–32 NLT

Today is Father's Day, and a good time to remember that God is your Father.

God's joy is to share His kingdom with you, but it's hard for you to receive it if you're running about in pursuit of your own goals and needs. Your mind will be filled with worries about your expenses and future plans, and you may worry about having enough. There are so many things to fear, from your family's safety to your own financial stability.

It's easy to convince yourself that your pursuit of job security or prosperity is noble and shows your care for your family, but along the way you can lose sight of your priorities, especially experiencing God's delight over you as a generous Father.

Today is a good day to ask yourself if you're worried or fearful about the future. Do you feel distant from God and the loving care of His kingdom? What would it look like to seek first God and His kingdom? Do you believe that His fatherly love extends to you as well?

Perhaps you can share God's kindness with others or see His goodness in your own father when you see God's fatherly love for you with greater clarity.

DELIVER US FROM SEEKING RICHES

*The disciples were astounded. "Then who in the world
can be saved?" they asked. Jesus looked at them intently
and said, "Humanly speaking, it is impossible.
But not with God. Everything is possible with God."*
MARK 10:26–27 NLT

What is it about money that obstructs the way into God's kingdom?

Perhaps for you, money may be a source of security, while others may see their wealth and status as personal validation. But the pursuit of wealth itself can take up your time, pulling you away from family, worship, and service to others. The accumulation of wealth can prompt you to buy things that require more time spent earning money so that you can afford them.

The more you're loaded down with the pursuit and management of money, the harder it becomes to free yourself to be present for God. Wealth can gradually take you captive, and the more you're surrounded by people who pursue it, the easier it becomes to justify the pursuit of "just a little more."

Jesus assures you that while wealth can wreck your soul, God can save you. Your only recourse is to fall on God's mercy and to trust Him fully for the salvation of your soul. Tempting as it is to say that wealth is a blessing from God, it may just as easily become your downfall if you aren't living by faith.

YOU ARE CALLED TO STOP

"Be still, and know that I am God! I will be honored
by every nation. I will be honored throughout the world."
PSALM 46:10 NLT

You can wear yourself out trying to bring glory to God. Ministry burnout is common, and many who attend church on Sunday feel like they can't add one more thing to their schedules. The idea of "being still" seems like a nice thought in theory, but who can truly be still?

Perhaps you struggle with being still and knowing that God is present because you believe that your world will fall apart if you stop working. You may have an exaggerated sense of your own importance or you may underestimate the power of God. Either way, being still before God puts you in your place, and, more importantly, acknowledges God's place over you.

Without your efforts and energy, God will still be honored throughout the earth. There is nothing you can give Him that He can't obtain without you. In fact, your ministry to others is merely an outflowing of God through you.

As you become still before God, you can see that He is *already* honored and exalted throughout the earth. The Lord is more than capable of handling your problems and concerns. You'll only see that with clarity if you learn to be still before Him (see Hebrews 4:9–11).

ADMIT YOUR DISAPPOINTMENT WITH GOD

Martha said to Jesus, "Lord, if only you had been here,
my brother would not have died. But even now I know
that God will give you whatever you ask."
JOHN 11:21–22 NLT

When have you felt hopeless or disappointed in God? Were you afraid to say exactly what you were thinking? Perhaps you didn't feel God would ever listen to your prayers again if you really told Him what you were thinking.

At her lowest point, Martha spoke her mind to Jesus. She didn't hold back. Her faith held the tension of Jesus' power and her disappointment. She could still believe in His care for her and His healing power, even if He hadn't shown up when she had requested.

Of course, Martha's story ends with a greater display of Jesus' power as He raised her brother Lazarus, but you don't always experience God's deliverance in such dramatic ways. Regardless of the results, Martha's faith after experiencing tremendous loss and grief shows that you can surrender your circumstances to God in faith, hope, and, most importantly, honesty.

Your honesty doesn't have to undermine your faith. Martha's spirit of surrender placed her future in Jesus' hands even as she faced her disappointment about the past. What do you need to speak to God about with complete transparency today? Is it possible that speaking about your disappointment in God could be a greater act of faith than holding yourself back from saying what you really think?

RECEIVING GOD'S MERCY

"I entered this world to render judgment—to give sight to the blind and to show those who think they see that they are blind."
JOHN 9:39 NLT

If you feel like you can't figure out how to draw near to God or if you struggle with particular sins, then you're right where Jesus can help you. In fact, the bigger problem is if you think you have your act together and have no need of His mercy.

Jesus came to reveal your true spiritual state. You can either resist His offer of mercy or you can fight it, claiming that you're good enough on your own and have no need for Him and His help. Ironically, the more you insist on your wisdom and·holiness, the less hope you have!

Your only hope is to stop pretending that you can see spiritually and fully admit your need for God's mercy. Jesus knows fully how blind and lost you are. He came to seek you out, to reveal that He's not interested in people putting on a brave face and acting as if they have things together.

If you come to Him with honesty and a complete dependence on His mercy, you're in the best position to receive His help and to experience true restoration.

TRANSFORMATION ISN'T UP TO YOU

But I will come—and soon—if the Lord lets me, and then I'll find
out whether these arrogant people just give pretentious speeches
or whether they really have God's power. For the Kingdom
of God is not just a lot of talk; it is living by God's power.

1 CORINTHIANS 4:19–20 NLT

Division and discord among Christians is nothing new, but perhaps Paul's approach to resolving it may surprise you. When facing a divisive and contentious church, Paul reminded them that their words held very little power for spiritual transformation. Whether relying on your own words or the teachings of others, the true power of God's kingdom is in the way His power takes hold in you.

Even your best attempts at encouragement may well fall flat if you aren't empowered by God. This puts the responsibility for your spiritual transformation on Him, so the pressure is off you.

You can't make people change and you can't change yourself. You can only submit to the power of God, and that process of surrender and submission will feel like a lot of work at times! However, the end result of seeking God's direction and influence is that you'll change into the kind of person who has something worthwhile to share with others.

GOD'S LIGHT ERASES YOUR DARKNESS

Remember, O LORD, your compassion and unfailing love,
which you have shown from long ages past. Do not remember
the rebellious sins of my youth. Remember me in the light
of your unfailing love, for you are merciful, O LORD.
PSALM 25:6–7 NLT

God's character defines how He interacts with you, not the other way around. If you had to be on your best behavior in order to receive God's mercy, you'd have no hope in the face of His holiness.

You can't hide your sins from God, but you can still approach Him with confidence because of His unfailing love and mercy. Today's psalm notes that in light of God's mercy, you have access to Him. You've never been able to be good enough, but He has always been good enough to receive you.

When God remembers you, He doesn't look at your failures, hypocrisies, and faults. He sees you with compassion as His beloved child. It's this love that changes and transforms you, renewing you and drawing you near to Him on the merits of His unfailing love.

You don't have to bring anything to God because He desires to show mercy and compassion to you. In the warm glow of His light your darkness is gone and you're free to be loved by Him.

YOU ARE GOD'S BELOVED CREATION

"What is the price of five sparrows—two copper coins?
Yet God does not forget a single one of them. And the very
hairs on your head are all numbered. So don't be afraid;
you are more valuable to God than a whole flock of sparrows."
LUKE 12:6–7 NLT

Do you fear that God sees you as expendable? Are you worried that you could be on the brink of being cast away by the Lord? Perhaps you've gone through some season of life where you've felt abandoned by God and you aren't able to pinpoint what has gone wrong.

God is intimately aware of you and your needs. Most importantly, this intimate knowledge of you doesn't turn Him away or result in your expulsion from His presence. In fact, this is a reason for you to have confidence that your Creator remains near to you and desires to be with you. The Lord is deeply invested in knowing you and in caring for you.

That isn't to say that you'll be spared hardships. Rather, you're assured of God's presence and comfort day after day. Just as the birds He created can never escape His notice, you can also take comfort in His ongoing awareness of you. If even the most common, seemingly inconsequential creature is known by God, how much more will He hold on to you?

WHAT'S THE RESULT OF FAITH?

Let your unfailing love surround us, LORD,
for our hope is in you alone.
PSALM 33:22 NLT

You can feel burdens of stress, of strained relationships, and of crammed schedules each day. You speak of feeling "weighed down" at times as challenges pile up, and as you're weighed down by fear, worries, and obligations, you may lose sight of God's provision for you.

While experiencing stress, fear, and aimlessness, you'll always grasp for answers, solutions, and anything that you can control. If you feel like you can't remove those burdens on your own, that's because you truly are hopeless on your own. Turning to God throughout the day gives you your only lasting relief from these burdens.

As you learn to trust in the Lord alone, you'll begin to see His lovingkindness for you with greater clarity. But being weighed down with your worries and cares may make it almost impossible to find God's concern for you. Your worries will become larger and larger the more you focus on them.

However, when you begin to place your trust in God, you'll see His patience and love for you with greater clarity, freeing you to see His love that has remained unchanged regardless of your circumstances.

SILENCE IS GOOD FOR YOUR SOUL

LORD, my heart is not proud; my eyes are not haughty.
I don't concern myself with matters too great or too awesome
for me to grasp. Instead, I have calmed and quieted myself,
like a weaned child who no longer cries for its mother's
milk. Yes, like a weaned child is my soul within me.
PSALM 131:1–2 NLT

Today's psalm reminds you that God nurtures and cares for you the way that a mother cares for her child. Perhaps you have a "tough love" picture of the Lord—you see Him as a God who demands much of you.

If you make the mistake of seeing Him this way, you may well become proud of your holiness, your commitment to Him, or your spiritual accomplishments. You may attempt to master "great matters" that distinguish you from others. The pride that comes with performing for God inevitably results in haughty glances at others. You imagine that they either don't measure up or are a threat to your own pursuit of false holiness.

However, if you see God as infinitely loving like a mother caring for a child, you can respond to Him with silence and rest. Your striving may cease, and you can truly trust in His protection and acceptance.

Then you can move into your days knowing the Lord's love that silences your doubts and striving. You will be humble and care for others since you have nothing to prove or to guard.

GOD IS ALWAYS GENEROUS

" 'Is it against the law for me to do what I want with my money?
Should you be jealous because I am kind to others?' "
MATTHEW 20:15 NLT

It's tempting sometimes to imagine that God is holding Himself back from you. You go through spiritual darkness or dry seasons, and *generosity* may be the last word that comes to mind. In fact, you may become so preoccupied with your own needs that you forget just how badly others need God's generous provision as well.

In the parable of the vineyard workers, some labored all day, while others only worked a few hours. Both received what they needed. As your own needs grow, you may not even be able to imagine that anyone else could need God's provision more. Perhaps you may be in a season of waiting for what you need from God, and it's particularly hard to see His blessings go to others. But remember, God is always generous—but not *just* to you.

Envy will dismantle the patience that God is growing within you, robbing you of the joy of His blessings when they finally come to you. The Lord is generous, but everyone experiences that generosity in different ways and at different times.

God's generosity won't spare you seasons of darkness and doubt. It's possible, however, that waiting will help you view His generosity with greater clarity.

LESS TIME THAN YOU THINK

"Watch therefore, for you do not know when the master of the house is coming—in the evening, at midnight, at the crowing of the rooster, or in the morning—lest, coming suddenly, he find you sleeping. And what I say to you, I say to all: Watch."
MARK 13:35–37 NKJV

Jesus gives a rather stern warning that your time on earth could be far shorter than you expect. Whether He returns during your lifetime or your life is cut short unexpectedly, you can't take your time for granted.

You may have plans that fill your schedule each week and prompt you to put off the things that truly matter. Perhaps you hope to get around to spending more time with your kids. You may be waiting on getting involved in a service opportunity in the community. There could be a spiritual growth meeting at church that should be a top priority.

Whatever you're putting off, your time on earth isn't unlimited. You may be surprised to see your carefully laid plans fall to pieces one day when a sudden change happens.

While Jesus isn't saying that you should never rest, there's a spirit of awareness and watchfulness that He wants His followers to adopt. You could well have less time than you expect, and that should change how you approach each day and make plans for the future.

CONQUERING EVERY POWER

*No power in the sky above or in the earth below—indeed,
nothing in all creation will ever be able to separate us from
the love of God that is revealed in Christ Jesus our Lord.*

ROMANS 8:39 NLT

You can't stop God's love for you. Nothing created on earth can alter His love. No spiritual power or authority can undermine the Lord's steadfast devotion to you. The ministry of Jesus reveals God's perfect love in its fullness, reaching out to you with healing, compassion, and sacrifice.

How often are you tempted to begin measuring this love by your difficult circumstances or deflated sense of security? How often have you believed that you've failed one too many times?

Your desires and failures lead you astray from within, and enemies constantly assail you from without. Paul saw the powers of this world aligning themselves against believers, with demons and rulers straining themselves to pry you away from the love of God.

Still, this love of God has been bonded to you in Christ Jesus who has forever linked you to God the Father. You are His child, and there's no force in this world that can change that. You can remain confident that your security in God is rooted in His unshakable love, not in your own circumstances or personal failures.

STABILITY IN UNCERTAIN TIMES

But you, O LORD, will sit on your throne forever.
Your fame will endure to every generation.
PSALM 102:12 NLT

When everything else appears to be shaking around you, you can still deal rightly with fear, anger, and uncertainty about the future. You can't control what tomorrow brings, but you can return to the one certainty that will endure from one generation to another and has remained from the very beginning of time: God will be with you.

Whatever else you may lose, the Lord can't be taken away. As despair sets in during a time of suffering or loss, you have a powerful opportunity to consider what you have placed your trust in. Have you placed your confidence in your health, your finances, your career, or some other material thing?

God is merciful and compassionate, empathizing with you when you're at your lowest point. However, your circumstances don't change the presence of the Lord; rather, your despair and grief can become opportunities to discover His never-changing mercy. While you aren't guaranteed the desires of your heart, you're given something far better: a loving God who will not abandon you and can never be moved.

There surely have been worse times, and tragedies are certain to come in the future, but none of this can disrupt God's presence.

SHOWING KINDNESS

And they [the men of Judah] told David, saying, "It was the
men of Jabesh-gilead who buried Saul." David sent messengers
to the men of Jabesh-gilead, and said to them, "May you be
blessed of the LORD because you have shown this kindness
to Saul your lord, and have buried him."

2 SAMUEL 2:4–5 NASB

After David was anointed king of Israel in Hebron, he learned
that the men of Jabesh-gilead had buried King Saul. Very likely
David inquired about Saul's body because he wanted to honor
him with a proper burial, or maybe the men of Judah wanted
to point the finger at the men of Jabesh-gilead, thinking David
might be displeased by their actions. But either way, David sent
a blessing back to them.

Regardless of how far Saul ended up going astray, he was the
Lord's anointed and was worthy of respect. David always had a
firm understanding of this concept, even when he was on the
run from Saul, fearing for his life. This is consistent with what
the Bible says about how God's people are to respect authority
and treat their enemies.

Proverbs 24:17–18 (NASB) says, "Do not rejoice when your
enemy falls, and do not let your heart be glad when he stumbles;
or the LORD will see it and be displeased, and turn His anger
away from him."

How do you respond when one of your enemies falls—either
literally or figuratively? How does that compare with today's verse?

COVENANT-KEEPING GOD

"Obey what I command you today. I will drive out before you the Amorites, Canaanites, Hittites, Perizzites, Hivites and Jebusites."
EXODUS 34:11 NIV

At this point in Israel's history, the Lord was establishing a covenant with His people, promising to "do wonders never before done in any nation in all the world" (Exodus 34:10 NIV). And He wasn't just promising to do such wonders in front of Moses, but rather, before *all* the people. This was a foreshadowing of God drying up the Jordan River (Joshua 3), His destruction of the walls of Jericho (Joshua 6), and more.

As if that wasn't enough, commentators point out that God listed the six enemies that He would drive out before Israel if they would obey what He commanded them that day. He then went on to list His terms, what He expected of them: they were to cut down the Asherah poles (v. 13), not worship any other god (v. 14), not make idols (v. 17), faithfully celebrate His festivals (vv. 18, 22), honor the Sabbath (v. 21), and more. They could only expect to receive the promises of God if they were faithful to Him.

What sort of enemies are you facing today? If you haven't seen any progress against them, take inventory of your obedience to God. While you won't always be able to understand His ways, He's still a God who covenants with His people, and therefore expects obedience.

EXPECT HARDSHIP

Can anything ever separate us from Christ's love?
Does it mean he no longer loves us if we have trouble or
calamity, or are persecuted, or hungry, or destitute, or in danger,
or threatened with death? (As the Scriptures say, "For your sake
we are killed every day; we are being slaughtered like sheep.")
ROMANS 8:35–36 NLT

When hardship comes, and it will, you'll find out how strong
your faith is. But how can God allow His own children to be
persecuted, or starve, or be threatened with death? Doesn't He
promise to protect His followers?

After all, Job 5:11 (NLT) says, "He gives prosperity to the
poor and protects those who suffer." And Psalm 12:7 (NLT) tells
you, "Therefore, LORD, we know you will protect the oppressed,
preserving them forever from this lying generation." And Proverbs
19:23 (NLT) promises, "Fear of the LORD leads to life, bringing
security and protection from harm."

In some instances, God does intervene—offering physical
protection to advance His kingdom. In other cases, He offers
spiritual protection against the advances of the enemy. And
sometimes, He allows hardship, while preserving your soul.

Today's verse quotes Psalm 44:22, and one aspect of it that's
hard to miss is this: Christians face death every day for the sake
of the kingdom. But hardship never separates you from the love
of Christ.

LIVE AS FREE PEOPLE

*Live as free people, but do not use your freedom
as a cover-up for evil; live as God's slaves.*
1 PETER 2:16 NIV

On Independence Day in America, it's appropriate to consider your understanding of freedom as it compares to the scriptures. In today's verse, Peter calls Christians to live as free people who don't use the freedom they have been given to secretly indulge in evil. In today's culture, that can be a constant temptation.

In 1 Peter 2:11 (NIV), the apostle Peter described self-indulgence as "sinful desires, which wage war against your soul." Bible commentator Adam Clarke says this about worldly people: "While others spend all their time, and employ all their skill, in acquiring earthly property, and totally neglect the salvation of their souls; they are not strangers, they are here at home; they are not pilgrims, they are seeking an earthly possession: Heaven is your home, seek that."

To live otherwise is to return to bondage.

Evaluate how you spend your free time. Make a list of your activities over the course of the next week and then total the amount of time you spent satisfying your whims and compare it to the amount of time you spent feeding your soul. You are called to live as one of God's slaves. Do your findings reflect that?

DOCTRINAL INTEGRITY

*Likewise, exhort the young men to be sober-minded, in all things
showing yourself to be a pattern of good works; in doctrine
showing integrity, reverence, incorruptibility, sound speech
that cannot be condemned, that one who is an opponent
may be ashamed, having nothing evil to say of you.*
Titus 2:6–8 NKJV

In today's verses, Paul addressed Titus, his partner and fellow
worker (2 Corinthians 8:23), telling him about the importance
of the older generation teaching the younger one. But they were
to go beyond teaching. They were to display a pattern of good
works, showing integrity, reverence, and incorruptibility in their
doctrine—so much so that even an opponent might not have
anything to say against them.

Doctrinal integrity doesn't mean perfection. It simply means
living out truth as best you understand it, without walking in
contradiction. If you know anger to be a sin, and you teach it
as such, but everybody knows you as a hothead, that's the type
of inconsistency that signals to the next generation that you
don't really believe what you're saying. It also shows that your
doctrine lacks power.

If you're older, say forty-five years of age or more, are you
teaching younger men in the faith? Do they see inconsistencies
in your life, or do they see a repentant heart? If you're younger,
how quick are you to accept the teaching of the older generation
while acknowledging your own weaknesses?

WORK, REST, AND PRAY

Be still in the presence of the LORD, and wait patiently
for him to act. Don't worry about evil people who
prosper or fret about their wicked schemes.

PSALM 37:7 NLT

Bible commentators point out that being *still* in the Lord's presence is about more than simply not moving. They say it's about silencing the tongue from all murmuring and complaint. It means to be resigned, content in Him. That doesn't mean you can't ask Him to act, but it *does* mean there should be times when you meet with Him without making requests.

The real test comes when evil people appear to prosper. Shouldn't a Christian fret then? Doesn't God call Christians to speak for the voiceless? Indeed, He does. But not always. Solomon said this in Ecclesiastes 3:1 and 7 (NLT), "For everything there is a season. . .a time to be quiet and a time to speak." If you're always speaking, or if you're always quiet, you haven't found the proper balance.

Either way, today's verse says don't worry about evil people. Instead, wait patiently for the Lord to act. That looks different in every circumstance, but isn't it nice to know that the success of His kingdom doesn't rest in your hands? Neither does toppling evil. You're called to work, rest, and pray—always trusting in Him.

STAY ALERT

Watch out that you do not lose what we have worked so hard to achieve. Be diligent so that you receive your full reward.
2 John 1:8 nlt

Deception has been an issue in every church age. At the heart of one deception was the denial that Jesus came in an actual physical body (2 John 1:7); this was, ultimately, a rejection of Christ. Jesus is always the sticking point with those who come in the spirit of the antichrist.

In this epistle, the apostle John warned the church to be on guard—to be diligent against such people. Otherwise, the Christian is in danger of losing his heavenly reward. John went on to say that anyone who wanders from this teaching has no relationship with God (v. 9). With such consequences, it's no wonder that he called the church to be so diligent.

If you knew your car might veer off the road and cause you to plummet off a mountainside at any moment, leading to your certain death, you'd be on heightened alert. Your radio would be off. Your hands would have a firm grip on the steering wheel. And your eyes would be giving the road their full attention.

Spiritual diligence works in a similar fashion. It includes keeping an eye out for deceivers, praying for discernment, and staying close to the Body of Christ so you can experience the process of iron sharpening iron (Proverbs 27:17).

SPIRITUAL EYES

*"The LORD will repay each man for his righteousness and his
faithfulness; for the LORD delivered you into my hand today,
but I refused to stretch out my hand against the LORD's anointed."*

1 SAMUEL 26:23 NASB

Sometimes, faithfulness means inaction.

That was the case in today's verse when Saul got wind of the
fact that David was hiding from him in the wilderness of Ziph
(1 Samuel 26:2–3). Saul took three thousand men in search of
him, but David outfoxed him. Then he showed up at Saul's camp
early one morning while everybody was sleeping. His cousin
Abishai wanted to kill Saul on the spot, but David recognized
that Saul was God's anointed, and restrained Abishai.

David's faithfulness to the Lord outweighed an opportunity
to kill his oppressor. The Hebrew word for *faithfulness* in this
verse means "moral fidelity." To kill Saul would have been the
equivalent of being unfaithful to God, and David wouldn't do
that. He had other moral failings over the course of his life, but
here he saw his situation through spiritual eyes and it made all
the difference.

Are you on the cusp of making a decision you'd feel justified
in making, yet you know deep down inside that it would mean
being unfaithful to God? Put off the flesh and look at the situation
through spiritual eyes.

LEAVING AN INHERITANCE

A good man leaves an inheritance to his children's children,
and the wealth of the sinner is stored up for the righteous.
PROVERBS 13:22 NASB

As you head off to work this morning, you may have a sense of weariness. Another work week is about to begin. But today matters. So does tomorrow. You're providing for your family, and hopefully being thrifty enough with your wages that you're storing up an inheritance for your children and even your grandchildren.

Bible commentator Adam Clarke goes a step further than simply providing materially in his exposition of this verse, saying that such a man "files many a prayer in heaven in their behalf, and his good example and advices are remembered and quoted from generation to generation. Besides, whatever property he left was honestly acquired, and well-gotten goods are permanent."

The point of today's verse is to think far beyond today, this week, this month, or even this year. Everything you do as a provider and leader of the home is to be done with future generations in mind—making physical and spiritual provisions that will last.

How are you faring in this? If this notion is new to you, that's okay. You can begin this day with a different mindset than you had last week. If you aren't sure where to begin, find an older man who has successfully laid the foundations for his children and ask him for advice.

FEAR GOD

"We have been rescued from our enemies so we can serve God without fear, in holiness and righteousness for as long as we live."
LUKE 1:74–75 NLT

You're in daily battles with three enemies: the world, the flesh, and the devil (Ephesians 2:1–3). All three are formidable, but in the eternal sense, you have already been rescued from all three. In the here and now, though, the battles will continue. And those battles can weigh you down, throw you off track, and cripple you with fear.

In today's verse, Luke mentions Zechariah's prophecy about the coming Messiah who descended from the royal line of David, just as God promised (Luke 1:69–70). He would be merciful and rescue God's people from their enemies. While Zechariah looked forward to the coming Messiah, you look backward, knowing He has already arrived. Your salvation has been secured. And even now, He's in the process of conquering your earthly enemies, while preparing a heavenly place for you.

But for now, live out your salvation. Don't fear persecution or even death for Christ's sake. Instead, fear God. Serve Him faithfully in the spheres of influence where He has placed you, being confident that His work will continue, no matter what His enemies do. Yes, they may prevail in some battles, but the war has already been won.

BOASTING COULD COST YOU

Do not boast about tomorrow,
for you do not know what a day may bring.
PROVERBS 27:1 NIV

In Luke 12:16–20, Jesus shared a parable about a rich man who had an abundant harvest. Presuming upon tomorrow, he decided to tear down his barns and build bigger ones to store his surplus grain. And he said to himself, "You have plenty of grain laid up for many years. Take life easy; eat, drink and be merry." Making such a presumption was a critical mistake because God said to him, "You fool! This very night your life will be demanded from you. Then who will get what you have prepared for yourself?"

The rich man's error wasn't in planning for the future or saving for a rainy day. It was in his boasting of having plenty of provisions and living a life of ease—but not caring about spiritual riches.

James 4:15–17 addressed the same problem. James instructed believers to say, "If it is the Lord's will, we will live and do this or that." He added, "As it is, you boast in your arrogant schemes. All such boasting is evil."

When you talk and plan for the future, do your words include anything that could be construed as boasting? If so, be careful. All your hard work and effort might be for naught.

A GENTLE DEFENSE

But sanctify Christ as Lord in your hearts, always being ready
to make a defense to everyone who asks you to give an account
for the hope that is in you, yet with gentleness and reverence.

1 PETER 3:15 NASB

You probably live for instances when someone genuinely inquires about your faith, asking you to give an account for the hope they see in you. But even during genuine inquiries, conversations can sometimes become heated—or become focused on one-upping the other person. Has this ever happened to you?

Peter says to give an account, but to do so with gentleness and reverence. This is much more difficult. But in Spurgeon's commentary, he explained why it's so important: "If they wish to know why you believe that you're saved, have your answer all ready in a few plain, simple sentences; and in the gentlest and most modest spirit make your confession of faith to the praise and glory of God. Who knows but what such good seed will bring forth an abundant harvest?"

A gentle, reverent response does a work that has the potential to bring forth great results. It's good seed because it isn't tainted by pride and arrogance. And it's good because the planter is seen as being in just as much need as the receiver. If this describes your evangelism, then carry on. If not, take Peter's words to heart.

FEED THE SPIRIT

Therefore put to death your members which are on the earth: fornication, uncleanness, passion, evil desire, and covetousness, which is idolatry.

Colossians 3:5 NKJV

If you have been raised with Christ, then you are to seek the things that are above (Colossians 3:1). One of the primary ways you can seek the heavenly is by putting the earthly to death. Jesus called His disciples to a life of self-denial. Matthew 16:24 (NKJV) records one instance: "If anyone desires to come after Me, let him deny himself, and take up his cross, and follow Me."

Easier said than done, though, right? What does self-denial and putting your earthly members to death actually entail? Romans 8:5 (NKJV) is the key: "For those who live according to the flesh set their minds on the things of the flesh, but those who live according to the Spirit, the things of the Spirit."

Your spiritual power will increase or decrease based on which aspect of yourself you feed the most. If you feed the flesh, you should expect your earthly appetites to get stronger. If you feed the spirit, your spiritual appetites will increase. Once your flesh's power source is cut off (or starved), it will decrease.

So, the obvious question is: Are you feeding the flesh or the spirit? What can you do to feed the spirit even more?

INTERNAL BATTLES

He that is slow to anger is better than the mighty;
and he that ruleth his spirit than he that taketh a city.
PROVERBS 16:32 KJV

For a split second, just before you either act or react to an event that might make you angry, you have the wherewithal to be measured and restrained, rather than erupt in anger. You might blow right past that internal check, feeling justified, but in so doing, you'll be showing an inability to rule your own spirit.

Being slow to answer shows the emotional fortitude it would have required to take a city back in the day. How so? The person who conquered a city overcame serious obstacles—the weather, a multitude of weapons, snares, and defenders. But the person who rules his spirit in the heat of the moment overcomes an internal battle—one in which the flesh makes demands but is vanquished by the spirit.

Are you quick to anger? If so, then you have some work to do, and that's okay. The Holy Spirit is at work in you. The next time you're tempted to display anger, view that internal check you feel as a gift from God and obey it. Use a soft answer to turn away wrath and the situation will become much less volatile.

GENUINE REPENTANCE

That is why the Lord says, "Turn to me now, while there is
time. Give me your hearts. Come with fasting, weeping,
and mourning. Don't tear your clothing in your
grief, but tear your hearts instead."

Joel 2:12–13 nlt

In Joel 2:1–11, the prophet speaks about a coming day of judgment when everyone should tremble in fear. Nothing will escape. "Who can possibly survive?" asks Joel (v. 11 nlt). And then the Lord provides the answer above.

Anybody who turns to Him now while there is still time can escape judgment. But this is serious business. God calls those who wish to escape the judgment to come with fasting, weeping, and mourning. When is the last time you took your sin that seriously?

But God goes even further, saying that He's not interested in the kind of repentance that is expressed outwardly. Instead, He wants godly sorrow to seep inside, all the way to the heart. David spoke about this in Psalm 51:17 (nlt): "The sacrifice you desire is a broken spirit. You will not reject a broken and repentant heart, O God."

If your heart is broken over your sin, then you've fully grasped what Joel and David are saying. Rejoice in your salvation. If you have never experienced such a broken heart over your sin, ask God to help you repent and find forgiveness.

WHAT THE HEART WANTS

"But the things that proceed out of the mouth come from the heart, and those defile the man. For out of the heart come evil thoughts, murders, adulteries, fornications, thefts, false witness, slanders."
MATTHEW 15:18–19 NASB

Many a man has gotten himself into trouble by embracing "the heart wants what the heart wants" mentality—as if Christians are to be slaves to their hearts' desires. The problem with this thinking is that out of the heart come evil thoughts, murders, adulteries, fornications, thefts, false witness, and slanders.

Genesis 6:5 says that every intent of the thoughts of a man's heart is only evil continually. And Jeremiah 17:9 says the heart is more deceitful than all else and is desperately sick. The heart does want what the heart wants, but that's the *problem*. You can't trust your heart. It only wants all sorts of evil. But that doesn't mean that all is lost.

In the parable of the sower (Luke 8:15 NASB), Jesus explains that "the seed in the good soil, these are the ones who have heard the word in an honest and good heart, and hold it fast, and bear fruit with perseverance." When your heart has the Word in it, it's honest and good. Have you fallen victim to obeying your heart without first bringing it under the authority of the Word?

PERFECT PEACE

Those who love Your law have great peace,
and nothing causes them to stumble.
Psalm 119:165 nasb

Darlene Rose, a missionary to Batavia, Java, arrived there in 1938 with her new husband, Russell. They ended up as prisoners of war during World War II and were taken to the mountains, where eventually all of the men were shoved into a truck. As Russell took his place, he spoke words of comfort to Darlene.

"Remember one thing, dear," Russell said, according to an article on the *Charisma Magazine* website. "God said He would never leave us or forsake us."

Darlene never saw him again. But she said that as the truck pulled away, she felt at peace because she believed Romans 8:28 (nasb): "And we know that God causes all things to work together for good to those who love God, to those who are called according to His purpose."

The article went on to say that over the next few years, Darlene and her fellow missionaries were forced to eat dogs and rats to stay alive. They were also in constant danger from pirates and savage murderers. Eventually, the missionaries were rescued by Allied soldiers. A few years later, though, she returned, spending forty more years in the jungles of Indonesia. Both she and Russell had perfect peace because they knew and trusted God's Word.

As you face hardship today, you, too, can experience perfect peace.

GOD IS WITH YOU

*David also said to Solomon his son, "Be strong and courageous,
and do the work. Do not be afraid or discouraged, for the LORD
God, my God, is with you. He will not fail you or forsake you until
all the work for the service of the temple of the LORD is finished."*
1 CHRONICLES 28:20 NIV

While Solomon seemed to experience little external opposition
while carrying out his father's wishes to build the temple, he must
have faced *some* sort of opposition, otherwise David wouldn't have
encouraged him to be strong and courageous in doing the work.
In fact, doing God's work *always* requires strength and courage.

Have you been called to start a Bible study at work or maybe
among your friends? Are you sensing that God wants you to
start volunteering at your local homeless shelter or maybe even
to start one? Maybe He's calling you into full-time Christian
work of some sort. Whatever the case, your primary opposition
is probably mostly internal.

Who are you to start a Bible study, or work in a homeless
shelter, or join the mission field, or become a pastor? You are
God's chosen—His anointed for this very task. And if He's telling
you to do something, don't be afraid or discouraged. Do the
work. God is with you.

PURSUING GODLY AMBITIONS

*My ambition has always been to preach the Good News where
the name of Christ has never been heard, rather than where
a church has already been started by someone else.*

ROMANS 15:20 NLT

You probably have several ambitions. Professionally, you have
your eyes set on a prize—maybe a promotion or ownership
of your own business. Personally, you're striving to become
a better leader in your home, and working on taking care of
yourself. What about your spiritual ambitions? Where do
your spiritual passions lie?

After his conversion, the apostle Paul had his sights set on
preaching the Gospel in places where the name of Jesus had never
been heard, and he spent the rest of his life doing so. He wasn't
disrespecting the work done in churches started by others. He
just left that work to someone else who had a godly zeal for it.

Do you have such clarity of thought? You don't need a
"calling" to pursue most of your godly ambitions. You simply
need to acknowledge that it exists deep inside your heart, and
then prayerfully seek ways to live it out.

Maybe your ambition is outside of the box—like starting an
online Christian news site in your city, or giving away everything
you own to the poor, or starting a ministry to mentally ill men
who have fallen through the cracks of society. Whatever it is,
jump into it.

WISDOM FROM ABOVE

But the wisdom from above is first of all pure. It is also peace loving, gentle at all times, and willing to yield to others. It is full of mercy and the fruit of good deeds. It shows no favoritism and is always sincere.

JAMES 3:17 NLT

In today's verse, the apostle James provides a filter for understanding whether the wisdom you follow is actually from God or not. Is the message pure? (Will it purify the heart?) Is it peace loving, rather than contentious? Is it gentle at all times? Is it willing to yield to others? Is it full of mercy and the fruit of good deeds? Does it show favoritism, or is it sincere?

Compare the characteristics of wisdom that's from above to earthly wisdom, which is at times helpful, but often tainted. Earthly wisdom says to look out for number one, to stand up for yourself, to get what you have coming. That's not to say you shouldn't stand up for yourself, but don't do it because you're motivated by pride or anger.

Jesus spoke only on the Father's authority. He was in constant communication with Him. The two go hand in hand. God does offer us guidance sometimes without being prompted, but even then, it usually happens as a result of being in close relationship with Him.

COMPASSION FOR THE LOST

Seeing the people, He felt compassion for them, because they were distressed and dispirited like sheep without a shepherd.
MATTHEW 9:36 NASB

As Jesus traveled, He encountered people in the synagogues who were sick, diseased, distressed (because of the yoke the Pharisees had placed on them), and helpless—wandering like sheep without a shepherd. The religious leaders of the day ought to have been guiding them properly, but instead, they were caught up in rules and regulations as a means for achieving righteousness. When Jesus saw that, He felt compassion for the people.

Does this describe the way you feel as you look around at work or in your personal life? Do you feel compassion for those who are trapped in religion rather than being in a relationship with Christ? Most of those people probably grew up in faith traditions that taught them that if their good deeds outweighed their bad deeds, then God would accept them.

In essence, they grew up without true Christian leadership, so they embraced the false doctrine, believing heaven could be earned. Have compassion on them. Unless you grew up in a Christian household, you were once just like them.

As you exhibit compassion toward them, you might get an opportunity to present the true Gospel of mercy and grace—one that no man can earn.

IN HONOR OF PARENTS' DAY

Children, obey your parents in the Lord, for this is right.
"Honor your father and mother"—which is the first commandment
with a promise—"so that it may go well with you and
that you may enjoy long life on the earth."
EPHESIANS 6:1–3 NIV

Parents' Day is a US holiday that's celebrated on the fourth Sunday of July "to recognize and promote parenting as a crucial part of families and the wider community," according to timeanddate.com. The website says it was signed into law in 1994 by President Bill Clinton.

If you had parents who raised you well by always placing your needs first, making huge sacrifices for you, and training you to become a God-honoring adult, then take some time today and let them know how appreciative you are. If your parents were less-than-ideal models, pick up the phone anyway, if they're still alive, and thank them for what they did right.

Honoring your parents generally leads to a longer life. This is how Henry Donald Maurice Spence-Jones and Rev. Joseph S. Exell explain it in *The Pulpit Commentary*: "Where obedience to parents is found, there is usually found along with it temperance, self-control, industry, regular ways of life, and other habits that tend towards prosperity and longevity."

DON'T WAIT

Then Caleb quieted the people before Moses, and said, "Let us go up at once and take possession, for we are well able to overcome it." But the men who had gone up with him said, "We are not able to go up against the people, for they are stronger than we."

NUMBERS 13:30–31 NKJV

The land of Canaan belonged to Israel. God had already promised it to them. But they still had to take possession of it. So, in obedience to God, they sent twelve spies—one from each tribe—who saw that it was indeed a land flowing with milk and honey (Numbers 13:27), just as God had promised (Exodus 3:8). But they also saw descendants of Anak there—people who were strong and tall—so they hesitated and issued an unfavorable report.

Caleb, however, wanted to go up at once to take possession of the land. His eyes weren't on the circumstances, but on the Lord and His promises. The Lord was with the Israelites, but they only trusted in their own might. Sadly, their fear lead to disobedience, even though they didn't see things that way. They believed they were being astute and practical.

How often have you allowed fear to lead you astray? To procrastinate? To put off the very thing God leads you to do? Today is the day to throw off excuses.

SEEK RECONCILIATION

Do not repay anyone evil for evil. Be careful to do what is right in the eyes of everyone. If it is possible, as far as it depends on you, live at peace with everyone.
ROMANS 12:17–18 NIV

Twenty-five years ago, Oshea Israel (who was sixteen at the time) killed Mary Johnson's only son (who was twenty) when they butted heads at a party in north Minneapolis. While Israel's case crept through the court system over the next couple of years, Johnson wanted to see him pay for what he'd done.

But, according to an article in the *Winona Post*, Johnson was a Christian and after reading a poem she came across in a book, and after much prayer, and after attending many worship services, the Holy Spirit did a work in her heart that she didn't expect. Johnson and Israel were eventually reconciled, with Johnson offering him forgiveness. They went on to become neighbors, and began traveling together, sharing their story with inmates, at schools, and on television.

Today's verse calls Christians to not repay anyone evil for evil, which is far easier said than done. But Johnson did it. Many others have as well. How about you? Are you at odds with somebody over an injustice they did to you or someone you love? Work through the process of forgiveness. Talk to a pastor or counselor. And seek reconciliation.

DETERMINED TO STAY OBEDIENT

But Daniel purposed in his heart that he would not defile himself with the portion of the king's meat, nor with the wine which he drank: therefore he requested of the prince of the eunuchs that he might not defile himself.

DANIEL 1:8 KJV

As one of the gifted Jewish youth taken by Nebuchadnezzar from Jerusalem to Babylon, Daniel had certain privileges, including a daily supply of meat and wine from the king's provisions (Daniel 1:5). But Daniel objected, purposing in his heart that he wouldn't defile himself in such a manner.

Commentators point to three probable reasons why he objected. The Babylonians had no regard for the Law of God and therefore would have eaten ritually unclean animals, as well as animals that had been strangled, and animals that had been offered to Babylon's false gods. Even in captivity, Daniel wanted to be obedient to God's dietary laws, and he was determined to remain as pure as possible—even going so far as to request a dietary change while in captivity. This surely came with a risk.

How would have you responded if you had been in Daniel's position? How determined are you to obey God's Word, and ultimately God? Is it your highest priority? What lengths will you go to in order to remain obedient?

PRESUMPTUOUS SINS

Keep back thy servant also from presumptuous sins;
let them not have dominion over me: then shall I be upright,
and I shall be innocent from the great transgression.
PSALM 19:13 KJV

In today's verse, David asked God to keep him from presumptuous sins—that is, deliberate, intentional sins, what the NIV calls "willful sins." He knew that when he indulged in disobedient acts willfully, they'd end up becoming habits that ruled over him. It's not that unintentional sins cause any less harm than intentional ones, but they don't flow as readily from a person's heart and mind.

The last thing David wanted was to be guilty of "the great transgression," which some believe meant pride or even apostasy.

David knew his wicked heart well. He was a murderer and adulterer, and he lied to cover up both. He might even have been considered slothful, given that he didn't go out to war at the time when kings go out to battle, choosing instead to stay behind in Jerusalem (2 Samuel 11:1). That's when he spiraled out of control.

How about you? How well do you know your own heart? What sort of gross, presumptuous sins is it capable of? Do you fear being guilty of the great transgression? Use David's prayer in today's verse and make it your own. Ask God to intervene, to rule your heart, and to keep you from stumbling.

UNUSUAL KINDNESS

Once safely on shore, we found out that the island was called Malta. The islanders showed us unusual kindness. They built a fire and welcomed us all because it was raining and cold.
Acts 28:1–2 NIV

Paul was a prisoner aboard a ship bound for Rome, and he was destined to stand trial before Caesar. But while they were sailing across the Mediterranean Sea, a storm arose with winds of hurricane force (Acts 27:14). The vessel was driven by the fierce winds for many days. After it ran aground and all the passengers made it safely to shore, they discovered that they had landed on an island called Malta.

Malta was inhabited by heathens. Some translations, such as the KJV, translate the word *islanders* as "barbarous people"— probably because they didn't embrace the Greek or Roman culture, though they were ruled by Rome. Either way, they were different than the shipload of people who had crashed on their island, but their first response was unusual kindness. They built a fire and welcomed everyone.

Your church may already exhibit this type of kindness to outsiders and strangers. If so, jump into the action. Find a way to help those in need. Maybe you could become an usher, or start an English as a second language (ESL) program there. If your church is lacking in this type of kindness to outsiders and strangers, talk to the leadership about finding ways to change that.

WALK IN A WORTHY MANNER

Therefore I, the prisoner of the Lord, implore you to walk in
a manner worthy of the calling with which you have been called,
with all humility and gentleness, with patience, showing tolerance
for one another in love, being diligent to preserve the
unity of the Spirit in the bond of peace.
EPHESIANS 4:1–3 NASB

The apostle Paul was a prisoner in Rome as he penned this epistle to the church in Ephesus. As such, he could have asked for any number of things—a visit, support, prayer—but, under the inspiration of the Holy Spirit, he had something else on his mind.

He wanted Christians in this church to walk in a manner that was worthy of their calling, and then he spelled that out for them. For what distinguishes the Christian from the world any more than humility, gentleness, patience, tolerance, love, and unity? And what better way to show the world what a redeemed life looks like?

Gentleness, humility, and patience are often viewed as being consistent with certain personality types; nevertheless, Paul said they were basic callings for every Christian.

How are you doing in these areas? If you've fallen short in your calling, confess that to the Lord and then rely on the sanctifying work of the Holy Spirit to change you.

FINDING JOY IN THE LORD

Even though the fig trees have no blossoms, and there are no grapes on the vines; even though the olive crop fails, and the fields lie empty and barren; even though the flocks die in the fields, and the cattle barns are empty, yet I will rejoice in the LORD!
HABAKKUK 3:17–18 NLT

The prophet Habakkuk foresaw a day of trouble coming, and he took to prayer. How much better is it to be in prayer before trouble begins so your heart can be prepared and resolved to endure it joyfully, than to be surprised by it and grumble?

Habakkuk saw a time of drought in which the trees, vines, and crops would fail, and most of the livestock would be dead. (This was likely the drought described in Jeremiah 14:1–6.) Yet, Habakkuk said he would rejoice in the Lord. In a preemptive strike against his own soul, he was filling himself up with faith and trust in God so bitterness couldn't creep into his heart when everything went astray.

Have you ever prayed a prayer like this? You probably aren't directly reliant on trees, vines, crops, and livestock, but you are reliant on your employer. If the economy takes a downturn and you're laid off, are you prepared to find joy in the Lord anyway? He is well able to place you in a new position. But will you praise Him during the interim time of uncertainty?

THE KINGDOM OF GOD

*For the Kingdom of God is not a matter of what we eat
or drink, but of living a life of goodness and
peace and joy in the Holy Spirit.*
ROMANS 14:17 NLT

If you've been part of a church for any length of time, then you know that strong differences of opinion sometimes arise over whether Christians should listen to certain styles of music, attend movies, eat or drink certain things, and any number of other issues. Paul wrote Romans 14 to keep believers from judging one another over such matters. The specific issues were different in his day, but the same sentiment continues to modern times.

But the kingdom of God is not a matter of what you eat or drink. It's about living a life of goodness and peace and joy in the Holy Spirit. Some Christians can enjoy the blessings of wealth without sinning, while others cannot. Some can listen to mainstream music without sinning, while others cannot. The same could be said for watching movies. However, flaunting such freedom is not in the spirit of today's verse.

In Romans 14:23 (NLT), Paul said each Christian is bound by his own conscience: "But if you have doubts about whether or not you should eat something, you are sinning if you go ahead and do it. For you are not following your convictions. If you do anything you believe is not right, you are sinning."

DON'T STOP NOW

Fight the good fight of faith; take hold of the eternal life to which you were called, and you made the good confession in the presence of many witnesses.

1 TIMOTHY 6:12 NASB

Timothy, who was called to minister, was to put off the cares of this world—namely the love of money that leads so many astray (1 Timothy 6:10). Instead, he was to fight the good fight of faith to advance the Gospel.

Timothy's vocational calling might have been different from yours, but his spiritual calling was quite similar. You're to be in the world, but not of it (John 17:15–17). You're to set your mind on things above, not on the things of this earth (Colossians 3:2). You're not to be conformed to this world, but be transformed by the renewing of your mind (Romans 12:2). As such, you're called to fight the good fight as well.

How is your fight going? If you don't sense a battle, then you probably aren't engaged in one. If, however, you feel the tension between this world and the next, and are actively engaged in overcoming your sinful habits and tendencies, then you're right where God wants you. Don't stop now. The world needs to see your witness. Wrestle, fight, and pray because eternity is at stake for all of humanity.

FIGHT FOR FREEDOM

Stand fast therefore in the liberty by which Christ has made us free, and do not be entangled again with a yoke of bondage.
GALATIANS 5:1 NKJV

The Slavery Abolition Act officially eliminated slavery throughout the British Empire on this day in 1834. Many of the men and women in England's Anti-Slavery Society were spurred to action by their Christian beliefs, notably William Wilberforce—who spent the last twenty years of his life fighting for abolition.

Slavery in the biblical world was a different matter than the kidnapping variety that conscripted free labor for growing empires in the second half of the past millennium. The Bible, however, specifically condemned kidnapping another person (see Exodus 21:16).

Now, the New Testament refers to believers as "slaves" to Christ several times (Romans 1:1; Ephesians 6:6; 1 Peter 2:16), but the imagery the Bible often uses, such as in today's verse, is of Christ setting believers *free* from bondage. Paul addressed this paradox when he wrote, "The one who was a slave when called to faith in the Lord is the Lord's freed person; similarly, the one who was free when called is Christ's slave" (1 Corinthians 7:22 NIV).

Jesus came to set you free from the "yoke of bondage," but then urges you to voluntarily join Him in serving others, saying, "Take my yoke upon you and learn from me. . . . For my yoke is easy and my burden is light" (Matthew 11:29–30 NIV).

STAY ON POINT

Be on the alert, stand firm in the faith, act like men, be strong.
1 CORINTHIANS 16:13 NASB

Four months after the Civil War ended, the Confederate cruiser C.S.S. *Shenandoah* accepted a British captain's report on August 2, 1865, that the South had surrendered. Although its crew had heard rumors of the war's end, they and their officers continued their mission, wreaking havoc on Union whaling ships. Eventually, Captain James Waddell navigated from the northern Pacific to Liverpool, England, where he surrendered his ship to British authorities on November 6.

What is *your* mission? That question works on two related levels—overarching and day-to-day. For the former, consider this: Who are you, apart from anything you do? If your career or roles define you rather than your sonship in Christ, your day-to-day work will be compromised by fear and doubt. Start here: you are His. The rest—relationships, work, ministry—follows this basic truth.

Your mission ends when Jesus returns—a moment about which He made two things clear: it could come at any time, so be prepared (Matthew 24:42); and when He comes, you should be going about *His* business (Luke 19:13)—living in such a way that seeking God's kingdom first is your highest goal. Keep at it until He comes back. That's when you'll know your mission is over, and your reward will be to hear Jesus Himself tell you, "Well done."

EYES ON THE PRIZE

*Thanks be to God who always leads us in triumph in Christ,
and through us diffuses the fragrance of His
knowledge in every place.*

2 CORINTHIANS 2:14 NKJV

Christopher Columbus set sail from Spain on August 3, 1492, driven by the offsetting dreams of fame and fortune and a passion for sharing his Catholic faith. He sought a faster passage to Asia, but his explorer's courage was canceled out by his navigational shortcomings, landing him in the Bahamas.

Records show similar contradiction in his personal behavior: a sailor who didn't swear (imagine that!) and conducted religious rites while en route also enslaved hundreds of natives and forced his beliefs on them. Columbus was a classic example of a "double-minded man" (James 1:8 NKJV), with the accompanying instability and hypocrisy.

It's easy these days to bash Columbus as some Old World imperialist, a product of the greed and legalism of his day, but it's not that simple. His malady goes much farther back in history, all the way to Eden. The apostle John described this problem as "the lust of the flesh, the lust of the eyes, and the pride of life" (1 John 2:16 NIV).

When you set your eyes on something you want—a wife, a job, a car—vet it through that lens. All truly great endeavors are stamped by God's ultimate glory, not your instant gratification. Everywhere you go and everything you do should, as a priority, promote His agenda.

MOMENTS OF CONNECTION

*Love each other with genuine affection,
and take delight in honoring each other.*
ROMANS 12:10 NLT

Jesse Owens won the second of his four Olympic gold medals in the long jump on August 4, 1936. In the final, Owens outjumped a young German, Lutz Long, who then joined him, walking arm in arm around the track as the crowd roared in support. War later separated the men, each loyal to his homeland, but never their friendship. Owens later said that moment in Berlin was worth more to him than all the medals and trophies he had ever won.

How are you at celebrating others' successes? Think of everything that goes into a moment of success—the dreaming, hard work, failures, sleepless nights, and small breakthroughs—and the lack of any sort of guarantee that you'll achieve your goal. Then, picture sharing that moment. Most champions would say that, after the cheering dies down and the euphoria wears off, the best part of winning is sharing it with someone.

Jesus honored His Father by giving His all to lift you up—and angels rejoice whenever someone chooses to receive His gift (Luke 15:7–10). To truly celebrate with someone, you have to know what they've been through to get there. Invest your talents in someone else's success. Look past worldly goals to godly ones—lifting others up, encouraging and admonishing with their highest good in mind. Their victories will become yours, and your victories, theirs.

THE LIBERATION WON'T BE TELEVISED

*"He has sent Me to heal the brokenhearted, to proclaim liberty
to the captives and recovery of sight to the blind,
to set at liberty those who are oppressed."*

LUKE 4:18 NKJV

August 5, 1944, was a day of liberation for 348 Jewish prisoners, as Polish insurgents stormed a Nazi forced-labor camp in Warsaw. The uprising lasted over two months, with the Polish gaining control of the city for a few brief days before German reinforcements and a lack of Allied help wore them down.

The urban combat you face today doesn't involve bombs and tanks, but it does include prisoners of war. Millions upon millions lead lives of quiet desperation—the abandonment of hope inscribed on Dante's version of hell's gates. Some have never known anything but hunger and cold and want, and most who have achieved a worldly version of success have found themselves wanting more. Whatever the case, each of us reaches a place where we can go no further—we've done all we can and it's not enough.

Freedom from tyranny has long been one of mankind's greatest rallying cries. If Jesus has liberated you from the tyranny of self and sin, join Him in the work of pointing others to His freedom. Don't be a good man settling for less in this life; be an honest man following a great God as He works in and through you to change the world.

PERSPECTIVE ON REJECTION

I have become all things to all people so that
by all possible means I might save some.
1 CORINTHIANS 9:22 NIV

Witnessing for Christ has always been a challenge. In the current climate of political correctness, where truth is often replaced by opinion and personal freedom is idolized, you face unique challenges. Sharing about Jesus requires letting go of preconceived notions while still clinging to God's truth. You have freedom in Christ to share His love and grace without the shackles of shifting expectations and demands.

At the same time, those things have shaped people's opinions of God, Jesus, the church, and Christians. Earning the right to tell people about Jesus is like solving a puzzle box—you have to watch, listen, probe, learn from failure, and keep trying.

Remember a few things as you go. First, everyone matters to Jesus. They may not ever receive His gift of salvation, but that's between them and God. Your job is to treat them as Jesus did. He met people where they were—amid pain, complacency, ignorance, busyness—and told them God's truth in a way that fit their circumstances.

Also, don't fear being an imperfect messenger. Listen first, trying to learn each person's story, situation, and experience with God. If it helps, share your story of salvation. Sharing your faith carries risk, but if you're rejected, take heart. Jesus was, too. Ask God for a wise and compassionate heart and for perseverance in the face of resistance.

THE MERIT OF BLOOD

"Greater love has no one than this,
than to lay down one's life for his friends."
JOHN 15:13 NKJV

George Washington created the Badge for Military Merit on this day in 1782, an award for "any singularly meritorious action" in battle. It was known as the Purple Heart. Soldiers have received it for being killed or wounded in action and for suffering as a prisoner of war. One recipient, Private First Class David Kenyon Webster, wrote, "Those things which are precious are saved only by sacrifice."

Blood as the ultimate cost required to conquer the effects of evil goes all the way back to Eden, when God replaced Adam and Eve's fig-leaf garments with animal skins. Later, Jesus fulfilled the requirements of Moses' Law, that "nearly everything was purified with blood. For without the shedding of blood, there is no forgiveness" (Hebrews 9:22 NLT).

True giving carries the idea of cost—giving not only when you're prosperous, but when you lack. David wouldn't build an altar on gifted ground, purchasing Araunah's threshing floor in an act of sacrifice that had been presaged by Abraham's offering Isaac and fulfilled by Christ's crucifixion, both of which also transpired on the mountains of Moriah.

When you give from your time, talents, and treasure, you honor a gift you can't repay. As a soldier in God's army, you can share in Christ's suffering by praying for peace, and giving all you can to see as many partake of it as possible.

WHO'S REALLY IN CHARGE?

The king's heart is like channels of water in the hand
of the LORD; He turns it wherever He wishes.

PROVERBS 21:1 NASB

When Richard Nixon resigned the office of the president on August 8, 1974, his successor Gerald Ford called it the end of a "long national nightmare." The Watergate scandal had eroded trust in both the president, specifically, and high-level government in general. In many ways, that trust has never quite been regained, and the public has a deeper mistrust of elected government officials than ever.

During times of political turmoil, remember that God is still in control. No ruler takes charge without His permission. God's orchestration of authority doesn't mean He approves of what people do with the power He allows them to exercise. As Daniel told Nebuchadnezzar, "He removes kings and establishes kings; He gives wisdom to wise men and knowledge to men of understanding" (Daniel 2:21 NASB).

Your political role as a believer is to stay involved, especially when it would be easier to check out and wait for Jesus to return. You submit to governing authorities because you're really submitting to God's sovereignty (Romans 13), but you need to know the issues and exercise the privilege of voting. Biblical values matter most, not a person or a party. And if God leads you to run for office, pray hard about it—you could be the man for such a season as this.

TAKE HOLD OF GOD'S PEACE

"You will keep him in perfect peace, whose mind is stayed on You, because he trusts in You."
ISAIAH 26:3 NKJV

As the spiritual leader of your family, the buck stops with you. While you're wise to discuss issues with your wife and seek the counsel of mature, experienced Christians, in the end, you're responsible for the big decisions. In those situations, how can you have peace?

When Jesus told His disciples, "Peace I leave with you, My peace I give to you" (John 14:27 NKJV), His peace was an actual thing, not an absence of something like conflict or confusion. Isaiah tied peace to trust, deliberately turning your thoughts toward God instead of your problems. Paul described peace as a shield "which transcends all understanding [and] will guard your hearts and your minds in Christ Jesus" (Philippians 4:7 NIV).

Furthermore, Paul detailed the types of thoughts you should be turning toward God—things that are true, noble, just, pure, lovely, of good report, virtuous, and praiseworthy (Philippians 4:8).

When you figure all of those into your decisions—thinking about what the cost might be or what it means to follow God in your circumstances—He will *give* you His peace. And it won't be the peace the world gives, the sort that leaves you doubting, second-guessing, and feeling more alone than ever. Once you grasp God's peace, you'll make the best decision possible, entrusting your cares to Him.

PRAISE HER

*Her children rise up and call her blessed; her husband also,
and he praises her: "Many daughters have done
well, but you excel them all."*

PROVERBS 31:28–29 NKJV

On August 10, 1877, Amanda McFarland became the first and only white woman to go to the mission field at Fort Wrangell, Alaska, a lawless town beset by enslavement of the natives and the widespread practice of witchcraft. Widowed a few years previously, McFarland also dealt with her own health issues and a complete lack of salary. Through it all, though, she won the respect and trust of both the local Indians and whites, raising support to build a boarding school, protecting the children in her care, and earning the title of "Alaska's Courageous Missionary."

There are few things more remarkable than a woman sold out to Jesus Christ. Whatever other qualities you could seek in a wife, that should top your list. You can trust that, throughout the various seasons of your life together, she will be faithful to do what's right in God's eyes.

That provides a spiritual barometer for you, a partner and sounding board for the tough decisions and situations you will face together. She will blossom under the shelter of your sacrificial love, and the two of you will create a true masterpiece—a unified life under God. If you're single, pray for such a woman; if you've already got one, let her know what a blessing she is.

A SAFE PLACE?

Even in laughter the heart may ache,
and rejoicing may end in grief.
PROVERBS 14:13 NIV

When Robin Williams was found dead of suicide on this day in 2014, people were shocked—both outside and inside the church. The man who made so many laugh and feel through his versatile performances finally succumbed to his struggles, including severe depression and the effects of his past drug addiction and alcoholism. And he hadn't been ready to share his health problems with the world.

One of the church's biggest failures is the need we feel to put on a perfect face. We're afraid we'll be judged when another believer finds out that we're struggling or hurting. By ignoring the fundamental truth of the Gospel—that we're all sinners in need of forgiveness and grace—we make the church feel unsafe.

Remember, Jesus was a man of sorrows, acquainted with grief (Isaiah 53:3). He wept over loss and the pain of sin's destructive path. He came to set captives free, but He knows none of us will be completely healed until He returns and completes the work He began in us at our salvation (Philippians 1:6).

Jesus is the best friend a depressed person could ever have, and we need to reflect that truth—that light, relief, and peace—both inside and outside the church. When the church is seen as the place of healing it's meant to be, people will flock to it, seeking the chance to begin to heal. Do your part to leave the doors open.

MAKE THINGS RIGHT

All things are of God, who has reconciled us to Himself through Jesus Christ, and has given us the ministry of reconciliation.
2 CORINTHIANS 5:18 NKJV

When New England Patriot receiver Darryl Stingley cut toward the middle of the field on August 12, 1978, searching for the pass coming his way, he never saw Oakland Raider safety Jack Tatum coming. Tatum, known for his vicious hits, jarred Stingley with his helmet and forearm, breaking the twenty-six-year-old's neck and rendering him a quadriplegic for life.

The hit was within league rules and considered tragic bad luck. However, not once did Tatum seek Stingley out afterward to apologize. Stingley, however, forgave Tatum, calling his predicament a test of faith. He asked himself, "In whom, and how much, do you believe, Darryl?" In the end, he was the one who was liberated as God released him from the burden of anger and grief.

Grudges are self-imposed burdens; they're not God's best for you. Once you consider the lengths God went to so you could be reconciled with Him, your perspective toward others should shift. You reflect well on Jesus when you make peace with those who have wronged you (or whom you have wronged).

Another part of the reconciling work God has for you involves letting people know how they can get right with God, and there's no room for bad blood in your life or theirs—only Christ's.

BREAKING DOWN WALLS

The LORD is a shelter for the oppressed,
a refuge in times of trouble.
PSALM 9:9 NLT

On this day in 1961, East German soldiers laid down the first barbed wire and bricks that would become the Berlin Wall, dividing the city and providing a global symbol for the Cold War conflict. Would-be defectors were often shot as they attempted to escape, ratcheting up tensions between the forces of freedom and tyranny.

The Wall is a perfect microcosm of the barriers created by sin. When Adam and Eve ate the fruit, their sin made them guilty and ashamed, and people have been building walls to defend themselves from sin's consequences ever since.

It's human nature not to show all your cards; it's hard to trust someone when you don't know their motives or agenda. Fear of the unknown drives behavior, and only perfect love can cast it out (1 John 4:18–19). God's love in Christ did just that. God reaches through your defenses, offering peace, forgiveness, and reconciliation.

That requires transparency on your part: you must be honest about your sin to come to Jesus—on both a general and daily basis. Being known for who you really are and still loved by the only One who has the right to condemn you breaks down fear's walls. Once there's no wall between you and God, it becomes easier to open up to others, and for them to be open with you.

OVERCOMERS

"But you, be strong and do not lose courage,
for there is reward for your work."
2 CHRONICLES 15:7 NASB

St. Louis Cardinals ace and Hall of Famer Bob Gibson threw the only no-hitter of his storied career on August 14, 1971, and prevented an old nemesis, the Pittsburgh Pirates, from getting a single hit the entire game. The Pirates had hit him hard over the years, including one batted ball that broke his leg. But overcoming adversity was old hat for "Bullet" Bob.

Gibson overcame several childhood ailments—among them rickets, asthma, and a heart murmur—to become a top-level athlete. Known as a ferocious competitor, Gibson never took credit for his abilities, saying, "It is not something I earned. . . . It is a gift. It is something that was given to me." God has given you talents, too, but they will be tested through trouble.

No one asks for trouble, but trouble comes anyway. When it does, as a Christian, don't be afraid to embrace it—not because you're glad for the problem but because God will be with you, strengthening your faith and endurance.

In fact, until you have overcome adversity, you can't truly appreciate God's gift of salvation. Tribulation reminds you of two important things: one, you need Jesus desperately; and two, His Spirit and power makes you an overcomer—*more* than a conqueror (Romans 8:37). Nothing should faze you because nothing can stand between you and God.

DOUBLE, DOUBLE TOIL AND TROUBLE

But to those who are selfishly ambitious and do not obey the truth, but obey unrighteousness, wrath and indignation.
ROMANS 2:8 NASB

On this day in 1054, Malcolm Canmore avenged his father, King Duncan I of Scotland, by slaying his killer, King Macbeth. (Yes, he was an actual historical dude!) Shakespeare's play dramatized the story, adding a sense of mystical destiny and downplaying the real Macbeth's promotion of Christianity, but the emotional heart of the account—unchecked ambition—didn't require much massaging.

So much of history is stories of kings building monuments to themselves and then being unseated or overthrown by other kings who do the same thing, over and over. For all their wealth and power, it's hard not to picture the broken head of the statue in the poem "Ozymandias," half-buried in drifting sands, carrying the ironic inscription of its futility: "Look on my Works, ye Mighty, and despair!"

How do you do something with your life that matters beyond your life? By focusing your ambition on God. Ambition isn't bad in and of itself; it depends on whom it's focused. That requires humility—the understanding that, no matter how much you accomplish, it's chump change compared to God's works.

When you overcome your self-oriented agenda with seeking God's greater glory, you'll find contentment. You can only do that by focusing your goals and energy on God's character and agenda, not yours. Anything less makes you a Macbeth.

BARE-BONES FAITH

Walk worthy of the Lord, fully pleasing Him, being fruitful in every good work and increasing in the knowledge of God.
COLOSSIANS 1:10 NKJV

"One! Two! Three! Four!" With a count-off that heralded the punk-rock revolution, the Ramones hit the stage for the first time on August 16, 1974, at CBGB's in Queens, New York. Seeking an antidote both for Woodstock's hippie-dippie psychedelia and the bloated excesses of mid-70s corporate rock, the foursome—clad in black leather jackets—hit the stage with a fast, furious wall of sound that struck in two-minute bursts.

The band's DIY ethos inspired a generation to get in the garage and start playing—whether they knew their instruments or not. Skill set aside, the Ramones took a deliberate approach to their art. Drummer Tommy Ramone described their philosophy: "Eliminate the unnecessary and focus on the substance."

That's a useful motto for Christians, too. Look past trends and movements and refocus on what following Jesus is about. Pray for a wise heart to know Him better. Then, as He leads, remove anything that muddies the living water—worldly relationships, churchy jargon, legalistic attitudes.

Stripped-down, bare-bones faith follows Jesus' lead: Jesus sought God's will first and always. He embraced society's outcasts, healed broken lives and hearts, taught God's Word, and prepared leaders. He didn't put up with hypocrisy but served rather than judged. Take a fresh look at Jesus' priorities, eliminating the unnecessary and focusing on the substance.

DANCING WITH WORDS

"Just say a simple, 'Yes, I will,' or 'No, I won't.'
Anything beyond this is from the evil one."
MATTHEW 5:37 NLT

We've all been in situations where it's easier not to tell the truth. We do it for a variety of what seem like good reasons—protecting ourselves or someone else, or maintaining someone's high opinion of us—or sometimes, just because it's easier. And while there are subtle shades of nuance in many situations, the bottom line question may very well be: *Would my words have passed Jesus' litmus test of intention?*

For Jesus, it wasn't enough to obey the Law externally; the motives and attitude of the heart were paramount. It was against Moses' Law to cheat on your spouse, but Jesus said that if you only looked at a woman with lust, you were just as guilty in God's eyes. God doesn't want outward performance without internal obedience.

There used to be a saying that a man's word was his bond. God even said He hates liars, but that He loves trustworthy people (Proverbs 12:22). Times have changed. Telling the truth these days often carries the consequences that lying used to, but God doesn't change. He keeps His word, and He expects you to do the same. Don't dance with words; tell the hard truth, and God will have your back.

LIVING WITH TENSION

*"So are my ways higher than your ways
and my thoughts higher than your thoughts."*
ISAIAH 55:9 NIV

On this day in 1590, John White, governor of England's colony on Roanoke Island, returned from a supply trip to find the settlement deserted. None of the hundred or so colonists he had left behind could be found, nor could any clues about why they had vanished or where to—save for a cryptic word carved in a tree, *CROATOAN*. Their disappearance remains a mystery to this day.

Faith provides clarity on one hand—the purpose of life and how to live it—and mystery on the other—the blessing and curse of free will in action. Christianity involves tension between the natural and supernatural, being in the world but not of it. You believe in permanent salvation and ongoing transformation, stability and growth, joy and pain, faith and works. It's all so clear and yet you see through a glass darkly.

God's plans for your life are not cookie-cutter, toe-the-line kinds of plans. He calls you to dive headfirst into grace *and* also to live a holy life, to fight for justice *and* to accept His sovereignty. These are paradoxes, not contradictions. Your Father knows the struggle between His Spirit and your flesh, and He's committed to the lifetime's work of preparing you for eternity. Faith is not about certainty but turning doubt over to God. Embrace with open hands that your God is and/both *and* either/or.

RESPONDING TO EVIL

"My prayer is not that you take them out of the world
but that you protect them from the evil one."
JOHN 17:15 NIV

On this day in 1934, after a whirlwind ascent hastened by political cunning and treachery, Adolf Hitler consolidated the two most powerful offices in Germany and became president of the new Third Reich. Underestimated by political enemies who had first sought to control and then minimize his reach, Hitler's reign of terror changed the world forever.

Remarkably, even though it seems that the world would never allow another leader like Hitler, history since World War II is full of such men. They seek a throne and a name for themselves, and they care little for the people they must crush to try and achieve their goals.

God in His sovereignty permits such leaders to rise to power. It would be foolish to try and figure out why, but God's grace is sufficient for you. That Jesus prayed for your protection from Satan and his devices—as opposed to your immediate rapture off the planet once you were saved—is proof that He still has work for you to do.

The way you face challenges and afflictions might be the greatest witness you'll ever bear. People are watching you, to see how you, as a Christian, react to hardship—a deeply personal loss or a national crisis. Study God's Word so you'll know what to say when such times arise.

PERFECT TIMING

"You shall be witnesses to Me in Jerusalem, and in all Judea and Samaria, and to the end of the earth."
Acts 1:8 nkjv

August 20 is a big day for far-reaching communication, with the sending of the first around-the-world telegram in 1911 and the launch in 1977 of Voyager II, with its phonographic message called *Sounds of Earth*. The first connected the world in a new way, and the second attempted to talk to any possible extraterrestrial life beyond the solar system. Both remind us of the most important message ever sent out to a huge audience—the Gospel.

God does an amazing job of arranging opportunities so His message can go out. Just look at what He did to set up the spread of the Gospel back in the first century. Alexander the Great hellenized the known world, making Greek the common tongue from southern Europe to India. Rome then solidified the region with paved roads and a common law. Christian missionaries could travel widely and safely and address any people they met in a common tongue. God's timing was perfect then, and it is now.

The imperfection of His chosen vessels, however, points to a fundamental truth: God loves everyone and wants as many as possible to be saved; all you have to do is share. The truth is simple, but it changed your life. Tell someone how. God orchestrated history so that you can play a key role in His story.

A MATTER OF INTEGRITY

If a house be divided against itself, that house cannot stand.
MARK 3:25 KJV

The Lincoln-Douglas debates began in this day in 1858. Much of the ammunition used in this battle for a Senate seat was supplied by a speech Lincoln had made two months earlier, when he characterized the issue of slavery in America as "a house divided." The biblical reference put Lincoln's arguments on high moral ground: "I believe this government cannot endure, permanently half slave and half free. . . . It will become all one thing or all the other."

Lincoln lost the Senate race, but his integrity played a key role in his election as president. His words then proved prophetic, as the South seceded and the Civil War began, four years of bloody, heart-wrenching conflict that saw the nation reunited under a single slave-free banner.

Jesus' "divided house" remarks were a prelude to His claim that whoever was not for Him was against Him (Matthew 12:30). No neutral ground exists in the battle between good and evil. As Matthew Henry put it, "There are two great interests in the world"—God's and Satan's. The heart of every person on earth is the battleground.

No enduring good can come from compromising God's truth. His words have integrity and the man who stands by them will, too. You'll avoid hypocrisy and know for sure that, though a battle may be lost, you'll be on the winning side in the war.

GOD'S ECONOMY

There is one who scatters, yet increases more; and there is one who withholds more than is right, but it leads to poverty.
Proverbs 11:24 nkjv

Compared to worldly views of wealth, God's economy seems built on paradoxes: to get, you must first give, but you shouldn't give to get (Luke 6:35). Jesus' encounters with the rich—Matthew, Zacchaeus, the rich young ruler—make it clear that you can have every material advantage in the world and still lack the thing that matters most. In fact, the more you have, the more you will be held accountable for (Luke 12:48).

Consider the following financial concepts: you're not an owner but a steward; give and you will be blessed; live within your means; save so you can invest in things with no tangible value. From God's perspective, they all make sense. If they make you scratch your head, you're living in the world's economy, not God's.

Since everything belongs to God (Psalm 24:1), His business should guide your finances. Give back to Him first—don't ever give up tithing, even if you're down to a widow's mite.

Remember, God's business is seeing as many as possible receive the gift of salvation. Christ purchased a gift for you that you can never earn or purchase; the only thing you can do is share it, with your words, deeds, and resources. No other religion has Christianity's track record of helping; your involvement carries on that great tradition.

A SURE BET

People with integrity walk safely, but those who
follow crooked paths will be exposed.
PROVERBS 10:9 NLT

Pete Rose, baseball's all-time hits leader, accepted a lifetime ban from the game on this day in 1989. Commissioner Bart Giamatti had strong evidence that Rose had bet on his own team, the Cincinnati Reds, breaking the rules of the game and tarnishing his Hall of Fame–level credentials. It took Rose almost twenty years to confess his gambling, but he did so in an autobiography, so his pleas for forgiveness were seen as tainted by a desire for gain.

But what about us? In childhood, we tended to operate under the principle that what our parents didn't know couldn't hurt us. We hid everything from bad grades to stolen bubblegum, and sometimes we got away with it. Believe it or not, that was the worst thing that could have happened. Every time we got away with sin, our flesh took it as a sign of approval instead of what it really was, evidence of a calloused heart.

At some point, though, maybe not until the Judgment Seat of Christ, the truth will come out. " 'There is nothing hidden that will not be disclosed' " (Luke 8:17 NIV). Confession is the best path, but getting busted might be next best. If that happens, take advantage of the chance to make things right. "He who conceals his transgressions will not prosper, but he who confesses and forsakes them will find compassion" (Proverbs 28:13 NASB).

WAIT NO MORE

*If anyone, then, knows the good they ought to
do and doesn't do it, it is sin for them.*
JAMES 4:17 NIV

In AD 79, around noon on August 24, the ancient Roman resort town of Pompeii came to a swift and sudden end when Mount Vesuvius erupted. Pompeii's citizens were instantly preserved in their final acts, a few thousand men, women, and children memorialized in hardened, muddy ash. Vesuvius is still active, and another eruption is expected.

Europe's only active volcano is a reminder that Jesus could come back any day. Scripture warns us to pay attention to the signs of the times, so we can warn non-believers and encourage other believers that "God has not destined us for wrath, but for obtaining salvation through our Lord Jesus Christ" (1 Thessalonians 5:9 NASB). You should be living each day for God, and every day like it might be your last.

But here's the problem: most people put things off. There's an ongoing battle between the part of you that knows how to make mature, responsible decisions and the part that wants to do that thing over there. Even the urgency of impending apocalypse pales before the tyranny of YouTube and Candy Crush.

In between "breaks," though, identify what it is that paralyzes you: indecisiveness, perfectionism, fear, or laziness. Once you've narrowed it down, then you know what to pray for. God will help you get focused and back on task.

A FAITHFUL FEW

A friend loves at all times, and a brother is born for adversity.
PROVERBS 17:17 NKJV

Accountability has become one of those trendy, buzzword kinds of church ideas that people either love or hate but don't really know how to do, or why. Too often, we get caught up in some of the issues surrounding accountability—good things like confessing sins and liberty in Christ—and lose sight of the most important things—obeying God's Word, the grace of the Gospel, and faithful, committed fellowship.

You need accountability because you still need God. Sanctification is a lifelong process because you're still susceptible to temptation and sin. You have blind spots, and you need to be told about them. You still struggle with the "old man"—old habits and patterns of thinking and acting that will cause you to fall away if you let them dominate you. This is much more likely to happen in isolation. For those reasons, you need fellowship—encouragement and accountability from your brothers in Christ (Hebrews 10:25).

Accountability isn't optional. It requires commitment, as well as compassion. Pray that God would show you the men with whom you can live life, not making idols of confession or obedience but embracing God's grace together on a regular basis.

If you find yourself resisting this, ask why. Make sure you're not harboring sin. "Bear one another's burdens, and so fulfill the law of Christ" (Galatians 6:2 NKJV).

EQUAL BUT NOT IDENTICAL

God created man in His own image; in the image of God
He created him; male and female He created them.
Genesis 1:27 nkjv

Men and women have equal standing before God. Paul observed that "there is neither male nor female; for you are all one in Christ Jesus" (Galatians 3:28 nkjv). However, God also designed male and female relationships to follow a pattern: God gave men the authority to take bottom-line responsibility for the welfare of women (1 Corinthians 11:3).

Both can show leadership and initiative, and they are "heirs together of the grace of life" (1 Peter 3:7 kjv), but there are certain responsibilities that fall to a man. And this is where too many guys have fallen short.

God meant for men and women to complement each other through physical and emotional differences. Respective roles are best defined and experienced in marriage, but they still play into everyday relationships. Even if you're not married, you can still look out for a woman's best interests and make her feel valuable, and she can still encourage you and show you respect.

If you're married, when you both submit to God and follow His design for your relationship (Ephesians 5:23–33), good things will follow. If you're single, practice emotional purity. If the woman you're friends with isn't going to be your wife, she may be another man's wife in the future. So while you can enjoy Christian fellowship, be sure to keep your relationship pure and in the proper perspective.

PRESSING ON

Let us not be weary in well doing:
for in due season we shall reap, if we faint not.
GALATIANS 6:9 KJV

The Battle of Brooklyn, the first major battle of the American Revolution, began on this day in 1776, but ended in defeat for the colonists. The British captured New York City a few weeks later and held it until the end of the war in 1783.

The revolution couldn't have gotten off to a more discouraging start. Washington had anticipated the British attack, but shortages of troops and military discipline, coupled with many New Yorkers' loyalty to England, left him susceptible to a surprise night attack from which his forces never recovered. But he never quit, and the war was eventually won.

Similarly, Jesus never guaranteed you a picnic, only an adventure, complete with trials and challenges (John 15:20). Before Jesus came, God had overlooked the ignorance that caused sin (Acts 17:30). But that still left the greater problem unresolved; so, to get the ball rolling, Jesus showed up and made people aware of their sin, making them accountable.

No one likes being told they're wrong, and they killed Him for it. But that served His greater purpose, too. Just when it looked like all was lost, Jesus in the grave and His followers scattered and afraid, God conducted the greatest countermove in history. The revolution of salvation continues this day, and even when it seems like we'll never get there, victory awaits.

FREE AT LAST

*And this is the plan: At the right time he will bring
everything together under the authority of Christ—
everything in heaven and on earth.*

Ephesians 1:10 NLT

On August 28, 1963, in front of a quarter-million people gathered on the Washington Mall, Martin Luther King Jr., seized a crucial moment in American history and gave his stirring "I Have a Dream" speech. King hoped that, by hastening racial harmony, citizens would "be able to speed up that day when all of God's children. . .will be able to join hands" and sing a true song of praise to God for His freedom.

The day to which he referred will be the kingdom age, when Jesus reigns on earth, establishing true global peace for the first time ever. It was a theme King touched on throughout his speech, quoting Old Testament prophets who looked forward to that time, too. "Let justice run down like water, and righteousness like a mighty stream" (Amos 5:24 NKJV).

God's plan from the foundation of the earth was to see His people gathered together and unified in worshipful living—a time King referenced: "The glory of the LORD shall be revealed, and all flesh shall see it together" (Isaiah 40:5 KJV). In the meantime, there is work to do, and God wants you to be a part of it—as a peacemaker and reconciler in the only name that puts all men on equal, valued footing: Jesus Christ.

A FORCE FOR LOVE

No one has ever seen God. But if we love each other, God lives in us, and his love is brought to full expression in us.
1 JOHN 4:12 NLT

On this date in 2005, Hurricane Katrina made landfall in New Orleans with devastating, Category 4 fury. Sustained winds of over 145 miles per hour severed power lines; battered homes, churches, and businesses; and left around 150,000 seeking cover on higher ground. It also provided a life-changing opportunity for Christians along the Gulf Coast and across the nation to step in and help—and they did so admirably.

Local congregations and groups from various national denominations were present before the federal government was, pushing themselves to the limit to deliver a hot meal and a ready ear. In the aftermath, the government recognized the unique capabilities that faith-based groups brought to the situation, including their knowledge of the community, the people, and their physical, emotional, and spiritual needs.

Christians have historically been at the forefront of providing hospitals, orphanages, shelters, schools, and relief efforts—and the impact goes beyond the immediate help offered. People who wouldn't give church a second thought are impressed that so much gets done in Jesus' name. It starts when people like you put their hand up and step forward. As one clergyman put it, "What our brothers and sisters in Louisiana and Alabama and Mississippi are suffering today is our suffering, too."

SITUATIONAL AWARENESS

I send you forth as sheep in the midst of wolves:
be ye therefore wise as serpents, and harmless as doves.
MATTHEW 10:16 KJV

On August 30, 1918, near the end of World War I, an American colonel discarded a false set of plans for a major Allied offensive, knowing that a German spy would find them. The misdirection, called the Belfort Ruse after the French town near where it occurred, was a last-ditch effort to capture key ground when all standard efforts had failed. The trick worked, the Germans pulled back, and the Allies were able to open crucial supply lines.

Sharing your beliefs sometimes requires similar cleverness—not deception but awareness of people and situations. The dove comparison sounds nice, with its associations with peace and problem-solving. The serpent, not so much. But Jesus would never tell you to emulate Satan's behavior, so He was clearly evoking a serpent's positive qualities, a shrewd sort of cunning that enables them to survive in hostile environments.

Jesus wasn't always gentle, and He used His wits to avoid being killed by His enemies for years. Paul followed His example. He stood up for himself, employing his legal rights as a Roman citizen to serve his ministry, and wisely considered his audience, whether it was Athenians or Pharisees. But he lived in good conscience before God and men and curbed his fleshly desires to protect his ministry.

Ask God to help you make the most of your Gospel-sharing opportunities, standing for truth with love and compassion.

WAIT FOR IT

Through patience a ruler can be persuaded,
and a gentle tongue can break a bone.
PROVERBS 25:15 NIV

Paul said, "Love is patient" (1 Corinthians 13:4 NIV). The Greek word for *patient* means "bearing offenses" or "persevering through troubles"—the idea being, that if you're being patient, you're suffering bravely.

That implies intention; you have to *want* to be patient, you have to be willing to put up with slings and arrows of outrageous fortune because you see a greater goal beyond them. Otherwise, your patience does no good. It drives you nuts, and an unappreciative recipient will just carry on as usual once the danger of your wrath is past.

In a parable, Jesus told of the king who forgave his servant a huge debt after the man begged him, "Be patient with me" (Matthew 18:26 NIV). But then the guy demanded payment from another servant who owed him far less than he had owed the king. When his pal asked for patience, he had none and had the guy thrown in jail. The king was stunned. His patience came to an end because the servant hadn't taken it to heart—didn't appreciate the gravity of his debt or the extent of his mercy.

God requires you to be patient—slow to boil, waiting for understanding. Fortunately, God offers patience as a gift of the Spirit (Galatians 5:22 NASB). You can love someone who is unlovable because God loved you first: He was patient.

GOD FORGIVES YOU

*LORD, if you kept a record of our sins, who, O Lord,
could ever survive? But you offer forgiveness.*
PSALM 130:3–4 NLT

Many men find it very difficult to forgive themselves for past mistakes and moral failures—particularly if they're living with the ongoing consequences of past actions. Daily reminded of their sins, they trudge on in condemnation and defeat, feeling that God has turned His back on them.

Though they experience His care and provision, they conclude that God is just putting up with them, barely tolerating them, but doesn't really love them. They may believe that they're saved, but often feel that they'll barely squeak into heaven.

If this describes *you*, you need to read Psalm 103:8–13 (NLT), particularly verse 12 which says, "He has removed our sins as far from us as the east is from the west." In Isaiah, He says, "I. . . will blot out your sins for my own sake and will never think of them again" (Isaiah 43:25 NLT). And in the New Testament, John tells us, "If we confess our sins to him, he is faithful and just to forgive us our sins and to cleanse us from *all* wickedness" (1 John 1:9 NLT, emphasis added).

If you've confessed your sins to God and turned from them, He has forgiven you. Now you must trust in the depth and power of His forgiveness, forgive yourself, and rest daily in His love.

LAY OFF BOASTING

Let someone else praise you, not your own mouth—
a stranger, not your own lips.
PROVERBS 27:2 NLT

This verse offers very basic advice, and if you follow it, it will save you much trouble, because few people enjoy listening to a braggart.

But have you ever run into a highly successful man who, despite his accomplishments, degrees, and reputation, is very humble and down to earth? If you didn't know from speaking with him how great he was, you only found out because someone took you aside and informed you. That's what this verse is talking about.

You may feel awkward that you're forced to "boast" on your résumé. You're required to make yourself sound as good as possible, and this includes boldly proclaiming every bit of education you've received, everything you've accomplished, as well as every commendation and award you've received. But if talking about yourself and how "great" you are *bothers* you, you probably don't have much to worry about. Your heart is already in the right place.

It's when you feel smug and enjoy having others admire you, and love to hear them gush over the great things you've done, that you begin to be puffed up like a bullfrog. If you plan ways to casually drop hints of how wonderful you are, then soak it in when others praise you, you're setting yourself up for a fall. Avoid this and you'll avoid trouble.

LABOR DAY

In all labor there is profit, but mere talk leads only to poverty.
Proverbs 14:23 NASB

In the United States and Canada, Labor Day is celebrated as a public holiday on the first Monday in September. It honors the labor movement and all that workers have done to make their country strong and prosperous. There are frequently parades, festivals, and speeches. Labor Day is considered the end of summer, so it has also become known for back-to-school sales.

The Bible also celebrates laborers, noting that "in all labor there is profit" (Proverbs 14:23 NASB), and observing that "the sleep of a laboring man is sweet, whether he eats little or much" (Ecclesiastes 5:12 NKJV). Paul advises the believer, "Let him labor, working with his hands what is good" (Ephesians 4:28 NKJV).

God has a special place in His heart for laborers. When working as a shepherd, the patriarch Jacob assured himself, "God has seen. . .the labor of my hands" (Genesis 31:42 NKJV).

The Bible celebrated the *first* Labor Day—not merely once a year, but *fifty-two times* a year, every *week* faithfully! God proclaimed, "Six days shalt thou labour, and do all thy work: but the seventh day is the sabbath of the LORD thy God: in it thou shalt not do any work" (Exodus 20:9–10 KJV). Next time you enjoy a day of rest, remember that it shows the Lord's love and care for you.

UNCONVENTIONAL TACTICS

So it was, when the Philistine arose and came. . .
to meet David, that David hurried and ran
toward the army to meet the Philistine.
1 SAMUEL 17:48 NKJV

One day a huge Philistine army marched up the Valley of Elah, but the Israelite army learned they were coming and blocked their advance at the town of Socoh. Then an enormous man named Goliath, covered in heavy armor, stepped forward and challenged any Israelite soldier to face him in single combat. Only David accepted his challenge.

Saul offered David his armor and sword, but after trying them on, David realized that he didn't stand a chance using conventional methods. So, grasping his shepherd's staff, he walked down to the brook, picked five stones, and slipped them into his pouch. Then he headed up toward the giant. The only weapon Goliath could see was David's staff, so he roared, "Am I a dog, that you come to me with sticks?" (1 Samuel 17:43 NKJV).

Suddenly David rushed the giant. Startled, Goliath grinned. *He really is gonna try to hit me with that stick.* At the last moment, David dropped his staff, thrust a stone into his sling, began swinging it, then let it fly with punishing force. Goliath never realized what David was about to do until it was too late.

When you face impossible circumstances, God can inspire you with crazy, unconventional solutions. Be open to them! They can work when nothing else will.

ALL THE WORLD'S A STAGE

Let everyone see that you are considerate in all you do.
PHILIPPIANS 4:5 NLT

When Paul advises you to "let everyone *see* that you are considerate in all you do," he's saying to make a conscious decision to be kind and thoughtful since others are watching you. Not that you're supposed to do it simply for show, but be aware that others are observing you and judging the Gospel by how you live it out in your daily life.

Jesus said something similar: "Let your light so shine before men, that they may see your good works and glorify your Father in heaven" (Matthew 5:16 NKJV).

Shakespeare declared, "All the world's a stage," and explained that everyone acts out the part given them to play. The world *is* a stage for Christians as well. "We have been made a spectacle to the whole universe, to angels as well as to human beings" (1 Corinthians 4:9 NIV). And how are you to act? Considerate.

In common usage, to be considerate means to show kindness and awareness for another person's feelings; it literally means to ponder, to carefully consider others and their needs. In the most intimate of relationships—marriage—the Bible advises, "Husbands, in the same way be considerate as you live with your wives" (1 Peter 3:7 NIV).

To act in a considerate manner, you need to be motivated by love.

THE MIGHTY POWER OF GOD

Finally, be strong in the Lord and in his mighty power. . .
so that you can take your stand against the devil's schemes.
EPHESIANS 6:10–11 NIV

A scheme is a methodical, calculated plan for reaching a specific goal or putting a particular idea into effect. To *scheme* often describes plans done in a devious way or with intent to bring about an evil result. The devil schemes to bring your life to ruin, and he employs time-tested methods such as hatred, fear, lust, covetousness, addictions, and so on. C. S. Lewis gave insightful descriptions of his schemes in *The Screwtape Letters*.

What's the best way to combat the evil one's schemes? To submit yourself to God and pray, "May your will be done" (Matthew 26:42 NIV).

For example, it was God's will that Jesus be crucified for the sins of the world, but Peter argued against it. So Jesus told him, "Get behind Me, Satan! . . .for you are not setting your mind on God's interests, but man's" (Matthew 16:23 NASB). Man's interests and "the will of the flesh" (John 1:13 KJV) often parallel Satan's will, because both are selfish.

How do you become "strong in the Lord. . .so that you can take your stand against the devil's schemes"? Simple. "Submit yourselves. . .to God." Then you will have spiritual strength. Then you can "resist the devil, and he will flee from you" (James 4:7 KJV).

WHOLEHEARTED OBEDIENCE

He did what was right in the eyes of the LORD,
but not wholeheartedly.
2 CHRONICLES 25:2 NIV

Amaziah, king of Judah, was *sort of* a good man. . .just like his dad. His father Joash had lived most of his life under the shadow of the high priest, Jehoiada, and had followed God as long as Jehoiada was alive. But after Jehoiada died, Joash quickly went astray. Amaziah, too, had been raised all his life to worship God but in his later years strayed into idol worship.

Many people raised in the church have a similar problem. They know all about God, know what is right, and even have a relationship with Him. But as they age, they gradually depend more and more on their own reasoning, follow their own inclinations, and eventually turn away from God. And their eventual backsliding largely stems from not following the Lord wholeheartedly to begin with.

It's wonderful to attend church faithfully, give to God, and read your Bible, but if you're mainly doing these things to put on a show, to please other people, and to be accepted as a "good Christian," eventually you'll run out of steam and come to a stop.

Don't let this be you. Remember the number-one commandment: "You shall love the LORD your God with *all* your heart and with *all* your soul and with *all* your might" (Deuteronomy 6:5 NASB, emphasis added).

AN EXAMPLE TO OTHERS

Be an example to all believers in what you say, in the way
you live, in your love, your faith, and your purity.
1 TIMOTHY 4:12 NLT

This verse may seem like a tall order. You might struggle with bitterness, question your faith at times, and have daily battles with lust. You don't feel like you're able to be an example to other believers. You're happy if you can hold your *own* act together enough to escape condemnation and self-doubt.

Don't give up on yourself. God hasn't thrown in the towel on you yet, and neither should you. Love and follow God today, and trust that He will continue working in your life and give you the victory in these areas as you cry out to Him to help you. Remember that when Jesus revealed God's power to Peter, the rough-hewn fisherman pleaded, "Depart from me; for I am a sinful man, O Lord" (Luke 5:8 KJV).

But Jesus *didn't* depart. He continued to work in Peter's life for the next three years. And even after all that time learning from the Master, Peter denied Him during a time of testing. But Jesus saw that coming, too, and said, "I have pleaded in prayer for you, Simon, that your faith should not fail. So when you have repented and turned to me again, strengthen your brothers" (Luke 22:32 NLT).

If there's hope for Peter, there's hope for you.

NATIONAL GRANDPARENTS DAY

A good man leaveth an inheritance to his children's children.
PROVERBS 13:22 KJV

In the United States many people, especially children, observe National Grandparents Day on the first Sunday of September after Labor Day. They draw pictures and tell stories about their grandparents. They also send cards to their grandparents and either visit them or invite them to dinner. This can be a very meaningful time and allows people to celebrate and appreciate their heritage.

If you're a grandparent, this day can be special for you even if your grandchildren are unaware of the holiday and aren't taught about it in school. You can be the one to initiate the phone call and use the opportunity to be a good grandfather to them. Take them out and treat them, and let them know how deeply you love them. Give them reason to be thankful for you and appreciate you.

Solomon said, "Good people leave an inheritance to their grandchildren" (Proverbs 13:22 NLT), and this need not only be physical possessions after you die. It's important that you pass down a trove of spiritual wealth and faith to your children and grandchildren while you're still alive. You can also tell them stories about your life, and make them aware of their family heritage. Both you and they will be happy you did.

PRAYERS OF PROTECTION

*Because he hath set his love upon me. . .He shall call upon me,
and I will answer him: I will be with him
in trouble; I will deliver him.*

PSALM 91:14–15 KJV

God tells the disobedient, "The LORD's arm is not too weak to save you, nor is his ear too deaf to hear you call," but "because of your sins, he has turned away and will not listen anymore" (Isaiah 59:1–2 NLT). When people are far from God, they can't claim His blessing or protection.

However, the opposite is true when you draw *near* to God. Then, you call upon Him and He *will* answer. He will be with you when you face trouble and protect you. This doesn't mean that He will spare you from *all* trouble, but it means that He will be *with* you.

Some people, however, question why God often *doesn't* seem to be with believers who love and obey Him. Does that mean this promise isn't true? No. What it means is that God is sovereign and has His reasons for sometimes allowing suffering.

Notice in Hebrews 11:35–37 that He allowed His righteous followers to be tortured, whipped, to languish in prison, to die by stoning, to be sawed in half, and to be killed with the sword. Many others were destitute and oppressed and mistreated. Yet we remember these people not as abandoned unfortunates, but as heroes of the faith.

NATIONAL PATRIOTS' DAY

They all plotted together to come and fight against Jerusalem and stir up trouble against it. But we prayed to our God and posted a guard day and night to meet this threat.
NEHEMIAH 4:8–9 NIV

Today, Patriots' Day, commonly referred to as 9/11, is an annual observance to honor the people who died or were injured during the terrorist attacks on September 11, 2001. Many people observe a moment of silence at 8:46 a.m. (Eastern Daylight Time), when the first plane flew into the World Trade Center. Some communities hold church services or prayer meetings. People who experienced the tragedies, or who lost loved ones in them, often lay flowers at the sites or visit memorials. The American flag is flown at half-mast.

The Bible tells you, "Be of sober spirit, be on the alert. Your adversary, the devil, prowls around like a roaring lion, seeking someone to devour" (1 Peter 5:8 NASB). The events of September 11 should serve as a perpetual reminder of the need to stay vigilant. Terrorists are still seeking openings to attack, and you are well advised to not let your guard down.

On a more personal level, you're wise to remember that the devil, the ultimate evil, is constantly seeking to tempt you in a moment of weakness or to cause you to compromise your convictions and fall. His goal is to bring about your ruin. So be on the alert! Don't give him any opportunity.

HELPING THOSE IN NEED

*As we have opportunity, let us do good to all,
especially to those who are of the household of faith.*
GALATIANS 6:10 NKJV

There are generally two ways God moves you to show kindness
to fellow believers. One is when you're aware of their need, are
thinking about it, and realize that you're in a position to help.
So you talk it over with your wife and arrange to do it. It's really
a logical conclusion, done out of love for others. Often you have
time to think it over and get counsel about it.

The second way is when you first become aware of their need
and right on the spot the Holy Spirit speaks, telling you exactly
what to do to help.

However God works to get you to loosen your purse strings,
and helping someone often involves finances. Yes, God may call
upon you to give to someone less fortunate than yourself, even
if you're a manual laborer earning minimum wage. Paul said in
Ephesians 4:28 (NKJV), "Let him. . .labor, working with his hands
what is good, that he may have something to give him who has
need."

James asked, "Suppose you see a brother or sister who has
no food or clothing, and you say, 'Good-bye and have a good day;
stay warm and eat well'—but then you don't give that person
any food or clothing. What good does that do?" (James 2:15–16
NLT). The answer is obvious.

INTIMIDATED BY GIANTS

*"There we saw the giants. . .and we were like grasshoppers
in our own sight, and so we were in their sight."*
NUMBERS 13:33 NKJV

When the Israelites arrived at the border of Canaan, Moses sent twelve spies into the land. When they returned, ten of them said, "The people who dwell in the land are strong; the cities are fortified and very large. . . .and all the people whom we saw in it are men of great stature" (Numbers 13:28, 32 NKJV).

They concluded, "We are not able to go up against the people, for they are stronger than we" (v. 31). Their negative report so discouraged the Israelites that they were afraid to invade Canaan, even though the Lord had promised He'd help them.

Does this ever happen to you? You're initially excited about a project and even though you're aware you'll face difficulties, you're buoyed by feelings of optimism. God has promised to be with you, and you know that He can do miracles. But when it actually comes time to launch out, you allow yourself to get discouraged by naysayers, get cold feet, and back out.

It's human nature to say, "There are giants in the land!" It's the default setting of the natural mind to see problems as huge and to feel grasshopper-size compared to them. But have faith in God. With His help you can overcome them, no matter how big they are.

BROKEN CISTERNS

"For My people have. . .forsaken Me, the fountain of living waters, to hew for themselves cisterns, broken cisterns that can hold no water."
JEREMIAH 2:13 NASB

Israel is dry most of the year, with rain falling predominantly in the winter, so water is a precious commodity. Then as now, the best sources were springs or fountains, as their supply was fresh and clean. Also, wells tapped into underground streams, another source of running water.

God referred to Himself as "the fountain of living waters," and Jesus called the Spirit of God "a well of water springing up to eternal life" (John 4:14 NASB).

When Israelite villages lacked sufficient water, they carved out underground reservoirs called *cisterns* to store water. They sealed the walls with plaster. Then they directed the winter rain into these cisterns. A great deal of mud ended up in the bottom of it (see Jeremiah 38:6). Also, Israel had many minor earthquakes, and the plaster was constantly cracking and the water draining away.

God pointed out how senseless His people were to choose broken cisterns with muddy, stale water over fresh spring water. Man's broken philosophies and stagnant religions are the same—far inferior to faith in the true God. Unfortunately, people today are still hewing out cisterns.

Ditch the stagnant water of man's philosophies and come drink of the water of life. "Let anyone who is thirsty come. Let anyone who desires drink freely from the water of life" (Revelation 22:17 NLT).

BOXING THAT BRUISES YOU

Everyone who competes in the games goes into strict training.
They do it to get a crown that will not last, but we do it to get
a crown that will last forever. Therefore I do not run like someone
running aimlessly; I do not fight like a boxer beating the air.
1 Corinthians 9:25–26 niv

The Olympic Games were held in Paul's day, too. The city of Corinth was also famous for the Isthmian Games, held every second year. Paul made many references to athletes competing in races, and here he refers to boxing, also popular in his day.

Paul had frequently seen boxers in training, shadow-boxing, striking out at nothing, and having no one strike back. He said, "I fight: not as one who beats the air. But I discipline [*bruise*] my body and bring it into subjection, lest. . .I myself should become disqualified" (1 Corinthians 26–27 nkjv, author's commentary added).

To Paul, the only kind of training that made sense was to fight an actual opponent, even though it meant taking repeated blows and getting bruised. It was far preferable to merely shadow-boxing. He didn't want to be disqualified during an actual boxing match because he wasn't tough enough to take physical blows.

Paul pointed out that athletes were willing to endure punishment to get a laurel crown that withered, so how much more willing should believers be to obtain an eternal crown?

THE DUTY OF A WATCHMAN

"As for me, far be it from me that I should sin against the LORD by ceasing to pray for you; but I will instruct you in the good and right way."
1 SAMUEL 12:23 NASB

God told Ezekiel, "I have appointed you a watchman to the house of Israel; whenever you hear a word from My mouth, warn them from Me" (Ezekiel 3:17 NASB). Watchmen stood on city walls, keeping their eyes open for danger, and sounding the alarm to rouse the people so the city wouldn't fall to the enemy. Men of God often watched over Israel. Samuel was one such man.

God declared, "I searched for a man among them who would build up the wall and stand in the gap before Me for the land, so that I would not destroy it" (Ezekiel 22:30 NASB). When the spiritual wall of a nation's defenses are weak, men of God are called to intercede for their people—to guard these gaps. You do this through intercessory prayer.

Samuel said that he'd be *sinning* if he ceased to pray for his people. Christian men today should also understand prayer as their duty. It's easy to just kick up your feet and relax after a day at work, and you *do* need rest, but it's *also* your duty to take matters to God in prayer. To do that, you must carve out some time in your schedule. Don't neglect this.

HONORED BY MEN

*"I know I have sinned. But please, at least honor me before
the elders of my people and before Israel by coming back
with me so that I may worship the Lord your God."*

1 Samuel 15:30 nlt

The prophet Samuel had just finished telling Saul, "Rebellion is as sinful as witchcraft, and stubbornness as bad as worshiping idols. So because you have rejected the command of the Lord, he has rejected you as king" (v. 23). Saul then admitted, "I have disobeyed. . .the Lord's command, for I was afraid of the people and did what they demanded" (v. 24).

Despite that, he *still* had the nerve to ask Samuel, "Honor me before the elders of my people."

Saul feared people, and being accepted and honored by them was all that mattered to him. He was not very concerned whether he pleased God. The religious leaders of Jesus' day were the same. "They loved human praise more than the praise of God" (John 12:43 nlt). As Jesus pointed out, "You gladly honor each other, but you don't care about the honor that comes from. . .God" (John 5:44 nlt).

The Lord understands the human need to save face and be respected. He *gets* it. Nevertheless, He insists that you seek to please Him above all. It can be difficult, but life would be so much simpler if people simply sought the praise of God first and foremost.

HOPE FOR HAPPINESS

*Make me hear joy and gladness, that the bones
You have broken may rejoice.*
PSALM 51:8 NKJV

In the ancient Middle East, a lamb that strayed from the shepherd and the flock put itself in great danger, since the surrounding wilderness was home to fierce animals. If a lamb continually strayed, a shepherd would break one of its legs. Until it healed, the lamb depended on the shepherd to carry it around and bring it grass. Once it healed, the lamb would usually stay nearer the shepherd than any other sheep.

Sometimes God allows accidents and misfortune to cause *you* to focus on Him and His doings. His desire is for your good and to draw you closer to Him, though it might not seem good at the time.

When he uttered the above verse, David was repenting for committing adultery with Bathsheba and for arranging for her husband to be slain. It almost seems inappropriate for him to pray, "Make me hear joy and gladness" and to ask that he might soon "rejoice." It seems he should have been pleading for God's mercy and forgiveness. That *is*, in fact, what he'd been doing in the rest of this psalm.

But David had tremendous faith in the Lord's lovingkindness. He knew that God was merciful, and he had the faith to look beyond his present distress to anticipate full restoration and the return of happiness. May you hope for the same.

THE SCAPEGOAT

"The goat on which the lot fell to be the scapegoat shall be presented alive before the LORD, to make atonement upon it, and to let it go as the scapegoat into the wilderness."
LEVITICUS 16:10 NKJV

Today is Yom Kippur, also known as the Day of Atonement or the Fast (Acts 27:9), and it focuses on atonement and repentance (Leviticus 23:26–32). On this day, two goats were selected. One was sacrificed to the Lord. The sins of the people were symbolically placed on the other goat, the scapegoat, which was then chased into the desert (Leviticus 16:1–26).

In modern usage, a scapegoat is a person who's unfairly blamed for causing a problem. While they may be responsible for *some* of it, they're blamed for the *entire* muddle. If you've ever been made a scapegoat for a family misunderstanding or a workplace mess, you know how unfair this can be.

If you're able to set the record straight, by all means do so. But you don't always have that opportunity, and even when you do, you're not always believed. That's why Paul said, "When we are slandered, we answer kindly" (1 Corinthians 4:13 NIV). The Bible tells you the attitude to have then: "For this is commendable, if because of conscience toward God one endures grief, suffering wrongfully" (1 Peter 2:19 NKJV).

Remember that Jesus Himself, though He was utterly innocent, was also falsely accused.

FEEBLE FOLK IN FORTRESSES

The conies are but a feeble folk,
yet make they their houses in the rocks.
PROVERBS 30:26 KJV

What, you may ask, are conies? The NIV translates this verse: "Hyraxes are creatures of little power, yet they make their home in the crags." The *Hyrax syriacus*, also known as a rock badger, is found in the Sinai Desert and cliffs along the Dead Sea. It's a small, shy, furry animal that resembles a guinea pig. It lives in rock crevices, safe from predators. Hyraxes feed in groups, watched over by sentries that sound an alarm when enemies approach.

They're reminiscent of the Ewoks, short furry bipeds in the *Star Wars* movies, who lived on the forest moon of Endor. They, too, were a "feeble folk" who proved to be mighty.

All believers are "feeble" in *some* area of their lives—weak, incapable, and lacking power. You may be ordinary, with no special talents, yet do things that compensate for your weakness. Maybe you're thrifty and good at saving, so despite a lack of good looks, strength, or other A-list abilities, you're able to provide a secure financial future.

"Remember. . .that few of you were wise in the world's eyes or powerful or wealthy when God called you. Instead, God chose things. . .that are powerless to shame those who are powerful" (1 Corinthians 1:26–27 NLT).

FLEE SEXUAL FANTASIES

"You have heard that it was said, 'You shall not commit adultery.'
But I tell you that anyone who looks at a woman lustfully
has already committed adultery with her in his heart."
MATTHEW 5:27–28 NIV

Many men think there's a big difference between lusting and actually having sexual relations. They fail to understand how if they continually think erotic thoughts, they'll eventually attempt to follow through on them. That's because they become addicted to the rush that fantasizing gives, and their brain needs ever more stimulation. Eventually, nothing short of the actual deed satisfies.

The Ten Commandments forbade both illicit sex and fantasizing about it. Exodus 20:14 (NIV) says, "You shall not commit adultery," and verse 17 says, "You shall not covet. . .your neighbor's wife." God knew that men had to arrest lust while it was still a thought.

Resist fantasizing before it becomes a habit. The patriarch Job knew that he, like all men, was aroused by visual stimulation, so he said, "I made a covenant with my eyes not to look lustfully at a young woman" (Job 31:1 NIV).

Paul wrote, "Flee from sexual immorality" (1 Corinthians 6:18 NIV), but if you're in the habit of intoxicating yourself with lust, you'll do the *opposite* on the day an opportunity arises. So ditch licentious thoughts now, so that on the day of temptation, you'll have the willpower to put physical distance between yourself and any alluring sirens.

ACCOMPLISHING ITS MISSION

*"As the rain and the snow come down from heaven, and do not
return to it without watering the earth and making it bud
and flourish. . .so is my word that goes out from my mouth:
It will not return to me empty, but will. . .
achieve the purpose for which I sent it."*
ISAIAH 55:10–11 NIV

God's Word is eternal, and is like buckets containing ever-fresh supplies of His Spirit. When you believe His promises and apply them to the different situations you face, it's as if you're pouring life-giving water on dry earth. This causes your situations to come to life like dormant seeds activated by water.

In the passage above, God promises that, just as water evaporates and returns as vapor to heaven, so His Word will return to Him—but not before it accomplishes the purpose He sent it to accomplish on earth.

You may sometimes wonder if the Word of God is truly effective, especially if you're claiming Bible promises for a very difficult situation. You can become discouraged if *years* go by without seeing promises fulfilled. But remember, explorers have found seeds in the deserts of Australia that have laid dormant, bone-dry, for hundreds of years, but after being watered, have miraculously and instantly sprung to life and bloomed.

If you're trusting God to do a miracle in your marriage, your finances, or your children, don't give up. God is powerful!

FIRST DAY OF AUTUMN

"While the earth remains, seedtime and harvest, cold and heat,
winter and summer, and day and night shall not cease."
Genesis 8:22 NKJV

For most people, autumn is a welcome season of cooler days after a hot summer. "Like the cold of snow in time of harvest is a faithful messenger to those who send him, for he refreshes the soul of his masters" (Proverbs 25:13 NKJV).

The leaves of the trees change to yellow, orange, and red, and swirl to the ground in a melee of beauty. Overhead, geese form great Vs and wing south. Gardens overflow with bounty. Fields of grain stand ready to be harvested. For this reason, most weddings in Israel happened after all the harvests were in. It was a festive, happy season. "You have enlarged the nation and increased their joy; they rejoice before you as people rejoice at the harvest" (Isaiah 9:3 NIV).

There are also natural periods of harvest in life, when God brings hard work to fruition. They make up for lean times, and allow you to catch up on your bills. Enjoy these times of refreshing.

There are also seasons of spiritual refreshing. The most important one is when God's presence first comes into your life. Peter told the crowds, "Repent. . .and be converted, that your sins may be blotted out, when the times of refreshing shall come from the presence of the Lord" (Acts 3:19 NKJV).

THE LORD'S FAVOR

For the LORD God is a sun and shield: the LORD
will give grace and glory: no good thing will
he withhold from them that walk uprightly.

PSALM 84:11 KJV

This beautiful passage tells you that the Lord is like the brilliant sun, giving warmth and light as you make Him your center, orbiting your life around Him. As you do so, He will bestow His radiant qualities upon you, filling your life with grace and favor, and causing you to reflect His glory. Furthermore, He's your strong defender, forming a protective shield around you.

Many people, however, fail to tune in to this overarching picture of God and His blessings, and focus only on the last half of the verse: "no good thing will he withhold from them that walk uprightly." They view God as some kind of galactic candy machine, and claim this truncated promise merely to get goodies.

Certainly God wants to bless you with your needs, but more than anything, He longs for you to walk close to Him, surrounded by and permeated by His presence. In turn, He wants you to shine His light upon the dark world. Only then, when you walk in the righteousness granted by His Spirit, will He be pleased to give you all good things.

A SURE SALVATION

But we are not like those who turn away from God to their own destruction. We are the faithful ones, whose souls will be saved.

Hebrews 10:39 NLT

You can't earn salvation by your own efforts. God gives eternal life to you as an undeserved gift. Also, once you're saved, it doesn't become *your* job to *keep* yourself saved; God keeps you saved (see John 10:28–29; Ephesians 2:8–9; Romans 10:9–10).

But some Christians suffer anxiety, worrying that they'll "lose" their salvation for some sin. After all, Jesus said in Matthew 24:13 (NKJV) that "he who endures to the end shall be saved." Some Christians also worry about 1 Corinthians 9:27 (KJV) where Paul speaks of disciplining himself to ensure that he didn't become "a castaway" (see also John 15:6).

However, Jesus said, "The one who comes to Me I will by *no means* cast out" (John 6:37 NKJV, emphasis added). Your salvation isn't like so much pocket change that you casually lose. Scripture indicates that people must knowingly, completely renounce their faith to be "fallen from grace" (Galatians 5:4 NKJV; see also Hebrews 6:4–6).

However, if you love God but constantly feel unworthy and worried about your salvation, be at peace. Remember that God has promised, "Being confident of this, that he who began a good work in you will carry it on to completion until the day of Christ Jesus" (Philippians 1:6 NIV).

TRYING TO FEEL YOUR WAY

*"That they would seek God, if perhaps they might grope for Him
and find Him, though He is not far from each one of us."*
ACTS 17:27 NASB

In Isaiah 42:19 (KJV), somewhat in exasperation, God asks, "Who
is blind, but my servant?" You may be faithfully serving God,
like Elisha's servant, but still struggle to sense the Lord and know
His will. You're unable to perceive exactly what He's doing. The
mountains might be full of horses and chariots of fire all around
you, but you can't see them (see 2 Kings 6:15–17).

Like many believers, you daily seek God and grope to discover
His will, much like the people in Isaiah's statement: "We grope
for the wall like the blind, and we grope as if we had no eyes: we
stumble at noon day as in the night" (Isaiah 59:10 KJV).

You may wonder why God made it so difficult to sense Him
and know what He's doing. But the most important thing to know
is that He's never far from you, and that He gently guides your
hands as you struggle to feel the wall that marks the boundaries
of His will.

Be encouraged! God promises, "I will bring the blind by a way
that they knew not; I will lead them in paths that they have not
known: I will make darkness light before them" (Isaiah 42:16 KJV).

NABAL'S FOLLY

His name was Nabal and his wife's name was Abigail.
She was an intelligent and beautiful woman,
but her husband was surly and mean in his dealings.
1 SAMUEL 25:3 NIV

Most men have their "Nabal days" when they're growly and ornery, like a bear that's been awakened too early from hibernation. But as your mother may have told you when you were a kid, "Don't scowl, because it could freeze on your face and you'll be stuck with it." (She never *told* you that?) Be on your guard against bad attitudes. Over time they can become habits.

Before he became king, David lived in the wilderness near Nabal's sheep farm. One day, one of Nabal's servants told Abigail, "David sent messengers. . .to give our master his greetings, but he hurled insults at them." The servant added, "He is such a wicked man that no one can talk to him" (1 Samuel 25:14, 17 NIV).

Do you get in moods where no one can talk to you? In Nabal's case, his attitude stemmed from the fact that he was wealthy and was used to bossing people around and getting whatever he wanted—including a beautiful wife. "The poor man uses entreaties, but the rich answers roughly" (Proverbs 18:23 NKJV).

Don't fall into that trap. You are to love your fellow man as you love yourself, and if you do, you'll treat him with consideration and be ready to listen to him.

SET FREE FROM CONDEMNATION

Christ Jesus came into the world to save sinners—
of whom I am the worst.
1 TIMOTHY 1:15 NIV

The Bible calls Satan " 'the accuser of our brothers and sisters, who accuses them before our God day and night' " (Revelation 12:10 NIV). So sometimes when God is purifying your heart and you contrast yourself to His holiness, you feel great guilt. As King David grew older, he was driven to pray, "Remember not the sins of my youth" (Psalm 25:7 KJV).

The apostle Paul was also reminded of his past sins, and this caused him to declare, "Christ Jesus came into the world to save sinners—of whom *I am the worst*" (1 Timothy 1:15 NIV, emphasis added).

Paul had done some horrific things. He confessed, "I persecuted [Christians] unto the death, binding and delivering into prisons both men and women" (Acts 22:4 KJV); "And when they were put to death, I gave my voice against them" (Acts 26:10 KJV). He tortured believers and demanded that they curse Christ, admitting, "I. . . compelled them to blaspheme" (Acts 26:11 KJV).

If you find that you're constantly beating yourself up over the same past sins, it's time to throw yourself anew upon the grace of God. John Newton, who wrote the famous hymn "Amazing Grace," referred to himself as "a wretch," because he'd been the captain of a slave ship. But God forgave even him. God has already completely forgiven you, too.

IN THE CAVE OF ADULLAM

David departed from there and escaped to the cave of Adullam.
1 SAMUEL 22:1 NASB

The title of Psalm 142 reads: "When he was in the cave. A prayer." David and his men had moved to Adullam when the winter rains began, when life out in the open became miserable. For a couple months, they hunkered down in the damp cavern near the city. In Israel, it often rains heavily for three days nonstop, and to David it was like a prison (Psalm 142:7).

He had been a much-loved hero of Israel. Now he was vilified, and King Saul and his army were hunting David, seeking to kill him. David had been forced to flee, leaving his wife Michal behind. It was in this context that he poured out his complaint to God. " 'You are my refuge, my portion in the land of the living' " (v.5 NASB). God was about all David had left. So he looked to Him for help.

David was deeply discouraged, yet he prayed, "When my spirit grows faint within me, it is you who watch over my way" (Psalm 142:3 NIV). He knew that God was with him. You, too, can be assured of this (Hebrews 13:5).

Are you going through a similar experience? Do you feel hemmed in and trapped, abandoned by God? Look to Him for help. In your darkest moments, He will be right by your side.

DISREPUTABLE DEALINGS

The buyer haggles over the price, saying, "It's worthless,"
then brags about getting a bargain!
PROVERBS 20:14 NLT

This proverb accurately describes events in an Eastern marketplace, but it also describes many dealings in the West. How many unsuspecting mothers have put their kids' entire comic book collections in a garage sale, asking fifty dollars for the whole box, only to have some unscrupulous collector chisel it down even further, then cackle with glee as he carries off the loot, knowing he'll earn thousands in sales.

This same principle is at play when greedy companies pay mere pennies per garment to sweatshops in third world countries where underage laborers work long hours for miserable wages, and when the manufacturers ask for more money, the companies moan, "You're cutting into my profit margin!"

Are there any areas of your life where *you're* living high on the hog, taking advantage of the poor or withholding from those in need? You might be surprised. For example, many waitresses in restaurants dislike the Sunday afterchurch crowds, because Christians are often cheaper tippers than regular customers. (Maybe the Sunday crowds feel that, after giving to God, they've *already* given their limit.)

Jesus repeatedly encouraged generosity in giving—and in all your financial dealings. It seems at times He simply wouldn't let up on the subject. He had a good reason for repeating Himself. He didn't want His followers to be known as cheapskates.

BEYOND THE BASICS

*Let us stop going over the basic teachings about Christ again
and again. Let us go on instead and become mature in our
understanding. Surely we don't need to start again with
the fundamental importance of repenting from
evil deeds and placing our faith in God.*

HEBREWS 6:1 NLT

You don't expect a high school senior to act like a preschooler.
Good fathers work to help their children grow up, demonstrate
what age-appropriate behavior looks like, and help that child
understand that adult maturity is the logical end result.

In the years following Jesus' time on earth there were
Christians who were satisfied to remain babies in their faith. There
was much to learn but they essentially said, "That's interesting,
but tell us our favorite story again." Where there was history,
psalms, law, and prophecy the people *could* have learned, they
only wanted to hear their introduction to the faith over and over.

Christians can be guilty of the same thing today. Perhaps the
struggle is that the more you know, the more responsibility you
have for acting on that knowledge. The apostle Paul recalled his
own struggle with this issue in 1 Corinthians 3:2 (NLT), writing,
"I had to feed you with milk, not with solid food, because you
weren't ready for anything stronger. And you still aren't ready."

God might need to nudge the complacent so they realize
that growing up into a solid faith is a vital next step for every
Christ follower.

CRUSHED—BROKEN—RESTORED

The LORD is close to the brokenhearted
and saves those who are crushed in spirit.
PSALM 34:18 NIV

You've had bad days, lived through moments marked by heartbreak and soul-crushing circumstances. You didn't enjoy it, sought a way out, and would have welcomed relief.

God's in the business of spiritual pain relief. He's been waiting for your call. God's ability to rescue isn't influenced by things like an attractive financial portfolio, your willingness to "owe Him one," or whether you think you deserve His help.

God has always done what you can't. He paid your sin debt, made you part of His family, forgave you, fixed your broken heart, and restored your crushed spirit. You could try doing everything on your own, but if you've tried that before, you know the results are less than ideal. Let God do what He does best.

Godly wisdom recognizes who does the work—and lets Him handle it. The God who heals loves to stand with those who need healing. He doesn't look down on those who hurt. This could be a new experience for you because, while mankind values perceived perfection, God desires honesty. Transparency with God is the best way to access His help.

Bad things happen. Wounds will be inflicted. Hearts are subject to breaking. Admit the hurt and God will step in. Accept the help and let the healing begin.

EMOTIONAL DESTRUCTION

Fools vent their anger, but the wise quietly hold it back.
PROVERBS 29:11 NLT

You're an emotional creature. Certain things make you sad, angry, anxious, or ashamed. None of these emotions are reliable indicators, however, of how God views you.

Many emotions can lead to negative and sinful responses. Unhappiness can lead to discontent, anxiety to a lack of faith, anger to a lack of love, shame to believing a lie about how God sees you, despair to self-injury, and jealousy to envy.

"Be alert and of sober mind. Your enemy the devil prowls around like a roaring lion looking for someone to devour" (1 Peter 5:8 NIV). Having a "sober mind" identifies someone whose thinking is in line with God's. The call to "be alert" means to be prepared and on guard.

Emotions are a by-product of your humanity, but to let them control you is like turning on a beacon helping your adversary find you. Negative emotions make you a *menu* option.

God's Word is filled with examples of how negative emotions led to sin. Moses couldn't enter the promised land because his anger led to disobedience (Numbers 20:12); David's lust led to adultery (2 Samuel 11); Saul's jealousy led to attempted murder (1 Samuel 19); and Peter's fear lead to multiple lies (John 18:15–27). Godly wisdom recognizes negative emotions, takes those thoughts captive (see 2 Corinthians 10:5), and refuses to entertain these destructive emotions for even one minute.

LIFE GUIDANCE

I have been crucified with Christ; and it is no longer I who live,
but Christ lives in me; and the life which I now live
in the flesh I live by faith in the Son of God,
who loved me and gave Himself up for me.
GALATIANS 2:20 NASB

If you decided to allow someone full control of your life choices, you'd want to be confident they could be trusted. You probably know people you wouldn't want applying for the job. Jesus offers full life guidance with every resource at His disposal. He owns everything, after all.

To take advantage of this offer, you simply put your own selfish interests aside and let Christ take over. If it sounds like an easy trade, you can be sure it's not. While Jesus will honor His side of the offer, you will struggle to let Him. There will be times when you'll want your own way, when your way conflicts with His plan, and when His plan makes no sense to you.

You need to embrace selflessness because it's the only way Jesus can work through you. You give up your rights in order to discover the new life He designed for you.

Godly wisdom allows you to say, "My old way of thinking is gone. Jesus lives here. I will serve Him because I trust the One who loved me enough to give everything for me."

CONTENT OR COMPLACENT?

I have learned how to be content with whatever I have.
I know how to live on almost nothing or with everything.
I have learned the secret of living in every situation,
whether it is with a full stomach or empty, with plenty or little.
PHILIPPIANS 4:11–12 NLT

What would make you content? You're probably thinking of things like money, a particular home, or maybe a certain vehicle. If you just had whatever you're thinking about right now, all would be perfect in your world and you'd discover ultimate contentment, right?

But every time you set your eyes on the next contentment-inducing object, the target shifts. When you have what you think you want, you discover something newer that promises greater contentment. Yet with each acquisition you schedule a new party for discontent.

The apostle Paul had almost nothing but knew contentment. He discovered contentment was the secret of living in varying circumstances. Contentment is being satisfied with where *God* places you. If He's with you, there's nothing to fear because you'll have exactly what you need.

Sometimes it's easy to exchange "contented" for "complacent." Someone who's satisfied in a circumstance he personally created is complacent. God can encourage him to move, but he doesn't want to take one step beyond the comfort zone he's made. Complacency is often found among those who've decided God can't be trusted to lead. With God in control, however, contentment can be found in multiple circumstances.

A TIME TO RETURN

For as the heavens are high above the earth, so great is His mercy toward those who fear Him; as far as the east is from the west, so far has He removed our transgressions from us.
PSALM 103:11–12 NKJV

Guilt is a peculiar thing. It can cause you to live in never-ending regret, disengage from meaningful relationships, and convince yourself to become exiled from God. However, guilt *can* serve a far better purpose.

Guilt is an internal indicator that you not only sin, but recognize you have caused hurt, demonstrated selfishness, and disobeyed God. Instead of treating guilt as a divine indictment leading to lifelong punishment, you can use the guilt to keep an appointment with God to tell Him about the sin, express sorrow, and accept forgiveness. Then? Stop feeling guilty.

Romans 8:1 (NKJV) offers this encouragement: "There is therefore now no condemnation to those who are in Christ Jesus, who do not walk according to the flesh, but according to the Spirit."

God doesn't send you a condemning voice that accuses and then is persistent in reminding you of past sin. That's something your greatest adversary does—often daily. It's important to recognize that guilt always invites you to come back to God. If you feel condemned then you've accepted a perspective that did *not* come from God.

Guilt offers a homecoming. Stop running away.

JUSTIFICATION ACCEPTED

Since we have been justified through faith, we have peace with God through our Lord Jesus Christ.

ROMANS 5:1 NIV

The term *justification* isn't commonly used outside a courtroom, but it's a great concept. To be justified means God views you as guilt-free. Justification doesn't require any extra work on your part, you don't have to argue your case, and infractions are removed from your *sin ledger*.

Justification is difficult to understand when you're convinced you need to work to pay for every sin. Justification is foreign to social norms. People are conditioned to believe that if you want something, you work for it. But God offers a real-life benefits package as a gift. If you could pay for it, you'd have to call it something else. Gifts can't be earned. God did what you could never do, and He simply asks you to accept it.

Romans 5 says you can have peace with God because by accepting what's already been done you can stand confident, clean, and forgiven before God. The resulting experience is a restored relationship.

Justification makes the unacceptable acceptable, the impure pure, and the stained spotless. It accepts the sacrifice of Jesus as payment for your sin. Justification restores what was lost, broken, and disbelieving. It softens hearts and changes minds. Justification is a perfect gift and the only solution for the charge of *lawbreaker*.

SO MUCH MORE

You hem me in behind and before, and you lay your hand
upon me. Such knowledge is too wonderful for me,
too lofty for me to attain.
PSALM 139:5–6 NIV

Christopher Columbus set out to blaze a new route to the West Indies. Instead of finding a new shipping route, this adventurer located a new continent. His undertaking is what is celebrated today.

Learning more about God is its own adventure. You might think of Him one way only to observe that He's much more. You might think He's a God of justice only to discover His mercy and grace. You might think He's a God who holds grudges only to learn He's ready and willing to forgive. You might think God is your cosmic buddy, but discover He's a holy deity worthy of profound honor and respect.

God is good and kind, but He's also powerful and just. He cares about your deepest needs while holding the world together. He extends grace, but asks for obedience. A journey with God is both the deepest blessing you'll ever know and a life of unexpected discovery. God is more than you dreamed of when you first believed. It shows great wisdom to spend time getting to know the One who made, loves, and understands you.

Unlike Columbus, your adventure with God leads to daily discoveries. Expect surprises. Be grateful. Express joy. Live knowing God's mercy is new every morning for the rest of your life. Rise, shine, and discover God.

STANDING IN THE WAY

*Not that we are sufficient of ourselves to think of anything
as being from ourselves, but our sufficiency is from God.*
2 CORINTHIANS 3:5 NKJV

The problem with self-sufficiency is *self*. This one little word makes the assumption that each individual can find a sense of completeness by simply following his own abilities, decision-making, and strengths. It also assumes that every individual has a complete understanding of what sufficiency means, looks like, and how to know when he's obtained it.

God made relationship a priority with and for mankind. Relationship is always improved when someone meets a need. Marriage meets many needs, but not all. Friendships meet needs, but not all. There's always something missing until you accept friendship with Jesus. You have needs that only God can meet. If you could meet all your needs there'd be no need for God.

You'll only be sufficient when you make room for God to begin His good work in you. He will complete it, and you'll find rescue, restoration, and purpose. Wholeness can only truly be achieved when you accept friendship with the God who actually knows where you're going and how to get you there.

When you're tired of trying to do life alone only to discover failure, it's time to remove *self* from sufficiency. Wholeness is available. Don't stand in the way.

CHOICE AND REASON

The commands of the LORD are clear, giving insight for living.
PSALM 19:8 NLT

Why did God supply a list of sins to avoid? Maybe you've thought He's simply trying to keep you away from things you'd enjoy. Maybe you've thought He just wanted to make Christianity a religion of rules.

Jesus summarized God's list of laws when He said to love God and then love everyone else (Mark 12:30–31). If love is the reason to follow God's laws then the choice to sin must be fueled by a *lack* of love for God and others.

While God's grace covers your sin, and His mercy might keep punishment away, the truth is, sin grieves God. His sadness is less about your inability to follow His commands and more about the potential damage you inflict on yourself and others when you sin.

God doesn't want you to sin because it damages your heart, mind, and soul. It also damages relationships. To be clear: avoiding sin doesn't keep you from something fun; it keeps you from grieving God, hurting others, and inflicting pain on yourself. Perhaps this thinking led the apostle Paul to say in Romans 6:1–2 (NLT), "Should we keep on sinning so that God can show us more and more of his wonderful grace? Of course not!"

God's words lead to life, promote healing, and can help restore relationships. They can serve as a warning signal and lead to rewarding life choices.

DON'T BE CONFUSED

God is not a God of confusion but of peace.
1 CORINTHIANS 14:33 NASB

God has His own way of doing things, and He thinks differently than you do (Isaiah 55:8), so if His Word seems confusing, maybe you came to Him confused.

God offers illumination for life's next step, perspective for your purpose in life, and directions for personal choice (see Psalm 119:105; Jeremiah 29:11; Proverbs 16:9). He's never been confused, and confusion is not a part of His plan for you either.

If you hear a perspective that differs from God's Word, refuse to be confused. Always rely on the clarity of what God has actually said. John 8:32 (NIV) was directed to those who follow Jesus: " 'You will know the truth, and the truth will set you free.' "

The reason God's truth may seem confusing at times is because it differs from what many accept as truth. Spending time with *common* thinking can result in a rejection of many scriptures. When that happens there's an unintended plan to rewrite the God-given concepts.

Following God's truth will challenge your thinking, but when you understand that any confusion you experience is a result of inaccurate thinking that doesn't include God, then it becomes easier to let what He has said change your opinions, behaviors, and allegiances. Man's greatest confusion comes in trusting his own thinking—or rejecting God's.

THE ANGER LIST

My dear brothers and sisters, take note of this: Everyone should be
quick to listen, slow to speak and slow to become angry,
because human anger does not produce the
righteousness that God desires.

JAMES 1:19–20 NIV

Anger increases your heart rate, makes your blood pressure rise, and consumes mental resources that could be used for more productive responses.

Anger can lead to bitterness, unforgiveness, and invisible barriers that keep others away. Anger is rarely rational, often visible, and always results in an internal storm warning. Anger is hard to reverse when you're quick to speak, slow to give a fair hearing, and reluctant to forgive. Anger infects those you come in contact with and can cripple those you live with. It greatly affects every aspect of living. Anger causes you to struggle to love.

Anger isn't always wrong, but shouldn't be your go-to response. " 'In your anger do not sin' " (Ephesians 4:26 NIV). And anger should always be resolved. As Paul said, "Get rid of all bitterness, rage and anger, brawling and slander, along with every form of malice. Be kind and compassionate to one another, forgiving each other, just as in Christ God forgave you" (Ephesians 4:31–32 NIV).

Maybe we're urged to keep a distance from anger because it's the perfect environment for compounding a laundry list of poor choices. Each additional rebellious choice will wound you as much, and perhaps more than, the objects of your anger.

TRUSTING THE OUTCOME

Those who trust in the Lord will find new strength.
They will soar high on wings like eagles. They will run
and not grow weary. They will walk and not faint.
Isaiah 40:31 NLT

You're not where you want to be. You'd hoped to be further ahead, someplace different, and on track to experience contentment. You believe you're stuck, and patience is hard to find.

But patience is an exercise plan in God's gym and He wants you to work out. Unlike a physical gym, this exercise can take place wherever you find yourself and in every circumstance. You'll need to develop patience when you're not where you want to be, when people seem to find great pleasure in getting on your nerves, and when it seems God is silent to your prayers.

One of the benefits of patience goes beyond exercise to a time of rest. You may not want it, but it helps prepare you for future activity God has planned. Psalm 37:7 (NLT) says, "Be still in the presence of the Lord, and wait patiently for him to act. Don't worry about evil people who prosper or fret about their wicked schemes."

It's hard to be patient when you see other people find the success you wanted for yourself. Keep in mind that patience is a fruit of the Spirit (Galatians 5:22). God believes you can progress from an impatient state to one that trusts His future—beyond impatience.

BOUND TO COME SOME TROUBLE

We are afflicted in every way, but not crushed; perplexed,
but not despairing; persecuted, but not forsaken;
struck down, but not destroyed.

2 CORINTHIANS 4:8–9 NASB

Adam's sin bent every man, woman, and child toward the choice to sin (Romans 5:12). This means people will make choices that intentionally or unintentionally bring trouble to their lives. Your own choices bring trouble. Trouble is found everywhere—and you're told to expect it. Jesus said, "In this world you will have trouble. But take heart! I have overcome the world" (John 16:33 NIV).

The apostle Paul experienced trouble. He was beaten, imprisoned, and lived knowing there were plenty of people who didn't like him. When trouble came Paul could say he wasn't distressed, didn't despair, didn't feel forsaken, and wasn't destroyed. Some who had witnessed Paul's distressing circumstances might have thought his words betrayed an advanced case of insanity.

The reason Paul could say these things is the same reason you can. Romans 8:28 (NASB) gives you the perspective: "God causes all things to work together for good to those who love God, to those who are called according to His purpose."

Paul loved God and had been called into service. He had absolute assurance that the God who accompanied him to the storm brought an umbrella. Wise men realize that the toughest of times are temporary when compared to eternity and that God never leaves and never forsakes His own (Hebrews 13:5).

BOXING GOD

*"No one can serve two masters. For you will hate one
and love the other; you will be devoted to one and despise
the other. You cannot serve God and be enslaved to money."*

MATTHEW 6:24 NLT

You've heard the term "putting God in a box." It's usually a reference to a person who believes God only works in ways that match his preconceived ideas. Today's verse provides a different example of putting God in a box. . .and leaving Him there.

God is often placed in a proverbial box marked, "Open once a weekend and only during times of absolute emergency." It's a comfort to have the box handy, but it's only intended for specific uses and is rarely opened daily. Other boxes are filled with an assortment of *life enhancements*. Usually these boxes are linked to enjoyable pursuits or personal possessions. You may find yourself drawn to these boxes because they hold a promise for immediate happiness.

You might tell others you believe God is important, but if it were a contest between which box you spend more time with, God might be hidden away in a box of your making while you keep drawing things from boxes that distract you from the neglected *God-box* in the corner.

You can only serve one. Splitting time between the boxes suggests a divided loyalty. Enjoy the things God has given you, but make sure He has your love, time, and heart. Let Him out of the box.

TOGETHER IS BETTER

*"Those who are the greatest among you should take the
lowest rank, and the leader should be like a servant."*
LUKE 22:26 NLT

Today you might chip in a few bucks for a Boss's Day gift. There
might be refreshments and a few well-wishes sent to the person
in charge.

It's possible you aren't sold on the idea of honoring someone
who doesn't seem to possess great leadership qualities. You might
even feel like you're going through the motions on a holiday you
never endorsed. On the other hand, maybe you'd celebrate *every*
day if you could. You feel like you have the greatest boss ever
and would attempt to move mountains if he asked.

National Boss's Day got its start in 1958. Patricia Haroski
registered the holiday with a specific purpose in mind. Yes, the day
was dedicated to bosses, but Patricia wanted to see improvement
in the relationships between employers and employees.

If you don't love your job, then bring love to your job. First
Corinthians 13:4–7 (NLT) says, "Love is patient and kind. Love
is not jealous or boastful or proud or rude. It does not demand
its own way. It is not irritable, and it keeps no record of being
wronged. It does not rejoice about injustice but rejoices whenever
the truth wins out. Love never gives up, never loses faith, is always
hopeful, and endures through every circumstance."

More can be accomplished when you work together.

IMPRACTICAL PRIDE

A man's pride will bring him low,
but the humble in spirit will retain honor.
PROVERBS 29:23 NKJV

Sometimes God's plan doesn't make sense, but there are practical reasons for His commands. Pride's a good example. God says He resists the proud (James 4:6). Other people recognize pride and turn away. God says pride leads to self-deception (Galatians 6:3). Other people believe those with blatant pride are delusional. God says pride leads to destruction (Proverbs 16:18). Proud but broken people make the news every day.

Pride causes an inflated view of yourself. It favorably compares personal accomplishments with others' and believes itself to be superior. Pride pays attention to personal success while minimizing personal failure. Pride has no place in God's plan because comparing personal skills and accomplishments with others is not the comparison God uses. He compares you with His Son, Jesus—and the comparison isn't in your favor.

By God's grace you're made acceptable (not superior) to God and others. He wants to use you, not to elevate you, but to advance His plan.

Proverbs 27:2 (NASB) says, "Let another praise you, and not your own mouth; a stranger, and not your own lips." Pride always has a motive for its actions. It demands to be noticed and is never really satisfied with each new accomplishment.

Honor is always a by-product of thinking more of others and less of self (see John 3:30).

HUMILITY'S FRIEND

True humility and fear of the LORD
lead to riches, honor, and long life.
PROVERBS 22:4 NLT

Humility provides a correct view of who you are and the impressive power of God. Pride offends God, but humility brings unexpected benefits. There's wisdom in refusing pride, but humility doesn't seem logical when society promotes self-marketing. We often believe that if people don't know who we are then we'll never get noticed and our talent will be wasted.

Humility promotes hard work with no demand for recognition, an advanced work ethic when no one's watching, and restful sleep because we've done our best. Humility doesn't refuse acknowledgment; it just doesn't chase it.

What Matthew 6:2, 4 (NLT) says runs parallel to humility: " 'When you give to someone in need, don't do as the hypocrites do—blowing trumpets in the synagogues and streets to call attention to their acts of charity! I tell you the truth, they have received all the reward they will ever get. . . . Give your gifts in private, and your Father, who sees everything, will reward you.' "

It's been said that humility isn't thinking less of yourself; it's not thinking of yourself at all. God knows what you do. He rewards you here or in heaven for acts of kindness and faithful service that don't seek a spotlight and don't demand applause. Humility refuses to do something positive in the name of God and then take all the credit for playing a supporting role.

FULL-TIME FAITH

God "will repay each person according to what they have done." To those who by persistence in doing good seek glory, honor and immortality, he will give eternal life. But for those who are self-seeking and who reject the truth and follow evil, there will be wrath and anger.

ROMANS 2:6–8 NIV

God was aware that His will, Word, and way would be manipulated, contorted, and misapplied. He encouraged His people to handle His Word correctly and be workers who had His approval (2 Timothy 2:15).

Some choose to learn what God says and readjust their thinking to conform to what He wants. Some take a mental marker and blot out sections they don't want to accept as truth. There's a reward for faithfulness and a reward for disbelief. They aren't the same reward.

God didn't hide His plan, conceal His will, or confuse His people. He offered generous helpings of truth and urged you to dig in, taste for yourself, and hold tight to the promise of being made a new creature (see 2 Corinthians 5:17).

Some stop short of accepting all truth and only look to God's Word for personally comforting quotes. But Christianity is more than a spectator faith with all the benefits of the fully engaged. The pursuit of a part-time Gospel was described in 2 Timothy 4:3–4 (NASB): "The time will come when they. . . will turn away their ears from the truth and will turn aside to myths."

Keep pursuing the reward of the faithful.

ACTS OF KINDNESS

*"If you lend money only to those who can repay you,
why should you get credit? Even sinners will
lend to other sinners for a full return."*

LUKE 6:34 NLT

Lending to relatives is generally considered a bad idea because hard feelings can develop when the loan isn't repaid. We're conditioned to believe good deeds *must* be repaid.

Jesus didn't seem to live by the phrase, "You scratch my back and I'll scratch yours." While cooperation was important, His life, words, and deeds suggest a different phrase: "I'll scratch your back because it's itchy and I can reach it." To expect a return on your time investment suggests you believe in the *wages of deeds* instead of the *gift* of time, talent, and finances.

Certainly you're entitled to lend money and expect repayment, but the bank doesn't consider that same service a good deed. It's simply a loan. If you help a friend, expecting they'll help you in return, that's less a kindness than an agreement for mutually beneficial services.

In most cases, truly good deeds go unheralded and are rarely repaid. The idea of doing good without return means you'll do something for someone for a better reason. This concept is critical to understanding that Jesus paid the ultimate sacrifice to offer salvation. You can't pay for it, earn it, or return the favor. You simply have to accept the greatest intentional act of kindness humankind has ever known.

HUMILITY'S ELEVATOR

Do nothing out of selfish ambition or vain conceit.
Rather, in humility value others above yourselves.
PHILIPPIANS 2:3 NIV

We can find a kernel of cynicism in some of the good news we read. Consider this story: A little girl takes the meal she's ordered at a restaurant and gives it to a homeless man on the street outside. It's a beautiful story that gets a little cloudy when her father follows her outside with his phone camera, capturing the moment and then uploading it to social media where it's shared repeatedly. Cynicism judges the motives of the father and the potential misuse of a child's good deed. It questions where the idea originated or whether this was a staged event.

Cynicism only sees what it wants to believe. However, cynicism can't get behind the outward gaze of the little girl who interacted with someone who had no ability to repay her. It doesn't take into account how this interaction may impact her life going forward.

If we reconstruct today's verse, it might read: "Motives associated with pride and selfish pursuits devalue others. Humility offers an opportunity for you to begin to see others with God's vision."

In God's playbook, personal ambition takes a back seat to helping others when they need help. Godly wisdom never steps on others to get to a place you want to claim, never overlooks someone because of perceived differences, and never elevates self while looking down on those with needs.

SOBER JUDGMENT

Do not think of yourself more highly than you ought,
but rather think of yourself with sober judgment,
in accordance with the faith God has
distributed to each of you.

ROMANS 12:3 NIV

Humility is the opposite of pride, but too often Christians are only willing to convert pride to false humility, which is just a different shade of pride. It intentionally shares personal faults with others. This information then begs to be refuted.

False humility prompts others to say something nice about you. This happens when you say things like "I'm not very good at that" or "I'm not sure why I ever tried." This side of pride can be even more insidious than blatant pride because it works hard to manipulate others into verbally affirming what you already believe you're good at, and you're secretly hoping an extended audience overhears people praising you.

God asks you to consider who you are with *sober judgment*. This means you don't think too highly—or too lowly—of yourself. You're made in God's image, but pride of any shade distorts the family resemblance. You're a servant of God, but also a son of God. True humility will be inclined to express gratitude for God's good gifts while false humility wants others to compliment *your* attributes.

Sober judgment means discovering how God sees you and then refusing to let your opinion of yourself climb a stepstool that doesn't resemble sober judgment.

WORK IN PROGRESS

Clothe yourselves with tenderhearted mercy, kindness, humility, gentleness, and patience. Make allowance for each other's faults, and forgive anyone who offends you. Remember, the Lord forgave you, so you must forgive others. Above all, clothe yourselves with love, which binds us all together in perfect harmony.

COLOSSIANS 3:12–14 NLT

True humility allows you to recognize you're a sinner saved by God's grace and no better than other human beings. You're a corecipient of God's grace, forgiveness, and love. You have fallen short of God's perfect standard (see Romans 6:23), yet God did the remarkable and offered a rescue plan so comprehensive it made you part of His family. He orchestrated His plan to encompass a restored relationship between a perfect God and an imperfect people.

Humility takes the clothing of sober judgment and offers others tenderhearted mercy, kindness, humility, gentleness, patience, forgiveness, and love. You're asked to model the behavior of your Father, God. He offers all of these things to you, so He's not interested in seeing you treat others in a way that's inferior to the way He treats them.

Christians are bound together by love, and it's the choice to love that inspires harmony between God's people. God didn't love you because you deserved it. He loved you—period. The same should be said of you. Love others because you see people differently, not as wretched and irredeemable, but as loved by God and as a work in progress. Just like you.

SHOW AND SAY

*How can they call on him to save them unless they believe
in him? And how can they believe in him if they have
never heard about him? And how can they hear
about him unless someone tells them?*

ROMANS 10:14 NLT

It's claimed that Saint Francis of Assisi said each man should always preach Christ and if necessary use words. The problem is no one can actually find these words (or anything similar) in his writings. Whether true or embellished, people have gripped this idea with a strong hand. Artwork has been made featuring these words. The quote has been shared in many small groups and Bible classes.

Nevertheless, the idea of letting your life convince others that you're different comes straight from the Bible. 1 Peter 2:9 (NLT) says, "You are a chosen people. . .God's very own possession. As a result, you can show others the goodness of God, for he called you out of the darkness into his wonderful light."

Your life *can* show there is a difference among those who follow Jesus, but some people will never ask why you're different. Perhaps that's why the apostle Paul said so dramatically in today's verse that people need to actually hear you *talk* about Jesus and what He's done. If they *won't* ask and you *don't* tell them, they miss opportunities to believe in the One who rescued you.

Let your life point to your faith. . .and let your mouth share what you believe.

FOR YOUR GOOD

As obedient children, do not conform to the evil
desires you had when you lived in ignorance.
1 Peter 1:14 niv

Dads know it takes time, patience, and plenty of reinforcement to get children to follow directions that reinforce obedient choices.

Imagine what it's like for God who wants to take His children from babies who don't understand much to mature believers who value godly wisdom. The early church in Corinth enjoyed their spiritual childhood a little too much. First Corinthians 3:2 (niv) says, "I gave you milk, not solid food, for you were not yet ready for it. Indeed, you are still not ready."

God knew it would be extremely easy to fall back to the earliest days of personal belief, which is why He asked for personal maturity. Hebrews 5:14 (niv) says, "Solid food is for the mature, who by constant use have trained themselves to distinguish good from evil."

Just like braces transform a smile, obedience transforms a life. As a dad you want your children to grow from babies to adults. You don't expect them to grow up overnight, but you do expect them to mature. God doesn't want you to stay living in ignorance either. He wants you to grow up. It's for your own good.

"When I was a child, I talked like a child, I thought like a child, I reasoned like a child. When I became a man, I put the ways of childhood behind me" (1 Corinthians 13:11 niv).

FORWARD WITH PURPOSE

*You say, "I am allowed to do anything"—but not everything
is good for you. You say, "I am allowed to do anything"—
but not everything is beneficial.*

1 Corinthians 10:23 NLT

When you come by faith to accept God's rescue there's *nothing*
you can do to earn His saving offer. You simply believe God can
do what you can't. Ephesians 2:8–9 (NLT) says, "God saved you
by his grace when you believed. And you can't take credit for
this; it is a gift from God. Salvation is not a reward for the good
things we have done, so none of us can boast about it."

You can't earn your place in God's family. This gift is not
for sale. He offers forgiveness long after you accept His rescue.
This can lead some to believe God doesn't care about behavior
or life choices. Ephesians 2:10 clears that up: "For we are God's
masterpiece. He has created us anew in Christ Jesus, so we can
do the good things he planned for us long ago."

God has *good things* planned for your life. Those plans didn't
include you sitting on the sidelines. He wants you to participate
in life transformation through obedience and new thinking that
aligns with His. God gave you liberty so you're free to do what
He created you to do. God gave you His Spirit so you could learn
to accept His best.

Come to God with nothing. Move forward with purpose.

SIMPLE, PROFOUND, AND WISE

Fear God and keep his commandments,
for this is the duty of all mankind.
ECCLESIASTES 12:13 NIV

If the God who made everything had a plan for your life, would you follow it? If the God who knew your name before you were born gave you a purpose, would it change how you live? If the God who's making a place for you in His future called you to active duty in your faith, would you do everything you could to follow the Leader? Well, He does have a plan, He's given you a purpose, and He calls you to active duty.

Today's verse is simple and profound. It contains impressive wisdom and divine directive. It contains the core of God's will for you.

While there's a *fear of God* that's connected to pending judgment (think Noah), the use of the term in this verse is positively reinforcing the view that God is awe-inspiring and worthy of the highest priority in your thinking and actions.

Keeping His commands points to your willingness to follow His leadership. By agreeing to follow, you're saying you believe He holds the key to truth and correct thinking.

By saying, *this is the duty of all mankind,* you can begin to see that even before the Bible said, "God so loved the world" (John 3:16), He had a plan for every woman, child, and man. The question isn't whether God has a plan; it's whether you'll follow.

LIVE THE ENCOURAGEMENT

Be joyful in hope, patient in affliction, faithful in prayer.
ROMANS 12:12 NIV

The ten Boom family worked to help oppressed Jews during the dark days of World War II. They harbored Jewish men, women, and children in hidden spaces in their home. When it was discovered what this family had been doing above their clock-making shop, they were arrested. Eight hundred people had been saved, but four ten Boom family members died for expressing their Christian faith by supporting the oppressed. Corrie ten Boom survived the concentration camps.

Corrie could have been bitter. She could have been angry with God. But Corrie found joy in the hope that God could rescue from such terrible circumstances, she was patient dealing with the worst of conditions suffered at the hands of her captors, and she was faithful in praying for her family and those who dealt with each day's horrors.

Corrie survived and spent more than three decades allowing today's verse to be revealed in her life story. That story has encouraged many.

Can you envision a future where others can point to moments where you joyfully expressed your hope in God, when moments of suffering were patiently endured knowing God's grace was enough (see 2 Corinthians 12:9), and where prayer defined your absolute trust in a good God?

This kind of life is worried less about why things happen and more about how God can be honored through the dark parts of your story.

HOLINESS

God's will is for you to be holy,
so stay away from all sexual sin.
1 THESSALONIANS 4:3 NLT

To be holy means to be set aside for special use, to be dedicated and blessed. It's a big deal. *Holy* is a term that easily applies to God, but it's a bit harder to embrace it for yourself. After all, you sin, go your own way, and are easily distracted (see Romans 3:23; Isaiah 53:6; 1 Corinthians 7:35).

When the term *God's will* is applied to biblical thought, it's part of His plan. In this case, God wants *you* to be holy. It's the next part of the verse that can seem troubling. How does sexual purity connect with God's will for personal holiness?

If you're set apart for God's use, then your greatest relationship will need to be with God. While God established sexual relationships within marriage, men sometimes take what He meant for their benefit and turn it into something that taints and subverts His plan. It doesn't show genuine love to the other person because it's mere physical desire. And it doesn't honor God's plan because it substitutes an enduring expression of intimacy and love for momentary satisfaction of lust.

It's not always easy to resist sexual temptation. But it's well worth the cost of refraining from sin to enjoy an unbroken spiritual relationship with God and a truly intimate, faithful relationship with your wife.

THE EXAMPLE

[Jesus] withdrew from them about a stone's throw, and He knelt down and began to pray, saying, "Father, if You are willing, remove this cup from Me; yet not My will, but Yours be done."
LUKE 22:41–42 NASB

Jesus was within hours of His death on the cross. This was God's plan from the beginning. Relationship with mankind would be restored and Jesus would defeat death, but in His human body there waged a war between the desire to live and the desire to honor His Father.

It can be a surprise to read that Jesus asked God for a second option. He prayed passionately. If Jesus' prayer ended with only a request for a way out we might leave confused, but Jesus ended His prayer with what has become the best response of all mankind: "Not my will, but Yours be done."

No wonder we're told that Jesus understands humanity (Hebrews 4:15). If God had granted Jesus' request, salvation either wouldn't be available or God would have needed a new plan to rescue mankind. But Jesus believed in the rescue plan. He was at a critical point. Jesus chose to follow His Father's plan. . .and mankind was offered rescue.

You may not always see the wisdom of God's will. It may seem an unnecessary hardship, a burden too big to bear, or something that no longer applies. As hard as it may seem to follow God's will, it's always been perfect.

DAILY DECISIONS

Whatever things are true, whatever things are noble,
whatever things are just, whatever things are pure,
whatever things are lovely, whatever things are of good report,
if there is any virtue and if there is anything praiseworthy—
meditate on these things. The things which you learned
and received and heard and saw in me, these do,
and the God of peace will be with you.

PHILIPPIANS 4:8–9 NKJV

Today is a day of conflicted perspectives. Some will approach Halloween abandoned to everything that's routinely celebrated while others refuse to participate in something they consider evil. While God doesn't speak directly to the holiday, He has given us a great list of things that we can apply to the day—and every other day. Take some time to read today's verses again.

Apply the attributes of truth, nobility, justice, purity, love, good reputation, virtue, and all that is worthy of praise to today's plans. A clean conscience is one that points you to a decision that leaves no guilt in the sight of God.

The decision each person makes about the day will be expressed in freedom or caution. It can also be the result of fear or something more thoughtful. Each decision will be personal and each decision-maker will deeply hold to the rightness of his choice. Whatever choices you as an individual make, don't allow it to divide you from other Christians (Romans 14:13–15).

LOSE THE PROFANITY

But now is the time to get rid of anger, rage,
malicious behavior, slander, and dirty language.
COLOSSIANS 3:8 NLT

The great Hall of Fame basketball coach John Wooden, who coached the UCLA Bruins to an amazing ten NCAA championships between 1963 and 1975, is remembered as a tough but loving disciplinarian who held his players to high standards of behavior, even at practice.

Wooden once said, "I had three rules for my players: No profanity. Don't criticize a teammate. Never be late." By today's standards, Wooden's prohibition against profanity seems outdated and square. In the world of big-time collegiate athletics, foul language is part of the everyday life of many coaches and players, even during games. You need only sit within earshot of certain coaches during hotly contested games to know that!

It might surprise some Christian men to hear this, but God has implemented the same rule for us today. Speaking through the apostle Paul in today's verse, He tells believers to "get rid. . . of dirty language."

Foul language can be a problem area for many Christian men, especially those who come from rough backgrounds where profanity was part of who they were. But with God's help through the Holy Spirit, you can have victory over bad language. Ask Him to help you do what you can't do yourself. When you do that, you please your Father in heaven. . .and also make yourself a better witness for Jesus Christ.

THE IMPORTANCE OF PREPARATION

Go to the ant, you sluggard; consider its ways and be wise!
It has no commander, no overseer or ruler, yet it stores
its provisions in summer and gathers its food at harvest.

PROVERBS 6:6–8 NIV

In the late 1980s and early 1990s, Mike Tyson was the most feared man in all of heavyweight professional boxing. But on February 11, 1990, a lightly regarded challenger named James "Buster" Douglas knocked out the then-undefeated (37–0) Tyson in the tenth round of a championship fight in Tokyo, Japan, to become world heavyweight champion.

Even the most casual sports enthusiasts still consider Douglas's win over Tyson one of the greatest upsets in sports history. But boxing insiders have since stated that Tyson lost, in large part, because he didn't take Douglas seriously and didn't train well for the fight. He didn't prepare properly.

The world is filled with supremely talented and gifted men who underachieved simply because they didn't put in the time and effort it took to accomplish big things. Among those men, sadly, are those God has called to do great things for His kingdom.

God has promised that He will give you everything you need to do the things He's called you to do. But that doesn't mean you shouldn't plan and prepare for what lies ahead. In fact, God calls you to do just that.

THE RIGHT KIND OF PRIDE

*I have spoken to you with great frankness; I take great
pride in you. I am greatly encouraged; in all our
troubles my joy knows no bounds.*

2 CORINTHIANS 7:4 NIV

Can you remember the last time you told a loved one or a friend
or coworker, "I'm proud of you!"? The word *pride* can make many
Christians nervous, because they know that God has stated
repeatedly that He hates the sin of pride. But nowhere in the
Bible are believers barred from speaking words of praise for a
person who has done something well, and sometimes it's even
fitting to use the word *proud* when you do so.

The apostle Paul gave voice to this expression of pride when he
told the Christians in first-century Corinth, "I take great pride in
you." The context of the apostle's kind words for the Corinthians
was how they had handled an especially ugly incident of sexual
immorality in their church.

There is absolutely nothing wrong with taking pride in
a job well done or in the words or actions of our children or
other loved ones. So when one of your children does something
especially noteworthy (such as a great report card or an act of
kindness toward another person) or when a coworker accomplishes
something great at work, don't hesitate to let them know that
you've noticed. You might even punctuate your recognition by
telling them, "I'm proud of you!"

WHEN YOU FALL, GET BACK UP

For though the righteous fall seven times, they rise again,
but the wicked stumble when calamity strikes.
PROVERBS 24:16 NIV

Jim Marshall was a key member of the Purple People Eaters, the imposing defensive front line for the Minnesota Vikings in the 1970s. At the time of his retirement in 1979, he owned NFL records for career starts (270) and games played (282). But Marshall's most memorable moment as an NFL player took place on October 25, 1964, when, in a game against the San Francisco 49ers, he scooped up a fumble and ran sixty-six yards *in the wrong direction*, leading to a safety for the 49ers.

The good news for Marshall and the Vikings is that he atoned for his embarrassing gaffe by forcing a fumble, which teammate Carl Eller returned for a game-winning touchdown.

Jim Marshall didn't give up after causing what many consider the most embarrassing moment in NFL history, and we shouldn't give up either when we make mistakes or stumble. Today's verse teaches us that a righteous man, a man who follows Jesus wholeheartedly, will stumble and fall but will always get up, dust himself off, and receive God's forgiveness.

How do you respond when you fall? Do you stay down and wallow in self-pity and self-condemnation? Or do you get back up and continue your journey with Jesus?

ACTING ON WHAT YOU KNOW

But don't just listen to God's word. You must do what
it says. Otherwise, you are only fooling yourselves.
JAMES 1:22 NLT

You can't be a part of our modern-day culture without knowing
a little something about what it takes to be physically healthy.
Almost daily you see and hear messages encouraging you to
eat right and get enough exercise to keep your mind and body
operating at peak efficiency.

Sadly, too many people know about these physical truths but
don't act on them. The results speak for themselves. Obesity and
the physical problems that accompany inactivity are at all-time
highs. As a whole, North Americans aren't very physically healthy.

Today's verse gives Christian men some very simple
instructions for getting and staying *spiritually* healthy. It tells
you that you're not just to read what the Bible tells you that
you should do, but you are also to put what you know into
action. Sadly, many Christians don't consistently put what they
know the Bible says into practice. The result is that they're in a
spiritually unhealthy condition.

God's written Word is filled cover to cover with all kinds of
truths, wisdom, and commands. And while it's a good thing to
read the Bible and learn what it has to teach you, that's only
the first step. The second step—and this means everything—is to
act on what you learn.

A BLESSED PRIVILEGE

*I urge, then, first of all, that petitions, prayers,
intercession and thanksgiving be made for all people—
for kings and all those in authority, that we may live
peaceful and quiet lives in all godliness and holiness.*
1 Timothy 2:1–2 niv

Sometimes to see the importance of things you take for granted, you need only look beyond the borders of the United States to see the plight of fellow brothers and sisters in Christ. One such example is that of the precious privilege American Christians enjoy—voting for their leaders, their representatives, and for specific issues facing them.

Think about this for a minute: many Christians today live in places where they have no say in picking the people who lead their countries. Some live in places where political parties are backed by factions in the military that fight it out to determine a new president or dictator, and others live in nations led by rulers who don't allow them to practice their faith openly and who treat women and minorities as second-class citizens. . .or worse.

As you prepare to cast your vote, start by expressing your gratitude to God that you live in a place where you have a voice in the direction of your government and your culture. Then prayerfully seek God's wisdom as you make choices that so many in our world today don't get to make.

THE TANGLED WEB OF DECEPTION

*Do not lie to each other, since you have taken off
your old self with its practices.*
COLOSSIANS 3:9 NIV

The goal of any fly fisherman is to catch fish by using hooks
adorned with fur, feathers, hair, and other materials in such
a way that they imitate an insect or other living creatures fish
like to eat. A good fisherman uses flies he knows can *deceive* a
hungry fish into biting.

While no one would criticize or condemn a fly fisherman for
practicing this form of deception, the Bible tells you repeatedly
that as followers of Christ you are to be completely honest with
others in how you speak to them and how you treat them—no
"white lies," twisted truths, or spin.

You live in a world in which politicians, marketers, and
many others regularly practice all sorts of deception in an effort
to get people to cast their votes or spend their money in a way
they want them to. But it should never be that way for believers.

As a Christian man, you damage your relationship with
God—and your witness for Christ—when you speak untruthfully
or when you behave in such a way as to deceive others. On the
other hand, when you make honesty a big part of who you are,
you please your heavenly Father and glorify Him in front of
those around you.

TOO FAR GONE?

*"So I will restore to you the years that the
swarming locust has eaten, the crawling locust,
the consuming locust, and the chewing locust."*
JOEL 2:25 NKJV

Have you ever looked at someone you know or some famous person and thought, *That person is just too far gone to ever turn to God*? If you have, then consider the story of Michael Franzese, a former New York mobster who ranked high in the notorious Colombo crime family.

In the 1980s, Franzese earned millions of dollars weekly for the Colombo family. At one point, his criminal activities made him a billionaire, but that all ended after he was indicted on fourteen criminal counts and later imprisoned for ten years. Now a free man, Franzese no longer serves the Colombo crime family. Now he serves Jesus Christ as a public speaker and author. (To hear his testimony, just search for his name on YouTube.)

Your job as Christian is not to judge people or their sinful actions. Your job is to love them and pray for them, asking God to do in their lives what only He can do.

If you were to tell Michael Franzese that someone is so far gone that they can never turn to Jesus for forgiveness, he'd likely tell you that believing that is to deny everything Jesus Christ did when He died for the sins of all humankind.

Wise words from a man who knows well about such things.

SEEK RECONCILIATION

If it is possible, as far as it depends on you,
live at peace with everyone.
ROMANS 12:18 NIV

Think about the last time you were in some kind of conflict with another person—maybe your spouse, one of your children, a close friend, or a coworker. These kinds of situations are always uncomfortable, sometimes extremely so, simply because you and that other person are not at peace with each other.

Even after Jesus saves you, you still have your sinful nature (at least until the day you start eternity with Him), so you're still bound to make mistakes and to engage in sinful speech and actions. That often means saying and doing things that hurt or anger others. That's a two-way street, because there may be times when someone hurts or offends you.

In either scenario, there's a loss of peace and unity. At that point, someone is going to have to step up and do what it takes to remedy the situation. The ball might not always be in your court, but when it is—even partially—the Bible instructs you to choose humility, to seek reconciliation and forgiveness.

So when you find yourself in conflict with someone close to you, don't let the situation fester. Instead, search your heart, evaluate your own words and actions, and then do what you must to be at peace with that person.

COMFORT IN TIMES OF STRESS

Trouble and distress have come upon me,
but your commands give me delight.
PSALM 119:143 NIV

New Christians, or those still working to become more mature in their faith, are sometimes shocked that the Christian life isn't free of trouble and stress. Some of them can even become disillusioned when they realize that many facets of their new life are like their old one in that they face a lot of the same problems they did before they were saved.

The plain biblical truth is that God never promised you an easy or trouble-free life. In fact, many scriptures promise you exactly the opposite. Take these words straight from the mouth of Jesus: "In this world you will have trouble" (John 16:33 NIV).

If life here on earth hasn't already affirmed that truth for you, take a closer look at today's verse. Notice that the psalmist doesn't thank God for keeping his life free of trouble and stress. Instead, he freely acknowledges that he's going through a rough time and that the troubles he's enduring are affecting him internally.

But this same psalmist ends his declaration that he's going through some difficulties with these words of hope: "Your commands give me delight." He had learned an important life lesson, namely that God didn't always keep his life free of problems but was always there for him, even in the most difficult of times.

LIVING IN FREEDOM

You, my brothers and sisters, were called to be free.
But do not use your freedom to indulge the flesh;
rather, serve one another humbly in love.

GALATIANS 5:13 NIV

Once a year, Americans commemorate a day set aside to honor and express gratitude to those who have served in the United States' armed forces. You honor those who serve because they do so to protect your freedoms.

Those freedoms—and the United States Constitution protects many for citizens of this land—include the freedom to plan your own course in life and the freedom to worship and serve God as you see fit. For protecting those freedoms, you should most certainly be grateful to the brave men and women in uniform. . . and to your God, who has declared you free through what Jesus Christ accomplished on the cross, and who has called you to live in that freedom.

The parallels between the freedom you enjoy as an American and the freedom you enjoy as a child of God are there for those who take the time to look at both. First of all, both freedoms were earned and are protected through the work of others, not your own. Secondly, neither freedom gives you the opportunity to do whatever you want regardless of how your actions affect others.

Jesus has made you free, and you are free indeed. Are you using that freedom to love and serve others?

A LIFE OF INTEGRITY

The integrity of the upright guides them,
but the unfaithful are destroyed by their duplicity.
PROVERBS 11:3 NIV

What would you do if your server brought your check at the end of a dinner at your favorite restaurant, and you noticed that your dessert was left off the bill? Or if you were overpaid for work you had just completed? Or if someone inadvertently gave you credit for a coworker's accomplishment?

Life is filled with all sorts of tests for that character quality called "integrity." Through big tests and small (relatively, that is) tests alike, you're constantly presented with opportunities to make sure you please God by doing what you know is right.

The Christian writer C. S. Lewis noted: "Integrity is doing the right thing, even when no one is watching." That's a great definition of integrity, isn't it? And it's also a great reminder to do everything you do, even in private, with an eye toward true integrity. Here's a question to test yourself and the level of integrity by which you live: Do you do what you know is right—even in the relatively "small" areas of life—even when you know no one is looking, even when you know there are no consequences?

When you walk in integrity in all areas of your life, you please your Father in heaven and also keep a clear conscience. That's a great way to live!

SEEING SCRIPTURE ANEW

Open my eyes that I may see wonderful things in your law.
PSALM 119:18 NIV

Have you ever sat down and watched your favorite movie, one you've watched several times before, and noticed something in that particular film you'd never noticed previously—maybe a line of dialogue or an action on the part of a key character that you somehow missed during past viewings?

The same thing can happen when you read your Bible. As you read, you can find yourself focused for the first time on a particular word or phrase that hadn't made much of an impression before. On that second or third (or fourth, fifth, or sixth) reading, it's as if God has opened your eyes to some truth or some piece of wisdom you'd never before picked up on.

This is why it's important to read your Bible daily, even if you've already read it cover to cover. And this is also why it's important to devote your time of reading to the God who authored every word of it. When you sit down and read your Bible, even if you're rereading a familiar passage, first stop and ask God to reveal what He wants to reveal to you in His Word that day. You might be amazed at how He'll open your eyes to a new truth (new to *you*, that is!) you'd never seen before.

THE LOVE OF MONEY

But those who desire to be rich fall into temptation
and a snare, and into many foolish and harmful lusts
which drown men in destruction and perdition.

1 TIMOTHY 6:9 NKJV

It's not difficult to see the proof of the destructiveness of greed in the world around you. The federal prison system is filled with men whose love of money led them to commit crimes so serious that they resulted in long—sometimes lifelong—imprisonments. Just do a quick internet search of the following names for some stark examples of the consequences of greed: Bernie Madoff, Jeff Skilling, Bernie Ebbers, Dennis Kozlowski, and John Rigas.

The Bible teaches that greed, or "the love of money," is the driving force for all sorts of evil and wickedness, and sometimes the ruin of men's lives of faith: "For the love of money is a root of all kinds of evil. Some people, eager for money, have wandered from the faith and pierced themselves with many griefs" (1 Timothy 6:10 NIV).

Money, in and of itself, is not evil, and neither is the desire to better yourself financially. Money is just a tool, one you can use to care for your family, to build yourself a better life, or to bless others. But you put yourself at serious risk when you make the acquisition of material wealth your life's focus.

PROPERLY MOTIVATED PRAYER

*And we are confident that he hears us whenever
we ask for anything that pleases him.*
1 JOHN 5:14 NLT

If you're on Facebook or some other form of social media, you've no doubt seen those posts promising amazing financial blessings from God if you'll just click on "Share" so seven of your friends can read the same post.

If you haven't already given that blessing plan a try, here's a little secret: It doesn't work, and it doesn't work because that's *not* the way God answers prayer. Your heavenly Father, as good and generous as He is with His blessings, isn't like an ATM—just shove in the right card and punch in the correct codes, and you get instant cash.

God wants to answer your prayers, and He wants to pour out His blessings on you, but, as today's verse point out, He hears you and grants your requests when you *ask for anything that pleases Him*. The apostle James put it very simply: "When you ask, you do not receive, because you ask with wrong motives, that you may spend what you get on your pleasures" (James 4:3 NIV).

In and of itself, there's nothing wrong with asking God to bless you—even bless you financially. But remember that this kind of blessing is contingent on two things: (1) are you asking with the right motives, and (2) does blessing you financially at this time please Him?

THINK BEFORE YOU SPEAK

Out of the same mouth come praise and cursing.
My brothers and sisters, this should not be.
JAMES 3:10 NIV

Ever had someone ask you if your ears had been burning? That's a humorous way of saying that they'd been involved in a recent conversation with someone else, and *you* were the subject.

Human beings seem to love talking about other people, don't they? And sometimes those conversations aren't what the Bible would call "edifying." It's probably safe to say that every man, if he really thought about it, can recall moments in the recent past when he spoke unkind or damaging words about another person—more often than not, out of that person's earshot.

God takes the words His people speak very seriously, and He isn't pleased when you speak negatively of another person—even when what you say is factually true. That's why the apostle Paul wrote, "Do not let any unwholesome talk come out of your mouths, but only what is helpful for building others up according to their needs" (Ephesians 4:29 NIV).

So think before you speak. If the words you're thinking build up another person and enhance his or her reputation, then by all means feel free to speak them. But if they tear another down and hurt that person's good name, then keep them to yourself. . .and then see if you can't think of something good to say instead.

STANDING FOR TRUTH

Everyone who wants to live a godly life in
Christ Jesus will suffer persecution.
2 TIMOTHY 3:12 NLT

The great British prime minister Winston Churchill, who led Great Britain through the darkest days of World War II, has been credited with saying, "You have enemies? Good. That means you've stood up for something, sometime in your life."

In today's world, many Christians seem more concerned with being accepted in modern culture than they are about standing for godly principles as they try to reach the world for Jesus Christ. And while you are to speak words of truth "with gentleness and respect" (1 Peter 3:15–16 NLT), you aren't to shrink from boldly speaking a truth many won't want to hear.

Jesus made His followers this promise, one many of them are uncomfortable reading: "If you belonged to the world, it would love you as its own. As it is, you do not belong to the world, but I have chosen you out of the world. That is why the world hates you" (John 15:19 NIV).

So boldly speak the truth to those who desperately need to hear it, and make sure you do it respectfully and humbly. But remember what Jesus told His followers: not everyone will want to hear it, and some (maybe even some you consider close friends) may turn away from you or persecute you because of it.

VICTORY OVER FEAR

The Lord is my light and my salvation—whom shall I fear?
The Lord is the stronghold of my life—of whom shall I be afraid?
PSALM 27:1 NIV

If you're honest with yourself, you'd probably have to admit that the future scares you on some level. Honestly, there seem to be legitimate reasons for experiencing some fear about the prospect of economic downturns, natural disasters, terrorist attacks, crime. . . . The list is seemingly endless.

This world is a scary place, and much of what happens in it gives you reason to be concerned. And while it's certainly no sin to feel some level of apprehension over the world around you and where it's headed, God tells you that you shouldn't allow fear to dominate you.

That's because you can rest in the assurance that your God isn't some distant deity but a loving heavenly Father who says, "Do not fear, for I am with you; do not be dismayed, for I am your God. I will strengthen you and help you; I will uphold you with my righteous right hand" (Isaiah 41:10 NIV).

When fear attempts to make its way into your heart and your thinking—and it most certainly will try at times—you can take comfort in knowing that you have a loving heavenly Father who is bigger and mightier than any reason for fear the world can throw your way.

THE HIGH ROAD OF FORGIVENESS

Make allowance for each other's faults, and forgive anyone
who offends you. Remember, the Lord forgave
you, so you must forgive others.

COLOSSIANS 3:13 NLT

We live in a time when it seems that even the slightest verbal barb or insult can start a war of words—on social media or through other forms of modern technology. The exchanges can be ugly, too; just think of the last time you read or heard of a "Twitter war" between two celebrities. One insult can start a seemingly endless string of messages, sometimes turning into a highly personal electronic game of "Can you top this?"

That's just fallen human nature, isn't it? In and of themselves, people aren't prone to just "take the high road" and let insults and "cuts" go without responding in kind. But God tells His people that it should never be that way with you. He challenges you in His Word to choose forgiveness, even when someone has intentionally or maliciously caused you pain.

So the next time someone cuts you off in traffic, the next time someone carelessly speaks hurtful words, or the next time you've been offended because of something someone did, take the high road and forgive that person.

That's the road God took when He extended forgiveness to you through His Son, Jesus Christ, and it's the same high road He wants you to take with those who have insulted or hurt you.

WHEN THINGS MAKES NO EARTHLY SENSE

By faith Noah, when warned about things not yet seen,
in holy fear built an ark to save his family.
HEBREWS 11:7 NIV

The unknown writer of Hebrews opens the eleventh chapter of his epistle by defining faith as "confidence in what we hope for and assurance about what we do not see" (Hebrews 11:1 NIV). He then goes on to show what that means through several Old Testament examples.

One of those examples is Noah, who, in obedience to God's command, built a giant ship called an ark to preserve him, his family, and representatives of every living creature from perishing during the Flood.

Noah's story is one of amazing faith on the part of one man. When you read God's instructions to him (see Genesis 6:12–22), you notice that not once did Noah question or test God. The end of this passage simply tells us that, "Noah did everything just as God commanded him." (Genesis 6:22 NIV). And because of his faith and obedience in the face of something he couldn't yet see, his family and all the animals were saved.

The apostle James tells us that even evil spirits believe in God—and tremble in fear! (James 2:19). Faith, therefore, means not just believing in God, but believing God when He speaks and then acting on His promises and commands even when they don't make any earthly sense.

SPEAKING WORDS OF HOPE

*Always be prepared to give an answer to everyone who asks
you to give the reason for the hope that you have.*
1 PETER 3:15 NIV

In the aftermath of the contentious 2016 national election, Ernie
Johnson, host of *NBA TNT Tip-Off*, spoke these amazing words:
"I never know from one election to the next, but I always know
who's on the throne. And I'm on this earth because God created
me, and that's who I answer to. I'm a Christian. I follow this guy
named Jesus. . .and the greatest commandment He gave me was
to love others. And scripture also tells us to pray for our leaders,
and that's what I'm gonna do. I'm gonna pray for Donald Trump."

In a time when a large number of people in the United
States felt hopeless and deeply anxious, Johnson spoke from
the heart a message of hope and peace. In doing that, he was
a flesh-and-blood example of what obedience to today's verse
looks like. When you encounter people who need to hear the
words of hope you call the Gospel of Jesus Christ, you should
always be prepared to tell them about the Source of your inner
peace and hope.

Have you ever struggled to find the right words to speak to a
friend whose heart was in turmoil, whose life had been turned
upside down? Then ask God to prepare you by giving you the
wisdom to gently speak words of peace into that person's life.

DAILY GRATITUDE

*"But giving thanks is a sacrifice that truly honors me.
If you keep to my path, I will reveal to you the salvation of God."*
PSALM 50:23 NLT

In 1789, George Washington, the first president of the United States, proclaimed a national day of thanksgiving, and that day was celebrated on and off until 1863, when President Abraham Lincoln proclaimed a national day of "Thanksgiving and Praise to our beneficent Father who dwelleth in the Heavens," which would be celebrated on the last Thursday in November.

In 1941, both houses of Congress unanimously passed a joint resolution establishing the national day of thanks, and, after some changes in the bill, President Franklin Roosevelt signed the resolution, making Thanksgiving Day a federal holiday.

Since then, gathering with friends and family to celebrate a day of giving thanks—and to enjoy a huge feast—has become a well-established tradition in America.

It's great to have a day set aside to gather with your loved ones to celebrate Thanksgiving Day, and it's even better when you take a break from your festivities to offer words of thanks and praise to the one who has blessed you with every good thing you have.

But make sure you don't forget to offer your expressions of gratitude to your God every day. When you give Him thanks from your heart, you draw closer to Him, honor Him, and move Him to bless you all the more.

BE CAREFUL WHAT YOU LOOK AT

"So if your eye—even your good eye—causes you to lust, gouge it out and throw it away. It is better for you to lose one part of your body than for your whole body to be thrown into hell."
MATTHEW 5:29 NLT

In today's world, seeing visual images that can trigger your mind toward lustful thinking requires you to do just one thing—have your eyes open. Television, magazine covers, the Internet, and just about any other form of communication are filled with sexually suggestive—and sometimes explicit—images that make it difficult for a man of God to keep his mind and heart sexually pure.

In today's verse, Jesus is emphasizing the importance of doing everything you can to keep your eyes from focusing on things that lure your mind toward lustful thinking. His point is the importance of ridding your life of things that can cause you to dwell on things that God deems impure and sinful. Far easier said than done in today's culture, isn't it?

Job, a man God lauded for his integrity, was onto something when he said, "I made a covenant with my eyes not to look with lust at a young woman" (Job 31:1 NLT). It's difficult, but not impossible, to keep your mind pure in the twenty-first century. It starts with simply making God, and yourself, a promise to get rid of the things that make sexually pure thinking more difficult.

CONFRONTATION TIME

But when Peter came to Antioch, I had to oppose him
to his face, for what he did was very wrong.
GALATIANS 2:11 NLT

Most men, if they're honest with themselves, have to admit that they dislike confronting another person, even when it's sorely needed. Confrontation of that kind makes most men very uncomfortable, and sometimes they choose the path of least resistance, leaving well enough alone rather than putting themselves through the trauma of speaking needed truth to another.

In today's verse, Paul recounts a moment of confrontation between himself and the apostle Peter, who because of his own fear of confrontation had behaved and spoken hypocritically concerning a thorny issue the early church faced (see vv. 12–13).

While it's highly doubtful that Paul took any pleasure in this face-to-face disagreement with Peter, what's clear is that he had the courage to say what needed to be said. In doing so, he set an example men of God can follow today.

When you find yourself in a situation that requires a face-to-face declaration of facts—with a friend, a family member, or a brother in Christ—ask God to give you the courage and wisdom to speak the words that address the problem. And when you speak, do so in a way that fosters love, reconciliation, and trust. Always seek to build up those around you, not tear them down.

HE KNOWS YOUR THOUGHTS

*May these words of my mouth and this meditation of my heart
be pleasing in your sight, LORD, my Rock and my Redeemer.*
PSALM 19:14 NIV

Professor Charles Xavier (also known as Professor X) is a Marvel
Comics character who has amazing superpowers: he can read and
control the minds of people around him. Imagine the advantages
in the superhero world of being able to read minds!

Of course, it's humanly impossible to know exactly what
another person is thinking, and honestly, being able to read
others' minds would probably create far more problems than it
would solve. But there is One who knows your every thought.
King David wrote of God, "You know when I sit and when I rise;
you perceive my thoughts from afar" (Psalm 139:2 NIV).

That's an example of the proverbial two-edged sword, isn't it?
On the one hand, you can be grateful that God knows everything
about you, even your thoughts, and still loves you anyway. On
the other hand, you probably have moments (no doubt lots of
them) when you'd prefer that God *didn't* know about your ugly,
angry, lustful, or doubting thoughts.

Knowing that He's aware of every thought you think is at once
a cause for gratitude for His unconditional love for His people and
also great motivation for you to heed the Bible's admonition to
"guard your heart, for everything you do flows from it" (Proverbs
4:23 NIV).

TEACH YOUR CHILDREN WELL

We will not hide these truths from our children; we will tell the next generation about the glorious deeds of the LORD, about his power and his mighty wonders.

PSALM 78:4 NLT

When you think of the words "a calling from God for ministry," your mind tends to focus on some kind of vocation such as preacher, missionary, or evangelist. But far more Christian men are called to a different kind of ministry, one that is arguably as important, maybe more so, than that of a preacher or teacher— fatherhood.

When God blesses you with children, He also gives you a set of profound responsibilities that comes with raising them. You must care for their physical needs (shelter, food, and clothing), their emotional needs (love and acceptance), and social needs (education and other basics). But He also tasks you with teaching your children to love and fear Him and to live and speak in ways that please Him.

This means imparting not just a belief that God exists, but a love for Him, for His written Word, and for spending time with Him in prayer.

As a father, you should never forget the importance of loving, disciplining, and correcting your children. But still more important is teaching them about the goodness and wonder of the God who loves them more than even you, as an earthly father, can comprehend.

LOVING THE UNLOVABLE

*"But I say to you who hear, love your enemies, do good to
those who hate you, bless those who curse you,
pray for those who mistreat you."*
LUKE 6:27–28 NASB

Have you ever thought about where humanity would be if God
had looked down on sinful, lost people and just said, "Fine! They
hate Me, they curse My Name, and live lives that offend Me in
every way. I'm through with them!"

The Bible teaches that you were once God's enemy (Romans
5:10), that you were alienated from Him and hostile toward Him
(Colossians 1:21). But it also teaches that while you were still a
sinner, Jesus, God's only Son, died for you so that you could be
reconciled to Him.

God is the perfect example of Jesus' command to love your
enemies and to do good to those who hate you. He tells you to
love your enemies, just like He did when He sent Jesus to die
for you. And He tells you to do good for those who hate you
and curse you, just like He did. But more than *telling* you to do
those things, He *showed* you what that kind of love and blessing
really looks like.

It's not easy to love and bless those who don't reciprocate.
But when you do just that, you give those who dislike you and
mistreat you a much-needed glimpse of what God's love is really
all about.

GIVE CREDIT TO WHOM IT IS DUE

Not to us, LORD, not to us but to your name be the glory,
because of your love and faithfulness.
PSALM 115:1 NIV

Samuel Brengle, a teacher, author, and commissioner in the Salvation Army in the early twentieth century, once responded to an associate's high praise for his work by writing the following: "The axe cannot boast of the trees it has cut down. It could do nothing but for the woodsman. He made it, he sharpened it, and he used it. The moment he throws it aside; it becomes only old iron. [Oh] that I may never lose sight of this."

This was not false humility on Brengle's part; rather it was his sincere reminder to himself that he was a servant, a tool in the hand of the God who had given him his ministry as well as the ability to carry out that ministry. When you train and educate yourself to prepare for what God has for you to do, it can be easy to forget that you are His creation and a mere tool in His hands. To paraphrase Samuel Brengle, "may you never lose sight of this."

When you accomplish something good—maybe even great—and people around you begin lifting up your name, be sure to thank them for their kind words. But also don't forget to give glory and thanks to your heavenly Father, who made you and gifted you so that you could glorify Him first and foremost.

SPIRITUAL JUNK FOOD

Anyone who lives on milk, being still an infant, is not acquainted with the teaching about righteousness. But solid food is for the mature, who by constant use have trained themselves to distinguish good from evil.
HEBREWS 5:13–14 NIV

Over the past few decades, people in America have become increasingly aware of the importance of a good diet. Now more than ever, you realize that the foods you eat have a huge impact on your longevity and on your general health.

But what about the "spiritual food" you consume daily? Living in the early twenty-first century, you're bombarded nearly every waking hour with images, music, television shows, and movies that not only don't enhance your spiritual growth but cause you to be stunted in your growth and generally unhealthy. Not only that, you can turn on your television or computer at any time of the day and find unsound teaching on any number of "Christian" broadcasts.

It's not always easy for the Christian man to consume a completely spiritually healthy diet. In fact, without a finely honed sense of spiritual discernment, it's nearly impossible. But you can give yourself a much better chance of good spiritual health when you put everything you watch and hear to two quick tests: (1) Does what I'm watching or listening to build me up in my relationship with the Lord, or does it tear me down? and (2) Does this line up with the truths God has revealed in His Word?

COMPARATIVE RIGHTEOUSNESS

*"The Pharisee stood by himself and prayed: 'God, I thank you
that I am not like other people—robbers, evildoers,
adulterers—or even like this tax collector.' "*

LUKE 18:11 NIV

Imagine for a moment that you had to appear in traffic court after
one of your locality's finest clocked you doing 55 mph in a 35
mph speed zone and then pulled you over and issued you a hefty
ticket. Instead of acknowledging your guilt and paying the fine,
you appear before the judge and offer this kind of alibi: "Hey, it's
not like I was driving drunk and caused a serious accident—and
I know someone who did just that. I didn't do anything as bad
as what *he* did."

Your mistake in this scenario is treating your own lawbreaking
in comparative terms. In other words, you thought, *Well, I'm not
as bad as this other guy, so. . . .* A quick word to the wise here:
that won't wash in traffic court.

It doesn't wash with God, either. All sins, even those you
might consider "little ones," are a serious offense to God, and
you won't find forgiveness and restoration by excusing your own
sinful thoughts, words, and actions by comparing yourself with
others whose sins you consider "worse." On the contrary, you
find forgiveness and restoration only by humbly confessing your
sins for that they are: falling short of the standards God has set
for His people.

THE PROMISE OF A HARVEST

So let's not get tired of doing what is good. At just the right time we will reap a harvest of blessing if we don't give up.
GALATIANS 6:9 NLT

If you've ever watched a tree bear fruit or tended a garden for a summer, you're familiar with the mundane, everyday tasks of watering, weeding, pruning, and guarding against pests. In the same way, it's not easy to live your faith every day without any harvest in the immediate future. There's only faithfulness and a future hope of a reward from God—a reward that you can't quite imagine.

God's promise to you may not be as tangible and in front of you as a garden, but it's certainly more reliable. If you continue to faithfully love others, seek justice, and obey the Holy Spirit's direction, there will be a harvest. Your daily faithfulness will pay off, but you may not see it for quite some time. In fact, it's possible that others will benefit far more from your daily faithfulness.

As you submit yourself to become a branch of God's vine, you simplify your daily tasks, only concerning yourself with obedience to what God has called you to do. You aren't in charge of the results. You aren't in a competition with anyone. You only have your small part to play as you trust God with your daily concerns.

PRAYING FOR GOD TO SET YOU STRAIGHT

*The LORD knows people's thoughts; he knows they
are worthless! Joyful are those you discipline, LORD,
those you teach with your instructions.*
PSALM 94:11–12 NLT

It's rare that you pray for discipline and correction, but living
by faith in an all-knowing God means learning to trust and to
even take joy in God's discipline. The last thing you want is to
go off course, making destructive choices that hurt you and those
you love. And so the best hope for you is to humbly know your
place and to take stock of your thoughts. Compared to God's
knowledge and wisdom, your own thoughts indeed are worthless.

Perhaps you can take comfort in knowing that despite being
aware of the best and the worst of your thoughts, God loves you
enough to seek you out for discipline. He has trusted you with
the scriptures to instruct and guide you. You have His Spirit
dwelling within you, assuring you that in spite of your "worthless"
thoughts, you're worthwhile. You are God's beloved child whom
He could never deny or abandon.

You can ask with confidence for His wisdom and instruction.
He delights in directing you toward freedom and life. The only
thing holding you back is your tendency to hold on to your
flawed thoughts.

YOU NEED GOD'S CORRECTION

*I know, L*ORD*, that our lives are not our own. We are not*
*able to plan our own course. So correct me, L*ORD*,*
but please be gentle. Do not correct me
in anger, for I would die.
JEREMIAH 10:23–24 NLT

How much of your life's direction can you control? While you're responsible for your day-to-day choices, the ultimate destination of your life isn't in your hands alone. In the midst of the destruction of his homeland, the prophet Jeremiah saw the fragility of life firsthand. So much remained out of his control, and under the crushing loss of his country, he entrusted himself to God.

You likely don't face that kind of devastation and heartbreak today, but you face the prospect of seeing your plans, hopes, and dreams unravel in an instant. One phone call can end a job you have relied on; one doctor's visit can change your future plans; and one bad decision can unravel many good ones. You're surrounded by people whose choices can dramatically impact the course of your life.

In the midst of this uncertainty, you can join with Jeremiah who placed his trust in God to direct his life. True, he couldn't plan his own course, but he could look to God for correction and instruction in the right path for his life.

GOD BEARS YOUR LOSSES WITH YOU

The LORD is close to the brokenhearted; he rescues those whose spirits are crushed. The righteous person faces many troubles, but the LORD comes to the rescue each time.

PSALM 34:18–19 NLT

As you remember those who made tremendous sacrifices for you, those who have suffered greatly, and those who have experienced great loss, you may wonder where God is. From family tragedies to financial difficulties to serious health concerns, there are words of comfort you can offer those who are suffering, but there's no way you can mend broken hearts and crushed spirits.

When you reach your lowest moments, God remains near to you. Having suffered to the point of death on the cross, Jesus is no stranger to heartbreak. He won't leave you by yourself, and while there are some things in this life that can't be undone, the promise of God's presence in the midst of sorrow and pain can't be unraveled by any conflict or disaster.

Rescue may not look like the things you expect or want. However, in the midst of your deepest sorrows, you may find that God's comfort and presence can reach even further down than you have known. Perhaps the holidays in particular open up old wounds for you and your family. An empty seat at the table may tap into a new wave of grief. In these moments of brokenhearted grief, God is near.

ALWAYS GIVE THANKS?

*And whatever you do or say, do it as a representative of the
Lord Jesus, giving thanks through him to God the Father.*
COLOSSIANS 3:17 NLT

It's striking to note that thankfulness is something that Paul
expected representatives of Jesus to regularly practice. You could
even add that you know who represents Jesus by looking for
people who are thankful. Why is thankfulness so important for
followers of Jesus?

For starters, thankfulness puts you in your place. You are a
representative of the Lord Jesus, serving His plans and His purpose,
and that requires you to live by faith. As you look to God for
guidance and direction, you'll soon experience His provision as
well. When you receive God's direction and provision, the only
appropriate response is gratitude.

Of course, a lack of gratitude could highlight some problems
to consider. Are you depending on your own wisdom and only
representing your own interests? Are you looking to other people
or things for your protection and guidance? The less you depend
on God or remain aware of His direction for your life, the less
likely you'll be thankful for His daily provision.

Then again, sometimes you need to ask God to help you see
the blessings around you. Thankfulness may only be a matter of
what you notice in the midst of your busy days.

THERE'S ALWAYS TIME FOR RENEWAL

Don't keep looking at my sins. Remove the stain of
my guilt. Create in me a clean heart, O God.
Renew a loyal spirit within me.
PSALM 51:9–10 NLT

Renewal isn't a one-time event in your life. The mere mention of a spirit being made new again, or "renewed," means that God *expects* you to hit low points, to wander, and to struggle. Your spirit can be made new again because God sees your potential—so long as you depend on Him.

As you seek to live in the wholehearted freedom of God's kingdom, you can't create your own clean heart. Breaking you free from sin and guiding you into a life of love and service is a creative act of God.

Most importantly, for your interactions with others, the harder you work to cleanse your own heart, the more likely you are to judge others—and to fail. Receiving a clean heart and right spirit from God as a pure gift is humbling and effective.

Those who recognize the depths of God's mercy live with gratitude and generosity, recognizing that all people are in need of this gift. May God's creativity reshape your life and model a right spirit for others to see.

HOW CHRISTIANS FIND UNITY TOGETHER

*I appeal to you, dear brothers and sisters, by the authority
of our Lord Jesus Christ, to live in harmony with each
other. Let there be no divisions in the church. Rather,
be of one mind, united in thought and purpose.*

1 Corinthians 1:10 nlt

There is no shortage of issues that Christians can become divided over, and perhaps unity seems hopeless some days. How in the world can Christians ever hope to find unity together today? Paul offers a few clues.

For starters, Paul's appeal for unity isn't just wishful thinking. He wants his readers to respond based on the authority of Christ. However, that authority of Christ isn't a top-down decree. Rather, Christ's authority comes from His Spirit dwelling within believers. He unites us together as His body.

Be that as it may, unity also doesn't necessarily mean uniformity, as there certainly will be times when Christians either misbehave or deviate from the truth. Paul admits as much elsewhere. Rather than demanding uniformity, he compels his readers to unite in their thoughts and purpose.

All Christians should aim to reach the same goals of knowing God and sharing His compassion with others. You should desire to think of God's love and salvation. In your worship and your actions you can find the unity that you may never reach in a doctrinal statement on paper.

BLESSED ARE THE UNDERQUALIFIED

*And Mary said: "My soul magnifies the Lord, and my spirit
has rejoiced in God my Savior. For He has regarded
the lowly state of His maidservant; for behold,
henceforth all generations will call me blessed."*

LUKE 1:46–48 NKJV

Who hasn't assumed at one time or another that God is surely
looking for someone more qualified or capable?

As Mary grappled with her holy calling, she saw that her
lowliness and lack of qualifications made her all the more
favorable to God. We don't know much about Mary beyond the
fact that she grew up in a relatively poor region, that the Jews
in Jerusalem looked down on her and her fellow Galileans, and
that she and Joseph could only afford the smallest of sacrifices
at the temple. She lacked reputation and resources, but these
very qualities made God all the more willing to bless her and
to include her in His plans to bless others.

The less Mary personally had to lose, the more she could
devote herself to the work of God. In this act of magnifying and
exalting the Lord with her life, she found a source of joy that no
one could touch. As she looked to God as her Savior, she could
find reasons for hope in the future despite her lowly place in
life and the turmoil that surrounded her day-to-day existence.

GOD FORGETS YOUR SINS, BUT CAN YOU?

Do not hold us guilty for the sins of our ancestors!
Let your compassion quickly meet our needs,
for we are on the brink of despair.

PSALM 79:8 NLT

Everyone has the burdens of their failures and struggles, but these need not hold you back from God. Your failures don't cut you off from His compassion and mercy. In fact, when you have confessed your sins to the Lord, they're as good as forgotten. While God chooses to forget whether or not you're "worthy," it's far more difficult for you to forget how unworthy you may be. You may cling to your past, remembering how you've fallen short.

The good news is that your failures are where God's compassion goes. His mercy meets you where you're weakest and at your most imperfect. He doesn't leave you hanging, wondering if you've gone too far this time. His compassion is swift and direct.

Is God's compassion something that you have to seek, beg for, or envy others for as you see them receive it? Do you imagine yourself as particularly sinful or cut off from God's compassion? If you struggle with guilt and shame, it may be that you're holding on to your sins. The Psalms assure you that God gives you more mercy than you may think you deserve.

ONLY ONE PATH TO CONTENTMENT

*Whom have I in heaven but you? I desire you more than
anything on earth. My health may fail, and my spirit
may grow weak, but God remains the strength
of my heart; he is mine forever.*

Psalm 73:25–26 nlt

Desire in and of itself can be good and healthy, but how often do
you suffer grief or disappointment because you have desired the
wrong thing or action? It's possible that you may think of such
desires as coming from the enemy, pulling you away from God.

God doesn't delight in thwarting or stifling your desires.
If you've grown up with a long list of religious rules to follow,
hearing that may be a shock. However, no one has ever found
God by amassing a list of things to do and stopping there. The
Psalms take us one step further.

Today's psalm invites you to rethink your desires—asking
where your desires are directed. Your desires can be directed
toward a God who passionately loves you and who wants nothing
more than to affirm your true self in union with Him.

There are a thousand ways to be discontent, lonely, and
disappointed. There's only one way to find the love and acceptance
that have been waiting for you since day one. The love and
acceptance you seek in a thousand ways on earth have always
been yours in the presence of God.

FIND JOY WHEN YOU STOP SEEKING IT

Satisfy us each morning with your unfailing love,
so we may sing for joy to the end of our lives.
PSALM 90:14 NLT

If you've ever had a difficult season or generally struggle to find joy throughout each day, you may wonder how to find joy during discouraging or difficult times. The short answer is: by *not* seeking joy!

This runs counter to advice from experts telling you to treat yourself to what you desire, to set aside time for yourself, or to create experiences that offer joy and fulfillment. While each of these actions may be fine in their place, taken at face value, they run counter to the wisdom of scripture.

Your joy is linked with the source of your satisfaction. In fact, the psalmist writes that you begin your days with the satisfaction of God's lovingkindness. When you find satisfaction in God's love and kindness, you find a stable foundation for the rest of the day.

Are you disappointed, bitter, or resentful? Perhaps consider where you have sought satisfaction. How you sought satisfaction in work, a hobby, entertainment, or a relationship that overshadowed the ever-present love of God?

God's lovingkindness gives you security and peace that no one can steal. You can only "lose" God's lovingkindness if you lose sight of it. . .but then its presence in your life doesn't rely on your seeing it.

GOD HASN'T ABANDONED YOU

"No, I will not abandon you as orphans—I will come to you.
Soon the world will no longer see me, but you will see me.
Since I live, you also will live. When I am raised to life
again, you will know that I am in my Father,
and you are in me, and I am in you."
JOHN 14:18–20 NLT

If you haven't wondered if your prayers are just bouncing off the ceiling or if you're the only one struggling with doubts, you'll most likely have a crisis of faith at *some* point. In fact, Jesus' disciples frequently struggled with doubts and confusion. You're in good company if you feel like living by faith each day is a bit beyond you.

Jesus recognized this struggle in His followers and assured them that He would remain closer to them than they could even imagine. While His followers feared being left behind like orphans, Jesus assured them that He would come live within them. This mystery isn't something you'll figure out from a sermon or a prayer retreat. This is a lifelong assurance that you can cling to and experience on deeper levels throughout the highs and lows of life.

Although you probably won't see Jesus walking alongside you, He is within you much like He and the Father are one. This union with God will one day save your faith—if it hasn't already.

DO YOU HEAR PEACEFUL WORDS?

I listen carefully to what God the LORD is saying,
for he speaks peace to his faithful people.
But let them not return to their foolish ways.

PSALM 85:8 NLT

There are many different voices speaking to you today from your relationships, television, radio, and computer. Even your own internal monologues can grow quite noisy and bossy. As you hear these many voices pushing and pulling you in several directions and toward various priorities, you're challenged to stop and ask: "Am I listening to what God is saying?"

Perhaps you should work backwards. Are you hearing words of peace? If you aren't hearing words of peace and hope, then it may be time to hit the pause button.

God doesn't speak fear to His faithful people. There may be people who claim to speak for God, but if they aren't speaking of God's faithfulness and peace to the faithful, then they aren't hearing from God. Even those who miss out on God's peace or who submit themselves to the many voices of this world are seeking the same thing: peace. The trouble is that so many counterfeits for peace exist in the world.

When you turn your heart toward God, you will find the peace that you crave and tend to seek in so many other places. God is already speaking peace to you. Are you listening?

WHAT SHOULD THE WEARY DO?

Then Jesus said, "Come to me, all of you who are weary
and carry heavy burdens, and I will give you rest."
Matthew 11:28 NLT

When you carry heavy burdens, when you grow weary, when you long for rest, and when you wonder if you can take one more step, Jesus calls you to Himself. He doesn't demand any particular action or mind-set. He knows full well that you're weary, so the invitation is spare and simple.

When Jesus calls you, He only tells you to come as you are. Isn't that a relief? Rather than telling you to get your act together or to wait until you're ready for a greater commitment, He tells you to come at your worst. When you're tired, hopeless, or weighed down with many worries, Jesus tells you to stop waiting around or trying to get your act together. Come as you are, right now.

While He doesn't guarantee solutions or the removal of your burdens, He assures you that coming to His presence will result in rest. If you come to Jesus, things will get better, even if you still bear your burdens.

You don't have to keep soldiering on. Weariness and many burdens become your "qualifications" in coming to Jesus for rest and restoration. Perhaps you'll only be prepared for transformation if you first come to the end of yourself.

YOU CAN'T ESCAPE WORRIES ON YOUR OWN

When doubts filled my mind,
your comfort gave me renewed hope and cheer.
PSALM 94:19 NLT

Seasons of doubt, fear, and even panic come up frequently in the Psalms. The writers of the Psalms voiced their uneasy thoughts to God in stark, unfiltered language. They held nothing back and let God know when life became unbearable or uncertain.

What is filling your mind today? There's no escaping your worries and cares. You can't distract them to the point that they disappear altogether. You must face them as they are and then surrender them to God. The longer you run from them or deny their existence, the more persistent they will become.

The Psalms help you face your uneasy mind. They teach you to cry out for help when you're overcome. Comfort and renewed hope can be yours, but you must venture through the valley of the shadow of death first, trusting that the Good Shepherd will guide you.

Your only hope is counteracting the noise of your worries and fears with the consolation of God, seeking His direction and restoration rather than wallowing in your cares. This isn't an easy process to begin, and perhaps it may feel short on consolation at first.

The Psalms assure you that God is present, offering you the peace you seek.

GOD IS COMMITTED TO YOUR RESTORATION

"Yet I will remember the covenant I made with you when you were young, and I will establish an everlasting covenant with you."
Ezekiel 16:60 NLT

After listing the shocking number of sins and transgressions that the people of Judah committed against the Lord, Ezekiel offered a message of consolation. After reaping what they had sown, the people had learned that God had planned something far greater and lasting than their unfaithfulness and sins. God's covenant with them was not contingent on their faithfulness.

This is precisely how God continues to treat you through the ministry of Jesus that gave you an everlasting covenant. God is committed to your restoration, even when that restoration must begin again and yet again.

When God thinks of you, He ultimately isn't focused on the ways you have let Him down. While sin must be dealt with, God's covenant stands. No matter how many times you let go, God won't abandon His people.

Perhaps you aren't shocked by God's mercy in the past, but you may have a hard time accepting it for yourself in the present. Is God *really* that merciful? There's no doubt in the pages of scripture that God's covenant stands, and you can only miss out on it if you walk away from it. The people of Israel started over again—and then started over again after that. God's mercies truly are new every morning.

THE HOW ISN'T UP TO YOU

*Mary responded, "I am the Lord's servant. May everything you
have said about me come true." And then the angel left her.*
LUKE 1:38 NLT

Comparing the responses of Mary and Zechariah to God's plan
for their future sons, you can surely relate to Zechariah second-
guessing the particulars. He and his wife were so advanced in age
that he didn't believe even an angel's word about having a son.

Zechariah had every reason to want the angel's words to be
true, but he could only imagine all of the ways that it couldn't
happen. You can certainly relate to that outlook today as you
face lesser challenges and still struggle to trust in God's provision.

Mary, on the other hand, placed herself fully in God's care,
trusting that a seemingly impossible plan could come true, word
for word. Her attitude appears to be especially important for her
act of faith. "I am the Lord's servant." Those who see themselves
as God's servants have nothing to lose when trusting themselves
to Him in faith. Their reputations and fears about the future are
God's concern, not theirs.

The "how" of God's plan isn't up to you, and Mary humbly
recognized that. As a servant of God, your place is to live by
faith, not to second-guess God on the details.

WHERE'S YOUR HEART TURNED TO?

"He will be a man with the spirit and power of Elijah.
He will prepare the people for the coming of the Lord.
He will turn the hearts of the fathers to their children,
and he will cause those who are rebellious
to accept the wisdom of the godly."

LUKE 1:17 NLT

As Zechariah learned about the miraculous birth of his son John, the angel also communicated an essential part of John's mission: turning the hearts of the fathers to their children. Throughout the stories of scripture, we see time and time again that the works of God must be passed from one generation to another.

The faithfulness of God had to be celebrated and remembered, and families played a critical part in hosting meals, showing hospitality to neighbors, and instructing their children in the ways of God. The people of Israel set up monuments as ways to help future generations remember what God had done.

In light of the prophecies about John the Baptist's future ministry, it's no mistake that changing the hearts of fathers is central. Perhaps fathers are concerned about their own status in the community, their earnings at work, or their own personal pursuits.

Today there are more than enough distractions to keep fathers busy. When God wants to change the course of history, one piece of the puzzle will be the fathers who commit to guiding their children.

TODAY'S TROUBLE IS TOMORROW'S BLESSING

As he considered this, an angel of the Lord appeared to him in a dream. "Joseph, son of David," the angel said, "do not be afraid to take Mary as your wife. For the child within her was conceived by the Holy Spirit. And she will have a son, and you are to name him Jesus, for he will save his people from their sins."

MATTHEW 1:20–21 NLT

Joseph's reputation was on the line as he learned about Mary's seemingly miraculous pregnancy. He could spare himself a lot of trouble by quietly walking away, saving them from speculation about their fidelity to each other, let alone his own holiness. This miraculous conception is celebrated by Christians today as good news, but for Joseph, it surely sounded like his life was about to become far more difficult.

Nevertheless, Joseph found courage to stay with Mary because of God's promise. Perhaps he woke up from his sleep second-guessing his dream. Perhaps he had a long list of reasons to second-guess the angel's words in his dream.

However, in the scope of salvation's history, you can see that Joseph's obedience and act of faith ensured that generations would enjoy God's blessing through Jesus. The hard times he endured as neighbors stared and whispered about him and Mary resulted in a legacy he could have never imagined.

DEALING WITH SIN THROUGH HOPE

"Comfort, comfort my people," says your God. "Speak tenderly to
Jerusalem. Tell her that her sad days are gone and her sins
are pardoned. Yes, the LORD has punished
her twice over for all her sins."

ISAIAH 40:1–2 NLT

While God loves you enough to let you make your own choices
and to reap what you sow in your life, His punishment doesn't
nullify His compassion and mercy. Even as you suffer the
consequences of your sins and faults, God is far from smug
or angry. He takes no delight in seeing you receive what you
deserve. In fact, God is eager to move on and to lead you into
renewal—the sooner the better.

As God spoke to the devastated people of Jerusalem, there
was only a heartfelt call for mercy and compassion for people
who were as guilty as anyone had ever been.

In the midst of failure or your own downfall due to sin, it's
hard to imagine that God would speak words of comfort. Far
from determining who is in and who is out, God's plan has
always been one of rescue and restoration. True, your sins have
terrible consequences and can't go unaddressed. However, God's
preferred way of dealing with your sins is pardon and restoration,
healing and hope.

FAITH ISN'T JUST FOR TODAY

Then the LORD took Abram outside and said to him,
"Look up into the sky and count the stars if you can.
That's how many descendants you will have!"
And Abram believed the LORD, and the LORD
counted him as righteous because of his faith.
GENESIS 15:5–6 NLT

Some days it's hard to see beyond the challenges and trials that are with you in the present moment. However, the story of Abram pulls you out of the present so that you can see God at work in you for the long term. There's much more at stake than the bills you pay or the conflicts you face. In fact, Abram's story teaches you that your faith today will impact generations for years into the future.

Perhaps the simple act of stepping outside to look at the stars at night can help you remember the vastness of God's power and the generations who will also follow you.

If you're feeling overwhelmed by your circumstances or a particularly difficult relationship, the best thing you can do may be to step back for a moment. In the vast movements of God throughout your life and the years that will follow, there's a good chance the one thing that will endure from today is your faith. How you choose to trust God today has the greatest chance of leaving a lasting impact for our own benefit and the benefit of others.

NEW LIFE WHERE THERE'S NO HOPE

*Out of the stump of David's family will grow a shoot—yes,
a new Branch bearing fruit from the old root. And the Spirit
of the LORD will rest on him—the Spirit of wisdom
and understanding, the Spirit of counsel and might,
the Spirit of knowledge and the fear of the LORD.*

ISAIAH 11:1–2 NLT

When the people of Israel believed that they were cut off and as good as dead, much like an old tree stump, the Lord promised new life and even fruit from this old stump that had been written off. How is new life possible when all seems lost? The answer is in the Spirit of God.

While you can't make new life spring forth from the supposedly barren parts of your life, you can trust that the Spirit of the Lord is present with you and more than capable of changing you. Jesus Himself embodied this story of resurrection, of new life springing from what appeared to be a dead stump. As He unites Himself with you, you, too, can take part in that story of new life, wisdom, and an awe-inspiring knowledge of God.

God's new life isn't going to match most of your expectations. Jesus certainly surprised most of His contemporaries with His message. As you look for God in this season, trust Him to bring new life and be prepared for your fruit to look different from what you'd expected.

GOD DELIGHTS TO BE AMONG YOU

"For the LORD your God is living among you. He is a mighty
savior. He will take delight in you with gladness.
With his love, he will calm all your fears.
He will rejoice over you with joyful songs."

ZEPHANIAH 3:17 NLT

Throughout the Christmas season you consider how God is with you, and perhaps you don't immediately see how wonderful that message truly is. Besides coming to earth for your salvation in the person of Jesus, God also takes great delight in you. You aren't just a reclamation project. God's deep joy and delight in you prompts Him to celebrate you and to respond to you with His generous love and kindness.

Perhaps you haven't thought of God's sheer joy and delight for you or His enthusiasm as He sings because you're one of His children. Perhaps you're so quick to move from the manger to the cross as you go from Christmas to Easter that you lose sight of God's deep affection that prompted Him to come live among us in the first place.

Jesus spent so much time healing and sharing meals with His people, not out of duty or obligation, but out of delight. And the same joy and delight that compelled Jesus to be present among His people is also why He's present for you today.

LIVING BY FAITH ISN'T A SURE BET

When they saw the star, they were filled with joy! They entered the house and saw the child with his mother, Mary, and they bowed down and worshiped him. Then they opened their treasure chests and gave him gifts of gold, frankincense, and myrrh.
MATTHEW 2:10–11 NLT

The wise men trusted the sign of the star in the heavens and traveled many miles with their valuable gifts to honor a newborn king. They endured great hardship and discomfort during their travels. They risked robbery and illness while traveling many miles through the deserts. When they arrived in the land of Israel, they were greeted by a violent, scheming king who intended to trick them into helping him commit murder. The risks and inconveniences they faced daily made for a treacherous, uncertain journey.

Finally, when they saw the star confirming that their journey had been successful, they offered their gifts to the newborn king. What did they think of the humble little town of Bethlehem at that time? Mary and Joseph weren't wealthy and hardly had the appearance of royalty.

Nevertheless, the wise men acted in faith, leaving their gifts with the family, rejoicing that they could celebrate the newborn king, and trusting that there was so much more to this king than their eyes could see.

A REASON TO HURRY

They hurried to the village and found Mary and Joseph.
And there was the baby, lying in the manger. After seeing him,
the shepherds told everyone what had happened and what
the angel had said to them about this child.
LUKE 2:16–17 NLT

There may appear to be many reasons to hurry and to rush. Many urgent tasks will come up, and the stress of the holidays can be particularly challenging at times. With the pressure and commitments you have at this time of year, you may not be able to see the ways that God is at work around you.

The shepherds offer you a helpful example of dropping everything in order to be a part of God's work. You may not know when God is going to offer you an opportunity to be a part of His work, and the timing may not be convenient. However, if you're willing to drop everything, you may find a deeper experience of God's salvation and a deeper connection with those around you.

Most importantly, as you seek to keep God at the forefront of the Christmas holidays, dropping everything in order to be present for Him will surely give you something to share. You may find renewed peace and joy that will be better than any gift you could purchase or make.

SEEING THINGS AS THEY TRULY ARE

Stephen, full of the Holy Spirit, gazed steadily into heaven and saw the glory of God, and he saw Jesus standing in the place of honor at God's right hand. And he told them, "Look, I see the heavens opened and the Son of Man standing in the place of honor at God's right hand!"

ACTS 7:55–56 NLT

The church remembers Stephen, a deacon in the early church who was martyred after accusing the religious authorities of killing God's Messiah. In his final moments before death, when it seemed likely that a mob would soon stone him, Stephen saw Jesus ruling in the place of honor at God's right hand.

He had faithfully shared the hard truth with great boldness. Filled with the Holy Spirit, he not only had great courage, but he also saw things as they truly were. While there may have been men standing in judgment over Stephen, God ruled in heaven with Jesus at His right hand. As he trusted his life to God, not pleading for deliverance from the mob, Stephen also had great compassion for his executioners. He pleaded with God to not hold their sin against them.

When you see yourself under God's rule, you recognize your great need for His mercy. You won't harbor illusions about what you deserve or your superiority to others. You'll see that your life depends on God not holding your sins against you.

THE GREATEST BECOME THE LEAST

Jesus called them together and said, "You know that the rulers
in this world lord it over their people, and officials flaunt their
authority over those under them. But among you it will be
different. Whoever wants to be a leader among you must
be your servant, and whoever wants to be first
among you must become your slave."
MATTHEW 20:25–27 NLT

John and James wanted to take a fast track of sorts to power and authority, and their mother wasn't shy in asking for Jesus to grant them the highest positions in His kingdom. We may associate greatness in a kingdom with status, authority, respect, and attention, but Jesus flipped their notions upside down.

There are no shortcuts or fast tracks in the kingdom. Jesus challenged John and James to pursue "downward mobility" instead of trying to leap over their fellow disciples into the most prominent places in the kingdom of God. John's later epistles reveal that he received this message and took it to heart, because in them he emphasizes love for one another rather than using his authority to order his fellow believers around.

Whatever John thought he could accomplish by receiving a powerful position from Jesus, he eventually found that loving service for others carried far more power. Most importantly, service disarms critics and bridges divisions. Jesus showed John and James a new way to lead and to use authority.

YOU GROW BY BECOMING CHILDLIKE

*"I tell you the truth, anyone who doesn't receive the
Kingdom of God like a child will never enter it."*
LUKE 18:17 NLT

Jesus holds up children to you as your teachers about the kingdom
of God. What is it about children that makes them so qualified to
teach you about receiving God's kingdom? Perhaps their simple
dependence and trust in their parents can show you what it's
like to live in the freedom of God's realm.

If you listen to enough interviews of adults who grew up in
poverty, you'll notice several trends emerge. In most cases, they'll
note that during their childhood they "never knew" they were
poor, or that their parents found ways to make things work out.
Even in some of the most challenging cases of need, children
found contentment and confidence in their parents. It turns out
that in many cases, a loving and present parent was more than
enough to compensate for the challenges of life.

Whether you're secure or in great need today, a childlike
dependence on God is where you'll find long-term contentment
and security. You often hear of growing in wisdom or maturity in
the Christian faith, and they certainly have their place. However,
Jesus also expects you to grow more "childlike" if you're going to
truly live in His kingdom.

MAY GOD SAVE YOU FROM WEALTH

Jesus replied, "Friend, who made me a judge over you to decide such things as that?" Then he said, "Beware! Guard against every kind of greed. Life is not measured by how much you own."
LUKE 12:14–15 NLT

In a culture where the firstborn son enjoyed immense benefits and privileges, a younger brother pleaded with Jesus for a more equal distribution of the family's inheritance. His argument certainly appears reasonable to us today, but Jesus wasn't looking at this matter from a financial standpoint.

Jesus saw that the younger brother had become obsessed with wealth, allowing greed to determine the value of his life. By refusing to arbitrate a settlement in this family, Jesus may have saved this young man from his desires. Tempting as it is to think that Jesus deprived this young man of something reasonable, Jesus most likely gave him the hard truth that he needed the most.

It's common to treat money as the solution to almost all of your problems today. Even if there's a risk that their desire for money will soon become a never-ending pit of greed and self-indulgence, people rarely treat money as a threat to their spiritual or relational well-being. Jesus didn't mince words in this story, treating greed as a threat that you must always remain aware of. Every time you pray for more money (or "provision"), you should also pray for God's protection from greed.

REFLECTING GOD'S RADIANCE IN A DARK WORLD

*"Darkness as black as night covers all the nations of the earth,
but the glory of the LORD rises and appears over you.
All nations will come to your light; mighty kings
will come to see your radiance."*

ISAIAH 60:2–3 NLT

Where do you find your hope today? Many look to politics or some mix of religion and politics in order to bring about change in our world. However, you must place your trust in a greater power that remains at work in God's people but will one day become visible to all. In fact, God assured Israel that all rulers would one day see God's radiance over His people.

You can begin to offer hope to a world struggling in darkness by first asking God to show His radiance in you. How can you surrender to God's plans and purposes today so that His radiance overshadows the darkness of this world? If you rely on your own light, you'll only become frustrated and discouraged.

Isaiah assures you that God's radiant light in His people will be undeniable. There's no mistaking the wholeness and redemption of God in this world when lives are restored and made whole. In the face of darkness, your first step is to present yourself to the Lord so that you can more fully reflect Him to others.

MAY GOD HOLD YOU CLOSE

Yes, the Sovereign LORD is coming in power. He will rule with
a powerful arm. See, he brings his reward with him as he comes.
He will feed his flock like a shepherd. He will carry the lambs
in his arms, holding them close to his heart. He will
gently lead the mother sheep with their young.
ISAIAH 40:10–11 NLT

When you think of God coming in power, do you imagine judgment or a settling of scores? While God's justice is a big part of scripture, perhaps you lose sight of how God manifests His power and justice among people. The restoration you're waiting for under God will reward you for the ways you have remained faithful to Him and will look like a shepherd finally bringing order to a flock of sheep that has long known suffering and disorder.

God's restoration will involve caring for the young and restoring families. Divisions and troubles will be resolved as the Lord brings His people together in harmony. Your fears of the future will be resolved as God Himself leads His people and cares for their daily needs.

Wrapped up in these promises from your heavenly Father is His deepest longing for intimacy with His people today, holding them close to Himself as a parent would hold a child. While you may suffer through adversity and uncertainty today, God remains present with you, willing and able to guide you through this coming year.

CONTRIBUTORS

Ed Cyzewski is the author of *A Christian Survival Guide: A Lifeline to Faith and Growth* and *Coffeehouse Theology: Reflecting on God in Everyday Life* and is the coauthor of *The Good News of Revelation* and *Unfollowers: Unlikely Lessons on Faith from Those Who Doubted Jesus.* He writes about prayer and imperfectly following Jesus at www.edcyzewski.com. Ed's devotions are found in June and December.

Quentin Guy writes from the high desert of New Mexico, to encourage and equip people to know and serve God. He currently works in publishing for Calvary Albuquerque and has cowritten such books as *Weird and Gross Bible Stuff* and *The 2:52 Boys Bible*, both of which are stuck in future classic status. A former middle school teacher, he serves with his wife as marriage prep mentors and trusts God that his children will survive their teenage years. Quentin's devotions are found in February and August.

Glenn A. Hascall is an accomplished writer with credits in more than a hundred books. He is a broadcast veteran and voice actor and is actively involved in writing and producing audio drama. Glenn's devotions are found in April and October.

Ed Strauss is a freelance writer living in British Columbia, Canada. He has authored or coauthored more than fifty books for children, tweens, and adults. Ed has a passion for biblical apologetics and besides writing for Barbour, has been published by Zondervan, Tyndale, Moody, and Focus on the Family. Ed's devotions are found in March and September.

Tracy M. Sumner is a freelance author, writer, and editor in Beaverton, Oregon. An avid outdoorsman, he enjoys fly fishing on world-class Oregon waters. Tracy's devotions are found in May and November.

Lee Warren is published in such varied venues as *Discipleship Journal*, Sports Spectrum, Yahoo! Sports, Crosswalk.com, and ChristianityToday.com. He is also the author of the book *Finishing Well: Living with the End in Mind* (a devotional), and he writes regular features for *The Pathway* newspaper and Living Light News. Lee makes his home in Omaha, Nebraska. Lee's devotions are found in January and July.

SCRIPTURE INDEX

16:24 – May 7
16:32 – July 14
17:17 – August 25
19:1 – January 5
19:20 – May 18
20:14 – September 30
21:1 – August 8
22:4 – October 18
24:16 – November 4
25:15 – August 31
26:11 – February 2
27:1 – July 11
27:2 – September 2
27:23 – February 11
27:23–24 – January 7
28:13 – February 20
29:11 – May 4, October 3
29:23 – October 17
30:26 – September 20
31:10, 28–29 – May 13
31:28–29 – August 10

Ecclesiastes
4:4 – March 4
4:9–10 – April 25
5:2 – March 3
7:8 – January 25
7:10 – May 15
10:12 – April 29
11:4 – January 11
12:13 – October 27

Song of Songs
2:11–12 – March 20

Isaiah
2:11 – May 22
11:1–2 – December 22
24:5 – February 26
26:3 – August 9
40:1–2 – December 20
40:10–11 – December 31
40:31 – October 13
52:7 – March 17
55:9 – August 18
55:10–11 – September 22
60:2–3 – December 30

Jeremiah
2:13 – September 14
10:23–24 – December 3
32:27 – February 7

Ezekiel
16:60 – December 16

Daniel
1:8 – July 25

Joel
2:12–13 – July 15
2:25 – November 8

Amos
5:24 – April 9
7:14 – May 20

Micah
6:8 – May 21
7:18 – May 8

Habakkuk
3:17–18 – July 29

Zephaniah
3:17 – December 23

Malachi
2:10 – February 13

New Testament

Matthew
1:20–21 – December 19
2:1–2 – January 6
2:10–11 – December 24
5:23–24 – June 10
5:27–28 – September 21
5:29 – November 23
5:37 – August 17
6:3–4 – June 9
6:24 – October 15
9:36 – July 21
10:13 – January 17
10:16 – August 30

11:28 – December 14
15:8 – February 16
15:18–19 – July 16
20:15 – June 27
20:25–27 – December 27
25:21 – March 2
28:19–20 – January 2

Mark
3:25 – August 21
6:34 – February 24
9:24 – May 16
10:26–27 – June 18
13:33–35 – June 28

Luke
1:17 – December 18
1:38 – December 17
1:46–48 – December 8
1:74–75 – July 10
2:16–17 – December 25
4:18 – August 5
6:27–28 – November 27
6:34 – October 20
12:6–7 – June 24
12:14–15 – December 29
12:31–32 – June 17
14:28 – February 27
14:33 – March 23
16:11–12 – January 9
18:11–12 – November 30
18:17 – December 28
22:15 – March 30
22:26 – October 16
22:41–42 – October 30

John
8:36 – March 6, April 5
9:39 – June 21
11:21–22 – June 20
12:13 – March 25
13:34–35 – May 5
14:18–20 – December 12
14:26 – April 17
15:13 – May 28, August 7
17:15 – August 19

Acts
1:8 – August 20
2:42 – May 29
5:29 – February 14
5:32 – March 15
7:55–56 – December 26
10:34–35 – January 15
13:38–39 – March 9
17:27 – September 26
28:1–2 – July 27

Romans
2:4 – February 25
2:6–8 – October 19
2:8 – August 15
5:1 – October 7
5:3 – February 17
6:23 – April 1
8:6 – January 30
8:35–36 – July 3
8:39 – June 29
10:11 – May 9
10:14 – October 24
12:2 – April 14
12:3 – October 22
12:10 – August 4
12:12 – October 28
12:17–18 – July 24
12:18 – November 9
13:14 – March 29
14:17 – July 30
15:13 – January 22
15:14 – January 31
15:20 – July 19

1 Corinthians
1:10 – December 7
3:14–15 – February 23
4:19–20 – June 22
9:22 – August 6
9:25–26 – September 15
10:23 – October 26
12:12 – May 23
13:4–5 – March 12
14:33 – October 11
15:10 – March 16
16:13 – August 2

2 Corinthians
2:14 – August 3
3:5 – October 9
4:8–9 – October 14
4:16 – March 26
5:18 – August 12
7:4 – November 3
12:9 – February 8

Galatians
2:11 – November 24
2:20 – October 4
3:28 – April 28
5:1 – August 1
5:13 – November 11
6:1 – April 10
6:9 – March 28, August 27, December 1
6:10 – September 12

Ephesians
1:10 – August 28
4:1–3 – July 28
4:31–32 – January 24
5:15–17 – April 15
6:1–3 – July 22
6:10–11 – September 6
6:13 – April 19
6:16 – March 5
6:18 – May 3

Philippians
1:20 – June 4
1:29 – May 14
2:3 – March 10, October 21
2:7 – February 19
3:7–8 – March 21
4:5 – January 27, September 5
4:6 – April 3
4:8–9 – October 31
4:11–12 – October 5

Colossians
1:3–4 – January 3
1:10 – August 16
1:16 – April 27
3:5 – July 13

3:8 – November 1
3:9 – November 7
3:12–14 – October 23
3:13 – November 19
3:17 – April 2, December 5
4:12 – May 2
4:18 – January 21

1 Thessalonians
4:3 – October 29
4:11 – February 5, March 19
5:18 – April 23

2 Thessalonians
3:3 – March 14

1 Timothy
1:15 – September 28
2:1–2 – November 6
3:5 – January 14
4:12 – February 18, September 8
6:6 – April 20
6:9 – November 14
6:12 – July 31

2 Timothy
2:3 – January 26
3:12 – November 17
3:16 – April 18

Titus
2:6–8 – July 5
3:1–2 – January 12

Hebrews
4:15–16 – June 3
5:13–14 – November 29
6:1 – October 1
6:10 – March 31
10:23 – April 30
10:39 – September 25
11:5 – May 17
11:7 – November 20
11:16 – February 4
11:39–40 – May 24

BIBLE READING PLAN
READ THRU THE BIBLE IN A YEAR

1-Jan	Gen. 1–2	Matt. 1	Ps. 1
2-Jan	Gen. 3–4	Matt. 2	Ps. 2
3-Jan	Gen. 5–7	Matt. 3	Ps. 3
4-Jan	Gen. 8–10	Matt. 4	Ps. 4
5-Jan	Gen. 11–13	Matt. 5:1–20	Ps. 5
6-Jan	Gen. 14–16	Matt. 5:21–48	Ps. 6
7-Jan	Gen. 17–18	Matt. 6:1–18	Ps. 7
8-Jan	Gen. 19–20	Matt. 6:19–34	Ps. 8
9-Jan	Gen. 21–23	Matt. 7:1–11	Ps. 9:1–8
10-Jan	Gen. 24	Matt. 7:12–29	Ps. 9:9–20
11-Jan	Gen. 25–26	Matt. 8:1–17	Ps. 10:1–11
12-Jan	Gen. 27:1–28:9	Matt. 8:18–34	Ps. 10:12–18
13-Jan	Gen. 28:10–29:35	Matt. 9	Ps. 11
14-Jan	Gen. 30:1–31:21	Matt. 10:1–15	Ps. 12
15-Jan	Gen. 31:22–32:21	Matt. 10:16–36	Ps. 13
16-Jan	Gen. 32:22–34:31	Matt. 10:37–11:6	Ps. 14
17-Jan	Gen. 35–36	Matt. 11:7–24	Ps. 15
18-Jan	Gen. 37–38	Matt. 11:25–30	Ps. 16
19-Jan	Gen. 39–40	Matt. 12:1–29	Ps. 17
20-Jan	Gen. 41	Matt. 12:30–50	Ps. 18:1–15
21-Jan	Gen. 42–43	Matt. 13:1–9	Ps. 18:16–29
22-Jan	Gen. 44–45	Matt. 13:10–23	Ps. 18:30–50
23-Jan	Gen. 46:1–47:26	Matt. 13:24–43	Ps. 19
24-Jan	Gen. 47:27–49:28	Matt. 13:44–58	Ps. 20
25-Jan	Gen. 49:29–Exod. 1:22	Matt. 14	Ps. 21
26-Jan	Exod. 2–3	Matt. 15:1–28	Ps. 22:1–21
27-Jan	Exod. 4:1–5:21	Matt. 15:29–16:12	Ps. 22:22–31
28-Jan	Exod. 5:22–7:24	Matt. 16:13–28	Ps. 23
29-Jan	Exod. 7:25–9:35	Matt. 17:1–9	Ps. 24
30-Jan	Exod. 10–11	Matt. 17:10–27	Ps. 25
31-Jan	Exod. 12	Matt. 18:1–20	Ps. 26
1-Feb	Exod. 13–14	Matt. 18:21–35	Ps. 27
2-Feb	Exod. 15–16	Matt. 19:1–15	Ps. 28
3-Feb	Exod. 17–19	Matt. 19:16–30	Ps. 29
4-Feb	Exod. 20–21	Matt. 20:1–19	Ps. 30
5-Feb	Exod. 22–23	Matt. 20:20–34	Ps. 31:1–8
6-Feb	Exod. 24–25	Matt. 21:1–27	Ps. 31:9–18
7-Feb	Exod. 26–27	Matt. 21:28–46	Ps. 31:19–24
8-Feb	Exod. 28	Matt. 22	Ps. 32
9-Feb	Exod. 29	Matt. 23:1–36	Ps. 33:1–12
10-Feb	Exod. 30–31	Matt. 23:37–24:28	Ps. 33:13–22
11-Feb	Exod. 32–33	Matt. 24:29–51	Ps. 34:1–7
12-Feb	Exod. 34:1–35:29	Matt. 25:1–13	Ps. 34:8–22
13-Feb	Exod. 35:30–37:29	Matt. 25:14–30	Ps. 35:1–8
14-Feb	Exod. 38–39	Matt. 25:31–46	Ps. 35:9–17
15-Feb	Exod. 40	Matt. 26:1–35	Ps. 35:18–28
16-Feb	Lev. 1–3	Matt. 26:36–68	Ps. 36:1–6
17-Feb	Lev. 4:1–5:13	Matt. 26:69–27:26	Ps. 36:7–12
18-Feb	Lev. 5:14–7:21	Matt. 27:27–50	Ps. 37:1–6
19-Feb	Lev. 7:22–8:36	Matt. 27:51–66	Ps. 37:7–26
20-Feb	Lev. 9–10	Matt. 28	Ps. 37:27–40
21-Feb	Lev. 11–12	Mark 1:1–28	Ps. 38
22-Feb	Lev. 13	Mark 1:29–39	Ps. 39
23-Feb	Lev. 14	Mark 1:40–2:12	Ps. 40:1–8
24-Feb	Lev. 15	Mark 2:13–3:35	Ps. 40:9–17
25-Feb	Lev. 16–17	Mark 4:1–20	Ps. 41:1–4
26-Feb	Lev. 18–19	Mark 4:21–41	Ps. 41:5–13
27-Feb	Lev. 20	Mark 5	Ps. 42–43
28-Feb	Lev. 21–22	Mark 6:1–13	Ps. 44
1-Mar	Lev. 23–24	Mark 6:14–29	Ps. 45:1–5
2-Mar	Lev. 25	Mark 6:30–56	Ps. 45:6–12